Resisting Racism
and Xenophobia

Resisting Racism and Xenophobia

Global Perspectives on Race, Gender, and Human Rights

Edited by
Faye V. Harrison

ALTAMIRA
P R E S S

A DIVISION OF ROWMAN & LITTLEFIELD PUBLISHERS, INC.
Walnut Creek • *Lanham* • *New York* • *Toronto* • *Oxford*

ALTAMIRA PRESS
A Division of Rowman & Littlefield Publishers, Inc.
1630 North Main Street, #367
Walnut Creek, CA 94596
http://www.altamirapress.com

Rowman & Littlefield Publishers, Inc.
A Member of the Rowman & Littlefield Publishing Group
4501 Forbes Blvd., Suite 200
Lanham, MD 20706

PO Box 317
Oxford
OX2 9RU, United Kingdom

British Library Cataloguing in Publication Information Available

Library of Congress Cataloging-in-Publication Data Available

ISBN 0-7591-0481-6 (cloth : alk. paper)
ISBN 0-7591-0482-4 (pbk. : alk. paper)

Printed in the United States of America

∞™ The paper used in this publication meets the minimum requirements of American National Standard for Information Sciences—Permanence of Paper for Printed Library Materials, ANSI/NISO Z39.48-1992.

Contents

Acknowledgments

$\mathscr{T}$his book has a history that can probably be traced, ultimately, to my formative experiences in the U.S. South—in Virginia, the state where George Washington and Thomas Jefferson launched their trajectories as fathers (and slave masters) of American democracy. I came of age and social consciousness during a time of turbulence and change, when a mass movement challenged the most flagrant violations of a racially subjugated people's civil rights and human dignity. Although race has been an issue that I have engaged throughout my life, my serious thinking about it did not begin until I was a graduate student studying race with St. Clair Drake, whose encyclopedic knowledge and encouragement I will always cherish. Drake was an Africanist and African diaspora specialist whose scholarship and teaching included a focus on the ideologies and structures of race and power. He underscored the analytical significance of power in its multiple modalities at a time when a great deal of race relations research was still limited by a preoccupation with prejudice.

More immediately, this book's history can be traced to a two-part workshop that I organized for the 2001 World Conference against Racism's NGO Forum held in Durban, South Africa. That workshop, which was sponsored by the International Union of Anthropological and Ethnological Sciences' Commission on the Anthropology of Women, brought together a dynamic and culturally diverse group of women to exchange ideas on racism, xenophobia, and the related problems of patriarchy and injuries of class. Our intense discussion had an emphasis—but not an exclusive focus—on how women negotiate these intersecting oppressions and confront them as violations of their human rights. Our experiences at the forum inspired most of us to continue working together to publish this collection, which brings issues of race, caste, class, gender, sexuality, nationalism, transnationalism, human rights, and global restructuring into a common frame of analytical engagement. After September 11, 2001, only days after the UN conference and forum had ended, we became even more determined to make the results of our respective research, and the important lessons we learned from Durban, available to the public. To strengthen and enrich our efforts, we solicited a few additional contributions that would help to extend our cross-cultural and geopolitical range.

I am thankful to my senior colleague Helen Safa for being the first person to express interest in the idea of a group of anthropologists participating in the NGO Forum. In fact, Helen was the only one who responded to the call for participation that I published in *Anthropology News*—in the Association of Black Anthropologists' unit news column that David Simmons edited at the time. David's enthusiasm about getting the word out about the forum and Helen's encouragement about participating in it led me to intensify my efforts to organize a session by inviting colleagues from around the world to present in it. Only twelve of the twenty or so people who submitted abstracts were able to travel to Durban. Once I began to work on the post–World Conference against Racism publication project, I invited all of the interested parties who were unable to be a part of the workshop in South Africa to submit chapters to the book.

I thank Fadwa El Guindi for agreeing to write a chapter from an Arab and Muslim perspective. She was not a part of the Durban group, but she had been involved in the commission's activities a few years earlier. After September 11, I thought that it was imperative to offer some much-needed clarity on the growing racial profiling of Arab Americans and on the political grievances of Arabs, especially Palestinians, in the Middle East.

I am excited that Cheryl Fischer's work is included here. She brings her considerable experience as an activist to the volume. Her ability to work at the grassroots level, as well as in international/transnational settings, is admirable, and I deeply appreciate the recommendations for antiracist action that she provides. She is someone who "practices what she preaches," and her knowledge is grounded in the trenches of everyday politics. I must also thank Cheryl's daughter, Dawn-Elissa, and husband, Donald, for their support. When an illness made it difficult for Cheryl to complete the revisions for her chapter by the deadline, they made sure that her revised chapter was included in the manuscript that I submitted to AltaMira Press. I especially want to express my thanks to Dawn-Elissa, who is a doctoral student in anthropology and who is doing incredible work. Dawn's enthusiasm for this project and for the future of an engaged anthropology has helped to keep me motivated.

It is also a pleasure to have worked with Mohamed Saleh, an activist and anthropologist whom I met at an international human rights conference in Copenhagen, Denmark, several years ago. Since then, we have exchanged news articles, human rights reports, and academic publications. One of his communiqués prompted me to invite him to present a paper on sexual violence at the Durban NGO Forum. He eagerly agreed to write a chapter with Fatma Jiddawi Napoli, who works on behalf of Zanzibari refugees in North America.

I must thank my friend Gina Ulysse for adding a provocative creative dimension to the book. Her poetry and spoken-word performances have become integral to her life as an activist intellectual and multitalented anthropologist committed to reaching a wider audience. I thank Gina for having the courage as well as the versatility not to make an either-or choice between her art and her social science.

I appreciate Devaki Jain's involvement in this project and would like to thank civil rights lawyer and legal scholar Barbara Sullivan for facilitating Jain's participation in the "Interlocking Dimensions of Difference" workshop. As a program officer at the Ford Foundation, Sullivan was supportive of the commission's request to have its Durban and post-Durban activities funded. Her positive personal assessment of our proposal did not result in financial support for the group. However, I believe she demonstrated her moral support and feminist solidarity by arranging for a veteran leader of the international women's movement to take part in our workshop.

Subhadra Mitra Channa has been a stalwart since she became active in the commission's core group seven years ago. I would like to acknowledge the instrumental role that her encouragement, occasional prodding, and exemplary intellectual vitality have played in helping me to sustain the drive that has kept me on track. On behalf of the commission, I would like to acknowledge the financial support that the Ford Foundation (through its New Delhi office) provided Subhadra, enabling her to travel to Durban, give a dynamic presentation, and come into meaningful contact with an extensive network of Dalit activists organizing against India's casteism. Esther Njiro became active in the commission around the time Subhadra came aboard. I am truly thankful to Esther for her warm collegiality over the past several years. I learned a great deal from her experiences as founding director of the Gender Studies Centre at the University of Venda. I also thank her for the kind hospitality she extended to me while I was in Pretoria, South Africa. Jan Delacourt has also been a member of the commission's core group since 1998, when we met at the International Union of Anthropological and Ethnological Sciences congress in Williamsburg, Virginia. I thank her for developing the first electronic communication network that helped to extend the commission's identity and field of praxis beyond the small core group. I especially appreciate Jan's sense of humor and the regular flow of positive reinforcement that made me feel more confident about this book and the commission's role in general.

Two others whom I would like to thank for helping to make this book a reality are Philomina Okeke and Maria Pedersen. Phil was one of several women who shared the space of the same bed and breakfast in Durban. Her lively and always insightful conversation, occasionally seasoned with pithy spiritual reflections, made our time together as enjoyable as it was thought provoking. I invited Maria Pedersen to join us in South Africa after Ann E. Kingsolver informed me about Pedersen's antiracist Aboriginal studies work, some of which she presented in a women's studies conference at the University of South Carolina. Maria found the means to travel to Durban with her sister, Ruth Bonner (who also presented a paper in our session), her children, and at least one of her children's friends. The conference was an event that strongly resonated with Maria's family and community's hopes and dreams.

My experience in Durban was particularly dear to me because I was able to share it with two women who have been both my friends and my students. Camille Hazeur pursued doctoral studies at the University of Tennessee, Knoxville, while she worked as an administrator in equity and diversity. Our mutual interests in the social construction of race have fueled fifteen years of traveling down parallel and intersecting paths. I thank Camille for her sharp intellect, her friendship, and for bringing so many interesting people together over such wonderfully nourishing meals. Melissa "Pooh" Hargrove is another student whom I have mentored. I have known her since she was an undergraduate and have had the privilege of witnessing her blossom into a full-fledged anthropologist. Melissa's trip to Durban was her first time outside the United States. I appreciate her for being honest, down to earth, and passionate about her scholarship and everything else she does. Working with her and Camille as well as with Nancy Anderson, Tracy Betsinger, Damien Borg, Scott Catey, Ana Cruz, Betty Duggan, Tanya Faberson, Brooke Hamby, Judith Hiscock, Lindsey King, Katherine Lambert-Pennington, Sarah Page, Shirley Rainey, Adam Renner, Joshua Schendel, Osagefo Sekou, Maria Veri, Marie Wallace, and others was absolutely the highlight of my years at the University of Tennessee.

There are many other people whose moral support, collegiality, conversations, and inspiration have made an important difference for me. I have shared important mutual interests with Willie Baber, Lee Baker, Angela Gilliam, Alan Goodman, Edmund Ted Gordon, Diana Hayman, Anne Francis Okongwu, Audrey Smedley, Arthur Spears, Frehiwot Tesfaye, Tony Whitehead, Ruth Wilson, and João Vargas. I thank Yvonne Jones for helping me get my first academic job and being a receptive sounding board. I want to express heartfelt appreciation to Pem Buck, Ann Kingsolver, Marilyn Thomas-Houston, and Gina Ulysse for believing in me and being in my "amen corner."

Louise Lamphere, an accomplished feminist anthropologist and a past president of the American Anthropological Association, has long been an important source of support and inspiration. Perhaps more than any of my un-dergraduate professors at Brown University, she encouraged me to follow my dreams. Her interest in my work has continued since she taught me in the early 1970s. I am sure that her presence on the *Annual Review of Anthropology* edito-rial committee had a great deal to do with why I was invited to write the re-view article on race that was published in 1995.

I also wish to acknowledge Yolanda Moses for her kindness and generos-ity. During her term as American Anthropological Association president, she widened the space within the profession for those interested in forging new directions in the study of race. Because of her influence, *American Anthropolo-gist* editor Robert Sussman invited me to guest edit the 1998 issue, *Contempo-rary Issues Forum: Race and Racism*. My conceptual overview for that collection of authoritative articles led to my being invited to an international conference on discrimination that the Danish Centre for Human Rights convened in 2000. I must thank Carolyn Fleuhr-Lobban for recommending me to George Ulrich, one of the conference organizers, and I thank George and his colleague Kirsten Hastrup, then director of the center, for giving me reason and oppor-tunity for shifting my research in a direction that locates racism and antiracism on the terrain of international human rights struggles. My preparations for, and attendance at, the Copenhagen conference made me aware of the significance of the 2001 World Conference against Racism and the complex politics sur-rounding the interpretation and enforcement of the international treaty out-lawing racial discrimination. In the midst of the Copenhagen conference and another human rights conference held in Atlanta, Georgia, later that year, I committed myself to going to Durban as both an advocate for social justice and as an anthropologist interested in investigating the workings of transborder al-liances dedicated to antiracist and antisexist activism in its various expressions.

I acknowledge the University of Tennessee for funding my travel to South Africa, and the University of Florida for giving me release time so that I could work on this book and another manuscript. The staff at AltaMira has been wonderfully patient and kind. I thank Rosalie Robinson, Sarah Scharf, Karstin Painter, and Scott Jerard for their professionalism and for making the publica-tion process both manageable and enjoyable. I would also like to recognize the role that Cathy Winkler played in getting this project off the ground by sug-gesting that I send the manuscript to AltaMira.

Last but certainly not least, I acknowledge the moral and intellectual sup-port that I have received throughout my career from my partner in life, William Conwill. For many years William has been developing antiracist and antisexist models for promoting mental health and healing. Our eldest son, Giles Harrison-Conwill, has been a refreshing source of stimulation and regeneration for both of us. Giles, now a graduate student in cultural anthropology, is teaching us a great deal about the discipline's current trends and new possibilities. I deeply appreciate his eagerness to share his intellectual explorations with his parents and his ambition to make his own footsteps rather than follow in mine.

My efforts at understanding the dynamics of resisting racism are more than an intellectual exercise, though intellectual objectives are certainly important. Resisting racism is, ultimately, about the concrete, politically grounded goal of making the world a better place for the next generation, which includes my sons Giles, Mondlane, and Justin. I hope this book will make a contribution toward that end.

Introduction

Global Perspectives on Human Rights and Interlocking Inequalities of Race, Gender, and Related Dimensions of Power

Faye V. Harrison

> I . . . noticed that the method of Anthropology—participant observation—was not very different from what I had used as an activist in community development work. I had to live among the people I worked with, observe what they did, why certain things made sense to them, and what motivated them. Participant observation is a prerequisite of any action which would try to change people's life circumstances.
>
> —Mamphela Ramphele, *Across Boundaries: The Journey of a South African Woman Leader*

*A*t a moment when anthropologists' interest in race and racism has been revitalized, it is important for at least some of our theory and practice as scholars, educators, and social critics to be informed and challenged by our having an ongoing dialogue with antiracist activists and advocates for human rights. For this reason, in 2001 several members of the International Union of Anthropological and Ethnological Sciences (IUAES) Commission on the Anthropology of Women (COTAW) went to Durban, South Africa, to participate in the World Conference against Racism, Racial Discrimination, Xenophobia, and Related Intolerance (WCAR), particularly its nongovernmental organization (NGO) Forum. We went because of our shared conviction that social scientific research on race's intersections with gender, ethnicity, national/transnational identity, and class can be enriched by the debates, social action, and political mobilization that occur in arenas influenced, in one way or another, by the international human rights system. We also believe that advocacy for women and racially subordinated peoples will benefit from the application of knowledge from the human sciences, especially the more holistic, interdisciplinary, and participatory varieties. Anthropologists who work on matters related to social suffering, inequality, and injustice are equipped to play an important role in this endeavor; however, we achieve these ends by positioning ourselves within interdisciplinary webs of connection and cross-fertilization—particularly those that blur the boundary between academic and nonacademic praxis.

The chapters of this book, including this introduction, have been inspired by this vision for a socially responsible and grounded anthropological praxis. Because that shared vision was reinforced and refined by the interactions and exchanges we had in Durban, it is worthwhile to address the significance of our experiences at the third international conference on racism organized by the United Nations (UN). I begin by recounting some of my own observations. From there, I examine the wider global context within which the WCAR and now the post-WCAR situation can be understood.

REMEMBERING DURBAN

During a late August afternoon in 2001, I stood in what felt like an eternal line waiting for my turn to pick up registration materials and then to be shown where I would have my photo ID made. That laminated badge would serve as my passport into the WCAR, the third such conference the UN had organized since an international convention (or treaty) had designated racism as a violation of human rights. I already had the identification I needed to participate in the WCAR NGO Forum that started a few days before the intergovernmental conference began. Once I got through that afternoon's registration process, I would have the main thing I needed to move back and forth between the two megameetings and, once the forum ended, to concentrate on attending the conference. I would remain in Durban even after my COTAW colleagues left for their respective homes in the United States, Canada, Italy, Australia, South Africa, India, and Japan. It was my intention to attend as much of the official conference as possible. I would also go to some of the post-WCAR activities, among them a symposium on racism and public policy sponsored by the UN Research Institute for Social Development. I would be able to do all this because I was the official representative of an international NGO, namely the IUAES, included on the UN secretary-general's roster and, as such, authorized to participate in UN conferences and the preparatory conferences leading up to them.

Like my colleagues and thousands of others, I had traveled to South Africa to witness and participate in the parallel meetings organized to bring the world's attention to racial oppression as a problem of global proportions and significance. Despite the confusion and disorganization that led the secretariat to lose my preregistration materials, I resisted letting my frustrations get the best of me. After all, I was pleased to have finally made it to South Africa with a group of twelve other wonderful women. My colleagues and I were in Durban as delegates of a commission that seeks to investigate and raise critical consciousness concerning the interlocking inequalities of gender, race, class, and national/transnational status. The women's commission, one of several units comprising the IUAES, provided an umbrella under which we had organized workshops for the NGO Forum. In them we addressed some of the ways that race in its mutually constitutive relationship with gender operates as a salient axis of power, conflict, and human rights abuse. We made a point to include nonanthropologists, activists, and practitioners so that our intellectual and cultural exchange would transcend the boundaries typically set by most academic discussions and so that it would be enriched by the perspectives and practical priorities of on-the-ground advocacy. That was our way to balance, complement, and integrate theory with practice and create some of the parameters for our shared praxis.

Because the IUAES commission values internationalism and advocacy, it participates in cross-cultural events that permit anthropologists to come into meaningful contact with people and organizations working for social transformation, specifically for forms of change that are consistent with principles of social justice and human rights. Toward that end, COTAW has found its way to UN forums and conferences where the predicaments and struggles of women and the racially oppressed have been addressed. In 1995 COTAW collaborated with a sister organization, the International Women's Anthropology Conference (IWAC), to organize workshops for the Fourth International Women's Conference in Beijing and the parallel NGO Forum in Huairou, a small town north of the capital. Among other things, anthropologist Eva Friedlander enlisted the assistance of the IWAC–COTAW network to serve as rapporteurs for the program of plenaries she was responsible for coordinating. Our rapid ethnographic "field notes" and, when possible, transcriptions of postplenary interviews fed into the reports and articles distributed to the thirty thousand delegates through the medium of a small but informative newspaper published daily during the NGO Forum. The plenaries on which I had been assigned to report had a major impact on my understanding of gender and such related inequalities as race and class within the contemporary, globalizing world. Due to the momentous impact that Beijing and Huairou 1995 had on me, I was confident that the WCAR would be as equally significant, especially for members of COTAW interested in working within the framework of a transnational feminism that is adamantly antiracist. Consequently, under the aegis of the IUAES, I invited colleagues from all over the world to participate in the ambitiously titled workshop, "Interlocking Dimensions of Difference and Power in Human Rights Conflicts: Racism in Culturally Diverse Gendered Experiences."

Our thirteen-person IUAES delegation participated in a truly significant global event in which more than three thousand NGOs from all over the world were involved. Among those NGOs were a critical mass of organizations that focused on the issues of racially subjugated women whose predicaments are shaped by gender and class as well as race. The WCAR NGO Forum therefore provided a setting for continuing and extending some of the discussions on "women's rights as human rights" held six years earlier in China. Those rights are spelled out in great detail in the Convention for the Elimination of All Forms of Discrimination against Women (CEDAW), a treaty that the United States has not (yet) ratified. The Beijing Declaration and Platform for Action adopted by the 1995 women's conference reinforced those rights and spelled out further mechanisms for their realization worldwide. The conspicuous presence of women's organizations at the WCAR signals at least two things: first, the extent to which women and those who depend on them for subsistence and well-being are suffering the brunt of racism's assaults and, second, the extent to which women are appearing in the forefront of local and translocal struggles against discrimination, which tend to be embedded in movements for democratic political participation; social, economic, and environmental justice; and more sustainable and humane forms of development. Women's activism is expanding the meanings and stretching the limits of antiracist and human rights politics. Their embodied knowledge and experience have a great deal to teach other activists about organizing against both racism and sexism. As Devaki Jain points out in her contribution here, Indian feminists who attended the WCAR recognized its potential for stimulating them to think in new ways about gender discrimination by exposing them to the harsh realities of racial discrimination.

Besides women's conspicuous voices, there were also other victims of discrimination who made their presence felt at the WCAR. While the international community expected the forum and conference to revolve around the grievances of the most paradigmatic racial subjects against white supremacy, the events in Durban challenged us all to expand the boundaries of racial discrimination beyond the traditional bipolarity (i.e., white–black binary opposition) to include the oppressions that are experienced by Indian Dalits, Eastern European Roma, Palestinians, and the much less-visible minorities in Central Africa we know as Pygmies. The discriminations these peoples experience are included in the UN convention against racism, which defines racial discrimination in broadly conceived terms. Anthropologist and antiracist activist Michael Banton has argued that:

> wherever there are encounters between persons who differ in respect of
> race, color, descent, ethnic or national origin, there is potential for racial dis-

crimination contrary to international law. The Convention offers protection to all of them, even to those who have earlier benefitted from the practice of racial discrimination. (1996, x–xi)

Durban expanded our awareness of the diversity of contexts within which, over time, various social differences may come to be "racialized" or to operate in ways that are very similar to "race" in its plural faces.

THE SIGNIFICANCE OF THE WCAR
IN THE UN HUMAN RIGHTS SYSTEM

At a moment when racialized conflicts appear to be escalating rather than declining in many places around the world, the urgent international relevance of the WCAR along with its declaration and program of action was, unfortunately, lost in the consciousness of most of the American public. This occurred in good measure because of how the conference was presented or misrepresented in the mass media. Its purpose was distorted in view of the United States government's opposition to its agenda. Months before the late summer event, news reports warned that the official American delegation might not participate because of objectionable positions included in the conference's draft declaration and platform for action. The most controversial issues were reparations for transatlantic slavery and colonialism and Israel's oppression of the Palestinian people. The United States took the position that the conference and forum were not appropriate settings for airing Palestinian grievances against Israel and U.S. foreign policy in the Middle East. In the government's view, the WCAR was "hijacked" by political "extremists" whom it refused to recognize as having legitimate voices. Yet, in spite of the official position, Americans, including members of the Congressional Black Caucus who were not there in their official capacity, attended the NGO Forum in large numbers. They, along with their international counterparts, represented a range of views and were not concentrated on an extreme end of the political continuum.

Unfortunately, the controversial issues that the WCAR attempted to bring to the public eye—as issues that implicate the faces of structural racism in many settings around the world—were abruptly erased from media attention by the tragic events of September 11 and how they have been interpreted within the United States'(and United Kingdom's) mainstream. The consequent preoccupation with fighting terrorism has, perhaps inadvertently, provided justification for a growing xenophobic patriotism that, in its worst cases, results in the "racial profiling" of "dangerous (Islamic) strangers."

The WCAR and its parallel forum were convened for the principal purpose of mobilizing support from governments, intergovernmental organizations, and NGOs for combating racist oppression and domination in their varied forms around the world (Harrison 2001). The fraternal twin meetings' immediate objective was to finalize the drafting of two sets of policy-relevant documents—declarations and programs of action collaboratively written from multiple and often conflicting perspectives. The writing of those documents was initiated in several preparatory conferences in the world's major regions and subregions that led up to the meetings in Durban, where the drafting was completed. The documents were the outcome of intense debate, pressures to compromise, and efforts to build some measure of consensus despite disagreements and even polarization over the most controversial issues—whose controversial character was magnified by the United States' threats and eventual decision to withdraw from the conference.

The forum and conference statements were meant to be twenty-first-century blueprints and guidelines for more effective strategies to combat and redress racism and the related intolerance that intersects it. As might be expected, the NGO Forum's declaration and program of action were more controversial than the documents that came out of the intergovernmental WCAR. Although not legally binding, world conference platforms have political import in that they are used by the most receptive, progressive states as guides or directives for legislative and institutional reform. Nongovernmental activists use them as leveraging tools, a resource for consciousness raising and popular education, and as international standards to which the actions of states and multinational entities can be held accountable. In the eyes of some sectors of the international community, the lobbying and negotiations that the preparatory conferences and the WCAR itself invested in these guidelines for action lend an important degree of legitimacy to the voices of change whose opposition to structural racism may make them vulnerable to the forces of containment and repression. However, legitimacy is not necessarily accompanied by the clout or "teeth" required to enforce compliance.

The WCAR and its NGO Forum—like the Fourth International Women's Conference and its parallel NGO Forum in 1995—were an extension of the UN human rights system. Within this system, there is an antiracism treaty—in theory, a legally binding instrument—called the International Convention on the Elimination of All Forms of Racial Discrimination (ICERD), which took effect in 1969. This convention, like others (notably CEDAW, which was adopted in 1979 and put into force in 1981), elaborates principles included in the UN Charter and in the Universal Declaration of Human Rights (UDHR). However, certain populations (e.g., women, children, the racially oppressed, refugees, and indigenous peoples) and policy areas (e.g., racism, development, environmental sustainability) were left in the realm of the implied and ambiguous in those original instruments. Hence, there has been a perceived need to make these rights—morally and legally defensible claims to just treatment—explicit in later generations of human rights codification (Messer 1993, 2002).

To promote the letter and spirit of the law expressed in ICERD, a committee is charged with monitoring compliance to ICERD, the Committee on the Elimination of Racial Discrimination (CERD). Since ICERD's adoption in 1969, there have been three world conferences (1978, 1983, 2001) and three decades to combat racism (1973–1982, 1983–1992, 1993–2002). The United States has refused to participate in all of the conferences, and the history of its lack of cooperation has been well documented in anthropologist Michael Banton's study (1996) of ICERD and CERD's monitoring activities, activities in which he himself participated as a committee member.

More recently, historian Carol Anderson (2003) offers provocative insights into the United States' highly ambivalent relationship to human rights instruments. She examines the beginnings of the UN and the political context within which the UN Charter and International Bill of Rights (i.e., the UDHR and the two covenants on political/civil and economic/social/cultural rights) were written. From the perspective of African American activists and the moderate and left-of-center organizations within which they worked, she shows how the human rights regime put into place in the wake of the Holocaust was compromised by the United States' concern with the boundaries of political expediency. Those boundaries were influenced by the government's wish not to offend or lose the support of its segregationist constituency, the Dixiecrat politicians and racist citizenry they represented.

Besides these domestic factors, the United States' role in organizing and setting limits on the UN was also influenced by its foreign policy objectives. Those objectives have led it to selectively apply human rights standards as a device to bring client states or potential client states into compliance with its geopolitical and economic regime. As I have written elsewhere,

> As the sole surviving superpower at the helm of the "free world," the USA has enormous economic, geopolitical, and military, ideological and cultural clout in the world today. It plays a leading role in human rights, but that role is circumscribed by the manner in which human rights are politicized as a propaganda tool for pursuing U.S.-centered interests. Paradoxically, as the purported paragon of democracy in the world, the U.S.A.'s domestic record of human rights leaves a great deal to be desired, particularly with respect to racism and the enforcement of criminal justice (e.g., prisoners of conscience, the death penalty) and women's rights (e.g., the Convention on the Elimination of All Forms of Discrimination against Women is still not ratified).

Although the U.S.A. signed the UN ICERD in 1966, its instrument of accession was not submitted until 1994, and it only submitted its initial report in September 2000. . . . Such slowly paced adherence . . . is due, in part, to "reservations" . . . expressed concerning some of the Conventions' articles, which appear to contradict the Constitution, particularly around interpretations of First Amendment rights. The U.S.A.'s record of compliance with other human rights treaties has been no less problematic. It has been especially recalcitrant concerning covenants on the social and economic rights that its neoliberal, neocolonial foreign policy violates. (2002a, 104–5)

From Banton's informative study, we know that when ICERD was adopted and later ratified, the signatory states were in accord that the treaty was imperative. Nonetheless, that consensus was based on their limited understanding of what racism was, beyond the most flagrant cases of Nazi Germany, South Africa, the United States (particularly in the Southern region of the country), and some aspects of the "tensions between" former colonial powers and newly sovereign states. Banton points out that the ratifying states that, in principle, agreed to the terms of the treaty did so for reasons having to do with foreign, rather than domestic, policy. They saw racism as a problem that belonged to "states other than their own" (Banton 1996, vii). In other words, ICERD was an ideological and legal device for completing the decolonization process and for exerting international pressure on other states (9). Beyond the paradigmatic cases, there was little understanding of the scope and diversity of racism, and there was resistance to the idea of applying the convention to states' own internal domestic conflicts, such as those related to indigenous peoples.

Much of CERD's work has involved expanding the international community's awareness of just how extensive racial discrimination still is and establishing the terms and mechanisms for holding states accountable to the standards set by international law. In many respects, CERD's work has been an uphill battle for more than thirty years. Contrary to naive or disingenuous claims, racism has not declined in significance. Indeed, in many parts of the world, it has intensified as well as morphed into new insidious guises (Harrison 1995, 1998). In some of these current configurations, ideas about "race" have shifted from those featuring biological criteria to culturalist notions that essentialize difference while denying the existence of biological races. In other words, it is not uncommon to find cases of "racism without races," or what I have characterized elsewhere as situations of unmarked racism (Harrison 2002a). Unmarked racism contributes to the ambiguity and confusion that complicate struggles to combat the symbolic and structural violence that peoples adversely affected by racial Othering are vulnerable to suffer.

RACE AND GENDER INTERSECTIONS:
IMPLICATIONS FOR THEORY AND PRACTICE

Race can be characterized as

> an ideologically charged distinction in social stratification and . . . a social
> and often legal classification applied to people presumed to share common
> physical or biological traits . . . [and/or] some socially salient ancestry . . .
> construed to be of social significance and consequence to the dominant so-
> cial order. . . . Racialized societies vary in the extent to which socially salient
> ancestry, appearance, and sociocultural status (e.g., education, income,
> wealth) are used as criteria for assigning race. . . . Social definitions and le-
> gal codifications of racial and related . . . distinctions have historically played
> a major role in "naturalizing" or representing as naturally produced and un-
> changeable the markedly unequal and unjust distribution of wealth, power,
> and prestige. (Harrison 2002b, 145)

Racism is often defined largely in terms of prejudice and belief; however,
a more holistic way of viewing it is as "a system of material relationships with
a set of ideas linked to and embedded in those material relations" (Frankenberg 1993, 70). It involves social practices, whether intended or not, that perpetuate an oppressive structure of power relations. In other words, racism can
be reproduced and sustained in the absence of race-centered prejudice. Moreover, even actions intended to be antiracist may unwittingly have racializing,
rather than deracializing, effects (Dominguez 1994; Wetherell and Potter
1993). Consequently, racism is an enduring social problem with serious implications for social and economic justice, political conflict, and struggles for human dignity. It is a problem that assumes diverse domestic forms as well as
global significance. As Karen Brodkin (2000) has reminded us, racial exploitation plays a central role in global capitalism. According to her analysis, along
with those of a number of feminist scholars (Alexander and Mohanty 1997;
Collins 1998; hooks 1984), race is an axis of difference, inequality, and power
that does not operate in isolation as a condition separable from other forms of
inequality—with gender, class, and ethnicity or ethnonational identity being
key among them. Many of the participants at WCAR were cognizant of how
entangled and embedded race is as one dimension among others in matrices
of power in which interlocking hierarchies become volatile sites of conflict
over needs, rights, and obligations.

Studies of women's identities, experiences, and social positionings are impoverished without nuanced, multifocal analysis of these kinds of complexities.
Intersectionality perspectives are among the conceptual tools that antiracist feminists, both scholars and activists, are finding useful for achieving that important

goal (Crenshaw 1991). An important implication of this approach is that the human rights system, which includes the UN along with an international network of NGOs and intergovernmental organizations, needs to look more closely at the potential points of convergence between advocacy groups deploying ICERD and CEDAW (S. James 2002). This conjoined space can potentially have important possibilities for coalition building and strategies for meaningful change that take into account the predicaments of women subjected to racist, xenophobic, and often class-biased patriarchy. As reflected in many of the workshops, plenaries, and caucus meetings in Durban, increasing numbers of race-cognizant activists are thinking along these lines. Models of intersectionality have as their origins the experiences of women of color who have felt compelled to craft alternative paradigms for making sense of and theorizing inequality, discrimination, and oppression. In the context of the United States, the homogenizing terms once used by middle-class white feminists to conceptualize women's oppression and those articulated by racially subordinate men to explain and transform racism have tended to neglect racially marked women and the particular ways they embody gender and race.

RACISM INTENSIFYING ON A GLOBAL SCALE

Political, social, and economic human rights violations—and the inequalities in power and resources that permit them—appear to be on the rise (Harrison 1995, 2002c). Within this context, there has been an intensification of those forms of discrimination and violence that target racially subordinated populations (Harrison 1995, 2002a). Women bear the brunt of much of the discrimination perpetrated against racially subordinated people. If we follow the reasoning of the feminist political theorist Cynthia Enloe (1990, 1993), we find that gendered assumptions and biases underlie the policies and processes (such as those associated with structural adjustment, welfare reform, and militarization) that contribute to the abuse of women. I would like to extend Enloe's claim by arguing that precepts concerning racialized gender and gendered race underpin the structural violence that assaults racially subjugated subjects (Harrison 2002c).

   Structural violence is a concept I define as being "the symbolic, psychological, and physical assaults against human subjectivities, physical bodies, and sociocultural integrity that emanate from situations and institutions structured in social, political, and economic dominance" (Harrison 1997, 457; also see Farmer 2003, 9). Paul Farmer argues that, until recently, social scientists have, for the most part, neglected to analyze "structural violence and the abuses it inevitably breeds" (2003, 12). He is especially critical of anthropology's "diverted gaze" and implores anthropologists to interrogate the "economically driven" "macrologics of power" that guarantee that human rights abuse will occur (9). The challenge before us is to expose and explicate those conditions "without sacrificing ethnographic depth."

HUMAN RIGHTS AND GLOBALIZATION

Many advocates and researchers argue that human rights appear to be in increased jeopardy under the conditions of globalization, especially the neoliberal form dominant today. As Alison Brysk points out, "the very blurring of borders and rise of transnational actors that facilitated the development of a global human rights regime may also be generating *new* sources of human rights abuse" (2002, 1). Before we proceed to question or substantiate this view, the key notions of human rights and globalization require further clarification.

Human rights may be understood to be the morally and legally justifiable claims to dignity, liberty, personal security, and basic well-being that all persons can make by virtue of being human. The safeguards delineated in declarations, covenants, and conventions represent international standards and principles that states are expected to uphold and protect. All members of the UN are supposed to comply with UN charter–derived instruments or doctrines, while the states that sign and ratify conventions—which are, in theory, legally binding treaties—are obligated to comply with them. This is the theory behind international human rights law. The reality, however, fails to live up to the ideal, a utopian vision for just and humane treatment for all human beings. Rights are defined as just, legally enforceable claims; however, most of the abstract norms or standards spelled out in human rights instruments are difficult to enforce, especially within the context of an international human rights regime without sufficient capacity to enforce its standards in a conflict-laden world where disparities of wealth, health, and power are widening.

Well beyond the formal and too-often self-serving acceptance of covenants and conventions, human rights represent an important set of ideals and goals for social change. In the aftermath of the Cold War, human rights have come to be the most globally intelligible and accepted political values in the world. In some important respects, the language of human rights fills the vacuum created by the "demise of [the former] grand political narratives" (Wilson 1997, 1). Of course, rights discourse is only one language of protest and power (Mamdani 2000). A major contender is "culture talk," which is often deployed to legitimize the state power of postcolonial elites in Africa and Asia. In those settings, collective and cultural rights figure prominently in national discourses in which the universal rights of individuals are problematized as impositions from Western cultural imperialism. However, individual rights cannot be reduced to this danger, for individuals, notably women, are often at risk of being abused within contexts in which sectarian power and privilege are naturalized by manipulating essentialist notions of culture and cultural authenticity.

Farmer (2003) also recognizes discourses that compete with human rights language elaborated around models of charity, liberation theology, and development. These discourses also provide vocabularies and strategies for redressing widespread poverty and indigent illnesses. These languages are not necessarily mutually exclusive. For example, although fraught with contradictions, development discourse, even that which the World Bank espouses, recognizes or pays lip service to human rights. Martin Chanock (2000, 33) describes the bank's nominal recognition of economic and social rights—"once the ideological preserve of communist and socialist rhetoric on rights." The logic is that with economic growth, a country's populace will benefit from "poverty reduction . . . [and] lending for 'human resource development.'" However, the bank's programs have rarely lived up to this supposed goal, and, as a consequence, economic and social rights have eroded through the destruction of state-based programs that provided safety nets.

Human rights, whose application is a transnational process, offer guidelines for consciousness raising and social praxis within global civil society. The language and instruments offer a normative discourse on human needs and dignity as well as a global vocabulary for addressing the discrepancy between ideals and realities. At their most effective, human rights are a moral and legal device for constraining the flow of unreasonable and illegitimate state power. They constitute a transnational field in which universal doctrine is translated, vernacularized, and transformed across time and cultural/political differences. This process of translation and transformation is integral to the universalization of rights. Universalization is a process requiring dialogue across nations as well as within them (An-Na'im 1992). This process is necessary for developing the legitimacy and efficacy of international human rights.

Ellen Messer (1997) advocates seeking a middle-ground position in debates over universalism versus cultural relativism in human rights. In her view, the evolving body of human rights instruments has plural sources and intersecting histories across four major phases or generations. The first generation produced the UDHR, which was drafted mainly by Western nations in the wake of World War II. This document emphasizes individualized political and civil rights as the cornerstones of human rights. Moving beyond the assumptions of liberal ideology, other philosophical traditions both within the West and outside of it took the view that while political and civil rights may be necessary, they are not sufficient for protecting human dignity and justice. Hence, the second generation of rights codification, influenced by socialist and welfare state–oriented nations, shifted attention to the rights that the International Covenant on Economic, Social, and Cultural Rights guaranteed. To a large extent, these rights are being eroded by current neoliberal policies, whose ideas are being globalized (Kingfisher and Goldsmith 2001).

The third generation shifted attention to development and collective rights, insisting that individual and collective rights be balanced against each other and rethought as being mutually reinforcing rather than mutually exclusive. We are currently in the midst of the fourth generation, in which the rights of indigenous people and refugees are being considered more closely. Instruments devoted to these rights are now being drafted. They are likely to push against the limits of the state-centeredness of most human rights doctrine because indigenous self-determination and control over economic resources and the transnational identity and long-distance nationalism of immigrants and refugees raise major challenges to the purview of states and the identities of nations. Jonathan Friedman (1994) has argued that the weakening and crisis of national identity are the outcome of cultural processes that global economic forces engender. To gain a clearer sense of this global context, we will examine what the global restructuring of economic relations entails.

The concept of globalization is used and abused in a number of different ways, sometimes muddling issues that urgently need to be clarified. Arguing that globalization has a history that goes back centuries, Ted Lewellen underscores the historical specificity of contemporary globalization. He defines the most current phase or moment of globalization as

> the increasing flow of trade, finance, culture, ideas, and people brought about by the sophisticated technology of communications and travel and by the worldwide spread of neoliberal capitalism, and it is the local and regional adaptations to and resistance to these flows. (2002, 708)

In Lewellen's view, the global order, with its cultural, ideological, political, and economic dimensions, is being restructured in accordance with a neoliberal logic. Neoliberalism can be understood as an ideology promoting unfettered marketization; privatization; a minimalist state that enables unregulated commodity exchange; a decrease in state expenditures for human welfare ("but sometimes paradoxically with increasing state interference . . . in social [and political] arenas"); and possessive, competitive individualism (Kingfisher and Goldsmith 2001, 716). Catherine Kingfisher and Michael Goldsmith, however, argue that neoliberalism is more than just an ideology. In their view, it is "a *cultural* system that makes certain claims about the economy, the proper role of the state, and the nature of personhood that, in turn, serve to organize society in highly gendered [and, I would interject, racialized and classed] ways" (716, emphasis mine).

The global spread of this logic has profound consequences for the direction that economic restructuring takes, especially in the aftermath of the Cold War, when debt-ridden countries have had few, if any, viable alternatives to the development policies that the International Monetary Fund (IMF) and World Bank impose. These institutions, along with agencies such as the United States Agency for International Development (USAID), "have a great deal of power . . . and they use it to push neoliberal principles and policies" (MacEwan 1999, 10). However, it is important to note that these policies are pushed and enforced selectively, according to a double standard or "an asymmetric practice" that the United States imposes on its competitors and clients (Amin 2003, 20). According to Egyptian political economist Samir Amin, the United States "would not be able to [retain its competitive advantage] were it not for the recourse to extra-economic means, a clear violation of the principles of [neo]liberalism the U.S. imposed on its competitors" (18).

Economist Arthur MacEwan claims that the contradictory neoliberal regime that dominant capital imposes on the world is a major obstacle to building a more democratic form of economic development. Significantly, his analysis underscores the importance of not limiting our understanding and expectations of democracy to elections and formally representative government, leaving the economic realm outside the reach of genuinely democratic debate and decision making, the kind of decision making that would challenge and counteract the forces of structural power as it is currently constituted.

Concerned particularly with the impact of "free," but not necessarily "fair," market policies on women, Manisha Desai (2002, 19) claims that the IMF, World Bank, and USAID are institutions that "prioritize the market rather than women's economic and social empowerment." She goes on to point out how the drastic budget-balancing acts, cutbacks, restraints on wage increases, and debt servicing associated with mandated structural adjustment packages have had patterned consequences for women both at work and at home. A racialized feminized proletariat has become a central component of the global labor force—both its formal and informal segments—and women's unpaid labor at home has increased as women are forced to make up for the government's retreat from safety-net provisioning.

The reasons that human rights abuses are escalating in so many parts of the world are complex. However, in part, this troubling state of affairs can be attributed to the virtual immunity with which transnational agents operate in relation to nation-states. Neoliberalism rationalizes, even naturalizes, this immunity. Under these circumstances, peripheral states, concentrated in the global South or the world system's periphery, are especially vulnerable. Their ability to protect rights to education, health, and humane work standards has been drastically compromised by internationally mandated policies and programs (e.g., structural adjustment) that give higher priority to corporate rights, the rights of transnational elites to accumulate capital, than to the basic needs and rights of the majority of human beings.

While the social contracts that states (that is, the more democratic states) may have once had with their populations have eroded, the repressive role of state power has clearly not. Indeed, in many cases, Western, particularly American, foreign aid packages include generous provisions for police and military upgrading (see, e.g., Harrison 2002c). Due to the free or unregulated market in arms, intergroup tensions are more likely to escalate into militarized and, at worst, genocidal conflicts. Of course, these problems are not restricted to the southern hemisphere or Third World, for they have northern variants as well. For example, while the IMF and World Bank prescribed structural adjustment programs throughout the debt-ridden South, in the United States and the United Kingdom, the 1980s Reaganomics and Thatcherism authorized the shift to safety-net slashing, market-friendly policies more or less equivalent to structural adjustment in their political-economic logic and effects. The far-flung search for cheaper supplies of labor and deregulated zones of manufacturing or processing has, in part, been played out in the serious expansion of the prison-industrial complex with its captive, "concentrated labor" force (Buck 1992) coerced into working for little or no wages. This late modern form of slavery disproportionately exploits men and women of color who are racially marked with the visible injuries of class subjugation (Buck 1992; Davis 2003; J. James 1998).

GLOBAL PERSPECTIVES ON RACE, GENDER, AND HUMAN RIGHTS

The chapters and poetry selection compiled in this volume represent the thinking and passions of a diverse network of women and a male ally. We live in the United States, Canada, France, Italy, South Africa, Australia, and India. Our international diversity can be extended even more, however, because the immigrants or transmigrants among us are originally from Haiti, Egypt, Nigeria, Kenya, Zanzibar, and Zimbabwe. Ten of us are anthropologists, mainly based in academic or other research settings as researchers, administrators, professors, and graduate students. The other six bring additional disciplinary and professional perspectives to the dialogue—women's studies, Chinese literature, Aboriginal studies, economics, and education. Five contributors were invited to participate in the project largely due to their knowledge and experience as activists. However, several more embrace some form of a scholar–activist identity, which has influenced the form and content of our scholarship.

Four of the authors did not participate in the Durban workshops. Cheryl Fischer, Gina Ulysse, and the coauthors Mohamed Saleh and Fatma Jiddawi Napoli were invited to participate in the workshops but were unable to because of extenuating circumstances. Fortunately, Fischer was able to attend the WCAR, although she arrived too late to be a part of the NGO Forum workshops. Fadwa El Guindi—a respected anthropologist, filmmaker, and public intellectual—was not part of the Durban group but was invited to contribute a chapter. We believed that it was imperative that an articulate and knowledgeable Arab and Muslim voice be included, especially given the post–September 11 climate.

The contributing authors provide provocative views on an array of topics and issues related to the racial, ethnonational, and gendered aspects of varied conflicts over social injustice and human rights. These wide-ranging issues are situated in both the global North and South, offsetting the tendency in so much of the literature to zoom in on human rights violations perpetrated in the South and East while neglecting the problems of the North. Even international human rights NGOs have followed this trend. Today, however, the international human rights community is well aware of the United States' failure to comply with many international standards.

Post-WCAR and Post–September 11 Reflections from the South

Devaki Jain, a prominent feminist economist, offers a perspective from India on the significance of the WCAR, especially from the perspectives of Dalits and feminists who saw the UN conference and forum as a space for "facilitating justice" and for linking their agendas with international alliances opposed to racial discrimination. She explores the problems, as well as the necessity, of building politically enabling identities and solidarities. The need for critical solidarity is especially significant in the post–September 11 context, which is marked by a growing unipolarity in world power and a troubling shift to a rhetoric of "clashing civilizations" and religions, an idiom more reminiscent of the Crusades than reflective of contemporary realities.

Jain brings an interesting perspective to bear on the multiple identities and struggles "at the bottom of the ladder of social exclusion and stigma." That convergent social bottom is a space of socioeconomic oppression. This is the space to which she directs much of her attention. She underscores the importance of grounding a rights perspective "in economic issues such as poverty" and—drawing on Arundhati Roy's speech at the World Social Forum in Porto Alegre, Brazil (2003)—grounding that sense of human rights in an opposition to the corporate globalization leading to the commodification of food, water, air, and even "the dreams we dream." She sees continued relevance in Gandhi's exemplary ethic for reducing social and economic distances by effacing "dif-

ference through absorption of the Other." To eradicate poverty—or by implication any other *ism*—activists should consider adopting a practice of identifying with the poor—that is, living among them, engaging in everyday forms of
pragmatic solidarity to promote the dismantling of discrimination and the assertion of justice.

Communities in Crisis and Struggle

Human rights, both their assertion and abuse, are not only ethical and politico-
legal concerns but also concerns that are often more abstract than concrete in
the manner in which they are represented. Human rights are claimed, embodied, and contested in the everyday lives of ordinary people in households and
communities, formal and informal workplaces, and public spaces of cooperative action or conflict.

Subhadra Mitra Channa follows up on some of the questions Jain raises
about Dalit mobilization at home and in the space of the UN conference in
Durban. In a sense, she has perhaps inadvertently taken up the Gandhian ethic
by immersing herself in the everyday life of the *Dhobis* individuals and families she has studied as an ethnographer. Going beyond stereotypes and mystifi-
cations, Channa illuminates the internal cultural logic of caste, untouchability
in particular, highlighting its most striking parallels with the social phenomenon of race. Although untouchability was outlawed upon India's independence, she demonstrates how it nonetheless persists in the fabric of civil society and in the complicity, if not the official legal stance, of the state. Her
intriguing interpretation of color symbolism and of the metaphors around
which the discourse of caste distinctions is expressed uncovers invidious assumptions strikingly similar to those underpinning the language of race in settings such as the United States.

Her analysis of the ways that caste and gender intersect in the everyday life
of Dalit women is especially insightful. Critical of most double- or triple-
discrimination arguments, she focuses instead on Dalit women's agency and self-
esteem, characteristics that often distinguish them from their less-independent
counterparts in more-privileged castes.

Before defining and mobilizing themselves as Dalits, untouchables shared
no unified identity among their widely dispersed communities. As both Jain and
Channa indicate, today Dalit identity denotes power and the exercise of rights
within a vibrant Indian democracy. At the WCAR, Dalits—including Dalit
women—were well represented, exhibiting their capacity to organize themselves across educational levels, gender, and region, differences that could very
easily divide them. Jain points out that the quest for unity was so intense that
many Dalit women's organizations placed greater discursive focus on caste than

on gender. Nonetheless, one might infer that Dalit women's ability to develop organizations focused on their problems as women suggests that both caste and gender are very much a part of their underlying practical consciousness.

J. Maria Pedersen, an indigenous social justice activist, takes us to Australia's Aboriginal communities where social inequality and unevenly distributed democratic rights have been strongly felt since early colonial times. She writes from the perspective of one who has experienced the compounded stigma of being Aboriginal, a woman, and a single mother in a community in which high unemployment, malnutrition, miseducation, racial profiling, police brutality, and youth suicide are prevalent. These are problems that Australia's dominant ideology naturalizes by claiming that Aboriginal criminality, sexuality, and fertility are driven by distinctive biological traits and pathologies, a threat that must be contained.

Pedersen resists this stigma in light of the knowledge gained from a critical rethinking of Australia's past. In this alternative history, Aboriginals have been vital agents struggling for the rights of self-determination and full citizenship denied them even in present-day Australian democracy. Relegated to the margins of that so-called democratic system, they have found ways to resist assimilationist policies designed to breed them out as though they were livestock rather than human beings. At the height of that colonial climate, mixed-heritage children were coercively taken out of Aboriginal communities. They and their indigenous kin were denied the means of family life and cultural identity integral to the International Covenant on Economic, Social, and Cultural Rights

Cheryl Fischer's discussion on the state of civil and human rights in the Ozarks region of southwest Missouri is written from the vantage point of an African American woman who has been involved in both grassroots and transnational politics for many years. She makes us acutely aware of the regional biases in media coverage as well as in the priorities of civil and human rights NGOs (e.g., the NAACP) in the United States. Gross human rights violations in the Ozarks, a region that she characterizes as the American "outback," have remained largely invisible despite efforts of activists such as herself to put them before the nation's public eye. She also criticizes the feminist movement for neglecting the issues that preoccupy the women with whom she works. Those women are largely African American and Latina along with Euro-American women with biracial families. They all have had to confront—or have had close relatives who confronted—hate crimes and discrimination at work, in school, in the criminal justice system, and within state agencies charged with providing children's services. Moreover, heinous hate crimes such as lynching are still occurrences with which communities of color in this part of the country contend.

In forthright practical terms, Fischer asks how the WCAR program of action can be relevant to the communities she describes. Not only does she raise this question, but she also goes to the next step by delineating a number of useful recommendations toward a concrete plan of action. She challenges us all to go beyond talking about human rights and justice to finding practical strategies for getting the work done and for building effective links between transnational arenas such as the UN and the everyday life of households, communities, and the organizations that serve them at the local level.

Helen Safa's chapter offers a compelling cultural critique of the sexual racist stigma endured by single mothers, particularly in African American communities but also in the Hispanic Caribbean. She brings considerable insights from her Caribbean work into her examination of racism in the United States, household dynamics, marriage, unwed motherhood, and significant shifts in welfare policy over the course of time. She provides the necessary historical context within which to think critically about the most recent trends in welfare reform, which emphasize personal responsibility and the work ethic.

Safa's analysis sheds important light on the social context in which what she calls citizenship rights, or the social and economic rights that have been respected in European social democracies, are profoundly underdeveloped if not altogether denied. Her analysis also illuminates a racial order that deploys ideas of sociocultural differences (namely, family dysfunction and deviance) rather than explicit notions of biological determinism. She convincingly demonstrates how the dismantling of the welfare state in the United States is a political process feeding on racialized meanings, relations, and practices. This process is not unlike that eliminating public safety nets in many other parts of the world. A common logic of state minimalism is at work (Kingfisher and Goldsmith 2001).

Sexual Matters

Matters of sexuality and power are inextricably entangled with the cultural politics and political economy of race and gender intersections. Women's bodies and sexualities are sites on which national sovereignty is fought, economic development strategies are pursued, and health crises negotiated. Melissa D. Hargrove begins the discussion on sexual matters by directing our attention to the human rights abuses that tourism engenders, particularly in contexts reorganized by structural adjustment programs and other neoliberal policies. She describes how the recolonization of "body, identity, and culture" that tourism promotes compromises women's health, work opportunities, and life chances in significant ways that deserve further scrutiny. The marketing of the "tourism experience" has become a global pattern of exploitation in which vulnerable populations, women in particular, are relegated to the ranks of exoticized objects of northern tourist consumption. Desperate to survive, often under circumstances of economic austerity induced by neoliberal policies, these women find themselves "drawn into an exploitative system based upon racial, gendered, and class inequalities," which are being reproduced and deepened under conditions of current-day globalization.

Although her range of vision extends to sites in Asia as well as those on the Internet, Hargrove focuses on the role of sex workers in tropicalized tourist zones in the African diaspora, namely the Caribbean and Brazil, where blackness and hypersexuality are marketed. In these illicit transactions, sex workers are demonized as promiscuous deviants rather than being viewed as workers who deserve to have their human rights respected. Although sex workers' rights are hard to protect because of the illegality of the occupation and the rampant nature of police brutality and government corruption, some sex workers have organized themselves to claim their rights "as women . . . workers . . . and citizens." Hargrove closes her chapter by insisting that it is not enough for anthropologists to document human rights violations. She urges them to find ways to "act upon the world," beginning in "our own back yards" and "in our own everyday lives."

Esther Njiro is a Kenyan anthropologist who acts on the world as an applied researcher in South Africa. Her contribution here is a timely examination of the gender and racial intersections that shape the present HIV/AIDS pandemic and its implications for social and economic development in South Africa and elsewhere on the continent of Africa. In her view, the difficulties that heterosexual women experience in enjoying safe, consensual sex is a significant human rights dilemma.

Her analysis provides an insightful cultural and political economy of African women's poverty, their economic dependency on men, and their risk for contracting HIV/AIDS. She underscores the significance of gender in conditioning power relations between women and men and in shaping the cultural dynamics and social norms fueling "the pandemic and influenc[ing] its impact."

Njiro sketches the historical development of apartheid and patriarchy in South Africa to highlight the major structural, as well as psychological, forces that have put women at a serious disadvantage. Given the gross socioeconomic disparities and migration patterns, women have often been impelled to exchange sexual services for "money, security, and favors." She challenges us to see that interventions in health care and health education require a holistic approach that confronts a complex web of causality going well beyond the personal responsibility of individuals to wider cultural dynamics and the workings of macroeconomic institutions.

Fatma Jiddawi Napoli and Mohamed Saleh are Zanzibari transmigrants and "long distance nationalists" (Glick Schiller and Fouron 2001). In their chapter, they examine the social suffering that Zanzibari women and their families face when women's bodies are sexually violated in the politically charged context of Zanzibar's struggle against Tanzania for sovereignty. The authors argue that sexual violence is a tactic deployed to intimidate and demoralize the Zanzibari people, inhibiting them from demanding their "inalienable human and democratic rights." In the immediate wake of British colonial rule, Zanzibar enjoyed formal independence. However, within only a month of independence, a coup d'etat propelled events that led to the small Indian Ocean archipelago being forced into a union with Tanganyika and becoming part of the United Republic of Tanzania.

In the authors' view, the tensions between Zanzibar and Tanganyika have a gendered character. Zanzibar has been feminized and denied a voice in a "forced marriage" consummated by "rape" rather than by a genuinely consensual union. Beyond the sexual symbolism of Zanzibar's political subjugation, there is also a sexual and racial politics of on-the-ground human rights abuse. For example, under the pretext of promoting "racial harmony" between "Africans" and "Arabs," marriages have been "arranged" by the state between older mainlander government officials and young girls of mixed African, Arab, and Indian descent without the young women's, or their parents', consent. This practice has been justified as being a retaliation for Arab men's having exploited African women as concubines in the past.

As part of a wider context of human rights abuse, the rape of women, and even that of children and men, has silenced many families, compelling them to abandon their political activities "for fear of reprisals" and public shame. Despite this intimidation, Zanzibaris—both at home and in the diaspora—have refused to retreat from the struggle for freedom and democracy. Not resigning themselves to victimhood, women are playing key roles in mobilizing against ethnocide and for their country's political emancipation. Napoli and Saleh express their belief that a truth-and-reconciliation commission would help their country come to terms with its history of disappearances, massacres, and rapes, as well as help it to "create conditions for a sustainable peace . . . based on principles of . . . forgiveness." The principled tolerance they attribute to the historic Zanzibari city-state and Swahili melting pot is what they envision for their nation's not-too-distant future.

New Diasporas: Refugees and Immigrants

Philomina Okeke's chapter takes us from the African continent to a transmigrant setting in Canada. Her analysis of a new diaspora focuses on the experiences of African women in Edmonton, the capital of the province of Alberta. She is particularly concerned with understanding their resilience and resourcefulness in the face of racism. Most of the women she examines belong to middle-class families that migrated to Canada in search of economic stability and improvement. They have also been fairly successful in establishing support networks and resistance strategies that meet their local needs as well as influence political and economic conditions in their home communities and nations in Africa.

She situates contemporary diaspora formation in the context of global restructuring and the population flows that it engenders, noting that these processes give rise to practices and policies that are racist and racializing. She aligns her analysis with postcolonial feminist critiques of development, highlighting the part African female scholars have played in developing theoretically appropriate modes of inquiry. This newer trend in the political economy of knowledge production is significant in light of earlier trends homogenizing and exoticizing African women as the Western feminist's Other.

Okeke argues that the transnational space linking diasporic sites to Africa is a central feature of immigrant life. Because of this, she insists on the difference between old-style immigrants, as they have been characterized in the literature, and transmigrants. Glick Schiller and Fouron (2001), however, encourage us to be more cautious about this distinction and the assumptions underlying it. They claim that earlier generations of immigrants also found ways to maintain their connections with and allegiances to the old country while busily planting roots in the United States and Canada. In light of this insight, the fluid, multiple identities and situations that Okeke observes African women negotiating may be consistent with their being both immigrants and transmigrants.

Okeke claims that the WCAR played an enabling role that enhanced antiracist activism within the new African diasporas. The UN conference gave diasporic activists a space in which to evaluate their experiences as new immigrants and transmigrants with distinctive problems. Okeke points out that in the United States and Canada, Africans are often placed in a stereotyped "black pool" without regard to the unique challenges they face vis-à-vis black communities with more distant African origins lying in the population dispersions during the transatlantic slave trade. The socially and culturally specific characteristics of different waves of black migrants (from the United States, the Caribbean, and Africa) have led to variable experiences of, and responses to, racism in Canadian society.

Jan Delacourt takes an interesting look at an immigrant situation in Northern Italy in which Kosovo refugees have settled, perhaps temporarily, in the town of Ivrea at the invitation of the town council. The support that local volunteers provided led to an outcome that has been deemed relatively successful compared to other instances of refugee resettlement. Delacourt conducted a dialogic style of fieldwork to explore the meanings of difference not only for refugees, asylum seekers, and immigrants but also for Northern Italians. She found many in the host community with personal histories that relate existential principles for "living [their] own differences." Delacourt levels the analytical plane by blurring the boundaries between citizens and aliens, natives and newcomers, Italian and non-Italian. Her investigation is organized around a dialogue between these categories of people, who "ask questions of each other's experiences," recognizing that valuable knowledge flows from both sides.

In her reflections on "differences that divide" and create unjust privileges and deprivations, Delacourt points to her own family's experiences in colonial Rhodesia as well as to Italians' experience with fascism and regional animosities between Northerners and Southerners (stigmatized as "Africans"). She argues that differences experienced through personal and interpersonal strategies of resistance and integration at home, work, and in civil society occur in a "third space," "neither the old margin nor the co-opted center." The third space is a locus where women's agency, inclusiveness, solidarity are exercised and where Otherness is converted into a space for building alliances and community. This space cannot exist without interrogating racial/national/gender privileges, particular those associated with "whiteness," often an unmarked dimension of European identity. Delacourt also urges listening "for and to the voices of those caught in the intersections of many forms of discrimination." Many of them are refusing their status and standing up for their rights.

We close this section on new diasporas with a selection that is not a chapter in the conventional sense. Instead, we present a poem written by an anthropologist, Haitian-born Gina Ulysse. Ulysse's career as an intellectual encompasses social scientific writing, filmmaking, and *ethnoperformance*. Ethnoperformance involves modes of creative expression that assume varied forms: spoken word, dance, and other kinds of creative productions. Ulysse is among those, including me (Harrison 1990), who advocate developing anthropologically informed performative practices as one among many strategies for reaching wider audiences and raising critical consciousness. Multigenre forms of artistic/cultural production are evocative of meanings, perceptions, and experiences difficult to express through the conventions of normal social science. These may be dimensions of knowing that resonate with potential audiences.

Ulysse's written poetry and spoken word art are more than an avocation or hobby. She is a versatile intellectual, cultural worker, and artiste with a remarkably extensive toolkit at her disposal. Her politics and poetics are recognized among Haitian Americans' most exemplary cultural expressions. For example, her poetry (Ulysse 2001) is included in *The Butterfly's Way: Voices from the Haitian Diaspora in the United States*, an anthology edited by the renowned writer Edwidge Danticat (2001).

Although the textualized presentation of Ulysse's poetry cannot do justice to the powerful cadences that can be appreciated fully only in the context of a live performance, "My Country in Translation" is nonetheless a poignant expression of her reflexive, autoethnographic perspective on Haiti and Haitian refugees in the United States. The poem touches on her experience as an immigrant struggling to come to terms with the social sufferings that Haitians bear. Those sufferings, however, do not end with migration. For the most part, Haitian refugees are not welcome in the United States, and their ambiguous and highly contested status as asylum seekers raises serious questions concerning the human rights of refugees and black immigrants. In her effort to assist and express her solidarity with her compatriots, she has volunteered to serve as an interviewer and interpreter for the Haitian Refugee Asylum Project. She understands that this service carries a heavy responsibility. Her translations, or *mis*translations, could have serious consequences, perhaps influencing whether the refugees are allowed to remain in the country or are deported. If deported, they may be sentenced to death by default.

Ulysse has lived in the United States since her childhood—long enough to speak English fluently without a foreign accent and to lose some of her competency in Kreyòl, a full-fledged language with its own regional and class dialects. Differences in vocabulary, idioms, and pronunciation complicate communication between newly arrived refugees and a diasporic Haitian whose everyday life demands that she speak English most of the time. Beyond sociolinguistic issues, there are other issues at stake. Haiti is not just the impoverished, politically corrupt country from which emigrants and refugees are lucky to escape. It is a beloved place they long for and dream of as members of the Tenth Department (*Dizyèm Depatman-an*). Haiti has nine departments, or provinces. In a speech marking his new position as democratically elected president in 1991, Jean-Bertrand Aristide designated the Haitian diaspora as the Tenth Department, acknowledging the integral role that the diaspora plays through remittances and other contributions to the impoverished nation-state (Basch et al. 1994, 1).

Ulysse is a part of that Tenth Department, and this transborder positionality gives her a useful vantage from which to interrogate and interpret the interrelationship among race, nation, migration, and human rights. She understands that assaults against Haitians' human rights both at home and abroad implicate a hemispheric and global regime that blames Haiti for its own problems and relegates it to the bottom of interlocking hierarchies of nations, cultures, and races (Farmer 1992). "My Country in Translation" evokes the intense dilemma of a Haitian in diaspora seeking to negotiate her Haitianness through the communicative practice of translation. Interestingly, translation is also a major function that anthropologists serve, but native anthropologists must confront their own particular complications and responsibilities.

Negotiating Diversity and the War against Terrorism

In the final section of this book, we direct our concerns with racism and anti-racism to U.S. society, where issues of difference, diversity, and human rights have acquired added layers of significance since September 11. Camille Hazeur and Diana Hayman begin the discussion with an insightful chapter in which they, a biracial team of collaborators, reflect on the trends in diversity initiatives and training programs, which have grown in number if not in popular acceptance since the 1978 *Bakke* decision. Their look at diversity training as well as some of the historical forces that have made it necessary takes place at a juncture when the meanings and implications of race and affirmative action policies are being heatedly debated. Not surprisingly, since September 11, national security has taken precedence over domestic human rights concerns, including those related to the climate of race and gender relations in workplaces, schools, and universities. These are contexts in which increasing levels and forms of diversity are being negotiated and managed, frequently by persons without adequate background, knowledge, or skills. Hostile climates foster conditions that compromise human rights, both constitutionally guaranteed civil rights and those defined in the International Bill of Rights as being economic, social, and cultural rights. Of course, the last set of rights are not consensually accepted as inalienable rights in the United States, especially at a moment when the dismantlement of welfare, affirmative action, and unionization are being rationalized by an ideology promulgating personal responsibility, economistic individualism, color blindness, and the valorization of "free" markets over human rights.

Based on their many years of working in educational arenas, Hazeur and Hayman present a critical assessment of the state of diversity and "cultural sensitivity" training. They also present their sense of what is needed to achieve the goal of reeducating the workforce and, in the context of educational systems, reeducating educators for working more effectively in desegregated and increasingly heterogeneous settings. The kind of training the authors envision would prepare trainees for racial democracy by exposing them to the social history of racial formation and gender subordination in the United States. They argue that an adequately delineated historical context for explaining racism will better prepare workers and educators to understand why power-evasive advocacy of color blindness, normative (and hence unmarked) white privilege, and white male privilege are issues that need to be redressed before racism can be confronted.

To their credit, Hazeur and Hayman recognize that reeducation takes much more time than is normally allotted in most training programs. Raising consciousness around sensitive concerns whose significance so many people are inclined to deny entails awareness not only of the historical and sociological facts but also of the cultural and psychological dynamics that fuel the backlash against affirmative action policies and diversity initiatives. Raising conscious-ness also requires awareness of the profoundly political nature of the effort. Hazeur and Hayman are aware of these complications and suggest that the po-tential effectiveness of a critical mode of diversity training may be its greatest obstacle. According to their criteria, effective diversity training should work to-ward subverting established power relations. But are corporations, school sys-tems, and universities committed to a transformation of this sort? What kinds of organizing strategies would be required to achieve a genuine racial and gen-dered democracy? Critical diversity training would be only one among them.

My own chapter addresses the political organizing strategies that a multi-racial network of activists in the U.S. South deploys in building a human rights movement with linkages across national and transnational space. In 2000, sev-eral of my students and I attended a human rights conference, a preparatory fo-rum for the WCAR, held at the historically black Clark-Atlanta University in Atlanta, Georgia. The conference was organized by a coalition of civil rights, feminist/womanist, labor, and environmental activists whom I call by the pseu-donym Southern Human Rights Activists Coalition (SHRAC). During that semester, I taught a course on social inequality and human rights. The South-ern regional conference presented an excellent opportunity for my students and me to extend our critical learning community beyond the classroom to a realm of human rights advocacy. Throughout the semester, questions had been raised about how the ideas we were engaging could be translated into concrete practices that could make a difference in the "real world" beyond academic texts and talk. The third biennial conference of SHRAC (SHRAC III) gave us a chance to find out how activists answer some of those questions.

My attendance at SHRAC III and, later, SHRAC IV prompted me to ask questions that could only be answered by taking a much closer look at SHRAC, the South, human rights, and the networks of activists employing the language, instruments, and organizational arenas of the human rights system, particularly that associated with the UN and its international conferences. The human rights–centered mobilization I have begun to examine is part of a worldwide trend that has blossomed since the demise of the Cold War. Al-though it is interpreted and appropriated in diverse and sometimes problem-atic ways, the language of human rights is globally intelligible. My concern is to understand exactly how activists interpret and apply abstract human rights principles in their culturally and politically specific contexts. What difference do human rights–based strategies make for what they are able to accomplish on the ground both locally and regionally? SHRAC not only has adopted hu-man rights language but has also situated itself as part of the global South and has begun building alliances that reflect this position. What is the meaning of this transnational praxis, and how does it affect organizational identity and efficacy? SHRAC and its SHRAC conferences are regional but with strong national and international connections. Hence, the activists' interpretation of and response to the war on terrorism transcended the parochial patriotism and xenophobia characterizing so many Americans' response to the tragedy.

We end the book with Fadwa El Guindi's powerful critique of the war on terrorism, which is written from the perspective of an Arab feminist and public intellectual. She offers provocative insights into the racial and religious profiling of Arabs and the problems of the Middle East, where the right to self-determination is being flagrantly denied to Palestinians and Iraqis.

According to El Guindi, the trauma that Americans have suffered after September 11 is comparable to that which many peoples experience in ground zeros around the world. She wants more of us to know that "Israeli and [U.S.] bombs and bullets . . . indiscriminately [kill] men, women, children, and elderly [people]," not restricting their targets to military sites. She is adamant that "colonized people have the internationally legal right to resist occupation." Hence, "all forms to resist occupation and to liberate one's land [are] legitimate." The characterization of freedom fighters as terrorists demonizes them and delegitimizes their struggle for human dignity, sovereignty, and justice. This ideological fabrication, with its racist underpinnings, makes it difficult for many Americans to have sympathy for the suffering of colonially subjected people in an intensely mystified and mythologized region of the world. The region of the historically and archaeologically salient "cradle of civilization" is now being labeled "barbarian" and "uncivilized." Moreover, the image of evil, uncivilized terrorists does not apply to individuals such as Timothy McVeigh, the Euro-American charged with the bombing of a federal building in Oklahoma.

El Guindi illuminates how the politically manufactured hysteria encourages "patriots" to target innocent Arab and South Asian immigrants, many of them American citizens, in hate crimes and acts of vengeful violence. The vengefulness also prompts the Department of Homeland Security to detain aliens, often without cause. The war on terror has become a war on immigrants, a serious assault against the civil liberties and human rights especially of Arab and Muslim Americans.

Besides her perceptive analysis of domestic dynamics, El Guindi provides a savvy view of the struggles and conflicts in the Middle East. Palestinians' right to self-determination has been flagrantly denied by a geopolitical and political-economic agenda that seriously implicates Israeli and U.S. policies. Whether Americans wish to face this reality or not, this is the wider context within which acts of protest, resistance, and armed struggle assume the form of what has now come to be defined as terrorism.

El Guindi elucidates the post–September 11 political climate and the processes involved in constructing the enemy and including within that category

both individuals and countries, "particularly [two that are] oil-rich or economically strategic," namely, Afghanistan and Iraq. She argues that the attack on Iraq
and its subsequent occupation was "preemptive, unilateral, unsupported by the
international community, [and] in violation of international law and universal
human rights." She is particularly critical of anthropologists and feminists for not
taking more of a public stand to clarify the issues at stake. Western feminists, often motivated by arrogant ignorance and myopia, fell into the trap of serving the
goals of U.S. militarism in the way in which they campaigned against the Taliban's repressive patriarchal policies, particularly that concerning the *burqu'*. She
insists that "U.S. feminism must liberate itself from the hold hegemony has on
it." Political leadership must also liberate itself from "a corporate-run bully out
of control." This is necessary before there can be any meaningful dialogue and
diplomacy with spokespersons representing the Middle East. Once this kind of
relationship is cultivated, the overly simplistic views of Islam and the Middle East
will give way to a willingness to understand their complexity and humanity. If a
give-and-take approach is not sought, the prevalently popular and spontaneous
resistance El Guindi describes as "Arab street" and "world street" will continue
to expand and explode beyond the bounds and control of official leaders, cells,
parties, or states.

CONCLUSION

This volume offers only a glimpse into the thinking, conversations, and activist
research agendas of one group of individuals concerned about the state of the
world as we witness it from our diverse vantage points as intellectuals and advocates for social justice and human rights. A few years ago, our shared interests and concerns led many of us to come together at the NGO Forum for the
WCAR in Durban, South Africa. The issues we encountered and pursued remain significant and urgent today. They warrant greater visibility than they
have received in the public eye. They are legitimate grievances that can only
be resolved if there is the personal and political will to remake the world for
the greater good of the mass of humanity. The world as we know it is replete
with injustice and violence, but there are also heartening signs of hope, including "world street" expressions of peaceful and humane alternatives to the
established global order.

We believe that racism, sexism, and other *isms* can be resisted and com-
bated through—among other things—reeducation, consciousness raising,
many different kinds of protracted concerted action, and a willingness on the
part of some to relinquish unearned privilege for the sake of acknowledging
and embracing, in meaningfully substantive ways, the humanity and human

rights of others, particularly those suffering the brunt of the politics and political economy of dehumanization and stratified personhood. Unfortunately, acknowledgment of others' humanity is easier said than done. It must be learned
and invented anew so that many more of us will be able to see ourselves in
others and others in ourselves. Without this basic sense of resemblance and
kinship, it will be difficult to transform the profound gulfs of pain, anger, oppression, and war that separate human beings into bridges and public commons
where new communities and solidarities can be built from the raw materials of
an alternative global restructuring based on the logics of dialogue, compromise,
mutual aid, shared dignity, and peace. These are the necessary values and conditions for reorganizing access to power and the means of sustainable life,
building more participatory forms of democracy, redistributing income and the
net assets that constitute wealth, promoting social justice and peace, and understanding that without justice there can be no peace.

REFERENCES

Alexander, M. Jacqui, and Chandra Talpade Mohanty, eds. 1997. *Feminist genealogies,
colonial legacies, democratic futures*. New York: Routledge.
Amin, Samir. 2003. Confronting the empire. *Monthly Review* 55 (3): 15–22.
Anderson, Carol. 2003. *Eyes off the prize: The United Nations and the African American
struggle for human rights, 1944–1955*. Cambridge: Cambridge University Press.
An-Na'im, Abdullahi A. 1992. Introduction. In *Human rights in cross-cultural perspectives:
A quest for consensus*, ed. Abdullahi Ahmed An-Na'im, 1–15. Philadelphia: University
of Pennsylvania Press.
Banton, Michael. 1996. *International action against racial discrimination*. Oxford: Clarendon
Press.
Basch, Linda, Nina Glick Schiller, and Cristina Szanton Blanc. 1994. *Nations unbound:
Transnational projects, postcolonial predicaments, and deterritorialized nation-states*. Lang-
horne, PA: Gordon and Breach.
Brodkin, Karen. 2000. Global capitalism: What's race got to do with it? *American Eth-
nologist* 27 (2): 237–56.
Brysk, Alison. 2002. Introduction: Transnational threats and opportunities. In *Globaliza-
tion and human rights*, ed. Alison Brysk, 1–16. Berkeley: University of California Press.
Buck, Pem Davidson. 1992. With our heads in the sand: The racist Right, concentration camps, and the incarceration of people of color. *Transforming Anthropology* 3 (1):
13–18.
Chanock, Martin. 2000. "Culture" and human rights: Orientalizing, occidentalizing,
and authenticity. In *Beyond rights talk and culture talk*, ed. Mahmood Mamdani, 15–36.
New York: St. Martin's Press.
Collins, Patricia Hill. 1998. *Fighting words: Black women and the search for justice*. Minneapolis: University of Minnesota Press.

Crenshaw, Kimberlé. 1991. Mapping the margins: Identity politics, intersectionality, and violence against women of color. *Stanford Law Review* 43:1241.

Danticat, Edwidge, ed. 2001. *The butterfly's way: Voices from the Haitian diaspora in the United States*. New York: Soho Press.

Davis, Angela Y. 2003. *Are prisons obslete?* New York: Seven Stories Press.

Desai, Manisha. 2002. Transnational solidarity: Women's agency, structural adjustment, and globalization. In *Women's activism and globalization: Linking local struggles and transnational politics*, ed. Nancy A. Naples and Manisha Desai, 15–33. New York: Routledge.

Dominguez, Virginia. 1994. A taste for "the Other": Intellectual complicity in racializing practices. *Current Anthropology* 35 (4): 333–48.

Enloe, Cynthia. 1990. *Bananas, beaches, and bases: Making feminist sense of international politics*. Berkeley: University of California Press.

———. 1993. *The morning after: Sexual politics at the end of the Cold War*. Berkeley: University of California Press.

Farmer, Paul. 1992. *AIDS and accusation: Haiti and the geography of blame*. Berkeley: University of California Press.

———. 2003. *Pathologies of power: Health, human rights, and the new war on the poor*. Berkeley: University of California Press.

Frankenberg, Ruth. 1993. *White women, race matters: The social construction of whiteness*. Minneapolis: University of Minnesota Press.

Friedman, Jonathan. 1994. *Cultural identity and global process*. London: Sage.

Glick Schiller, Nina, and Georges Fouron. 2001. *Georges woke up laughing: Long-distance nationalism and the search for home*. Durham, N.C.: Duke University Press.

Harrison, Faye V. 1990. "Three women, one struggle": Anthropology, performance, and pedagogy. *Transforming Anthropology* 1 (1): 1–9.

———. 1995. The persistent power of "race" in the cultural and political economy of racism. *Annual Review of Anthropology* 24:47–74.

———. 1997. The gendered politics and violence of structural adjustment: A view from Jamaica. In *Situated lives: Gender and culture in everyday life*, ed. Louise Lamphere, Helena Ragoné, and Patricia Zavella, 451–68. New York: Routledge.

———. 1998. Introduction: Expanding the discourse on "race." *American Anthropologist* (Contemporary Forum: Race and Racism) 100 (3): 609–31.

———. 2001. Imagining a global community united against racism. *Anthropology News* 42 (9): 22–23.

———. 2002a. Subverting the cultural logics of marked and unmarked racisms. In *Discrimination and toleration: New perspectives*, ed. Kirsten Hastrup and George Ulrich, 97–125. The Hague: Martinus Nijhoff.

———. 2002b. Unraveling "race" for the 21st century. In *Exotic no more: Anthropology on the front lines*, ed. Jeremy MacClancy, 145–66. Chicago: University of Chicago Press.

———. 2002c. Global apartheid, foreign policy, and human rights. *Souls: A Critical Journal of Black Politics, Culture, and Society* (Race and Globalization) 4 (3): 48–68.

hooks, bell. 1984. *Feminist theory: From margin to center*. Boston: South End Press.

James, Joy. 1998. *The Angela Y. Davis reader*. Malden, Mass.: Blackwell.

James, Stanlie. 2002. Racialized, gendered/gendered racism: Reflections on black feminist human rights theorizing. In *Black women, globalization, and economic justice: Studies from Africa and the African diaspora*, ed. Filomina Chioma Steady, 151–61. Rochester, Vt.: Schenkman.

Kingfisher, Catherine, and Michael Goldsmith. 2001. Reforming women in the United States and Aotearoa/New Zealand: A comparative ethnography of welfare reform in global context. *American Anthropologist* 103 (3): 714–32.

Kingsolver, Ann E. 2001. *NAFTA stories: Fears and hopes in Mexico and the United States*. Boulder, Colo.: Lynne Rienner.

Lewellen, Ted. 2002. *The anthropology of globalization: Cultural anthropology enters the 21st century*. Westport, Ct.: Bergin & Garvey.

MacEwan, Arthur. 1999. *Neo-liberalism or democracy? Economic strategy, markets, and alternatives for the 21st century*. London: Zed Books.

Mamdani, Mahmood, ed. 2000. *Beyond rights talk and culture talk: Comparative essays on the politics of rights and culture*. New York: St. Martin's Press.

Messer, Ellen. 1993. Anthropology and human rights. *Annual Review of Anthropology* 22:221–49.

———. 1997. Pluralist approaches to human rights. *Journal of Anthropological Research* 53 (3): 293–317.

———. 2002. Anthropologists in a world with and without human rights. In *Exotic no more: Anthropology on the front lines*, ed. Jeremy MacClancy, 319–37. Chicago: University of Chicago Press.

Ramphele, Mamphela. 1995. *Across boundaries: The journey of a South African woman leader*. New York: Feminist Press.

Roy, Arundhati. 2003. Confronting empire. In her *War talk*. Cambridge, Mass.: South End Press.

Ulysse, Gina. 2001. A poem about why I can't wait. In *The butterfly's way: Voices from the Haitian dyaspora in the United States*, ed. Edwidge Danticat, 209–20. New York: Soho.

Wetherell, Margaret, and Jonathan Potter. 1993. *Mapping the language of racism: Discourse and the legitimation of exploitation*. New York: Columbia University Press.

Wilson, Richard A., ed. 1997. *Human rights, culture, and context: Anthropological perspectives*. London: Pluto Press.

I

A POST-DURBAN AND POST–SEPTEMBER 11 VIEW FROM THE SOUTH

1

Finding Strategic Identities in an Unequal World: Feminist Reflections from India

Devaki Jain

In this chapter, I propose to use the World Conference against Racism (WCAR) as a reference point to torchlight the nuances, the differences in perception of the hierarchies of issues, the distances as well as the intersections between various struggles against discrimination. This will lead to an examination of the impact of September 11, which unfortunately arrived almost immediately after the conference, on some of the issues of building solidarity in identity—crucial to internationalizing injustice and universalizing human rights. I argue that, post–September 11, there was a change in the power structure ruling the globe—namely, the emergence of a unipolar political force backed by coalitions against terror. Furthermore, I argue that there was also both a peaking of economic control (Jain 2002a), as expressed in George Bush's threats to withdraw or ban financial deposits if "you are not with us" (Said 2003; Roy 2002), and a change in the categorization of the peoples of the world—for example, the suggestion of the clash of civilizations (Huntington 1996), with "civilizations" being a mask for religions and something negative (not positive).

What then are the dilemmas that emerge in evolving solidarity on a common identity that will upturn the hierarchies of power, melt discrimination, and provide compensation to the earlier historically violated social categories?

The WCAR offered a space to unwind some of these tangles. Overall, the conference exposed a great deal about the nuances and issues around the concept of racism as well as the ideas and analysis of the intersections among gender, class, caste, and race. To listen to the types of language and the sense of pain and anger that pervaded the discourse, which had a salutary effect, one was brought back again to some of the earlier concerns of feminists, namely, that they need to identify themselves with the "worst off." The worst off were those who were caught in the intersection of all the *isms*, including those in poverty.

It is difficult for those not in situations of struggle, not in situations of discrimination and poverty, to understand how meaningful these exposures to internationalism, as represented at the WCAR, are to such groups. Recall how the first World Conference on Women, held in Mexico in 1975, became a defining moment not only for women but for governments, too—including the Indian government, which has since not only set up structures and policies exclusively for women but has also learnt to listen and respond to women.

The WCAR showed once again that there is a case for looking at the United Nations with eyes wide open, as a space that can in fact bring together voices of the enslaved (i.e., their descendants) as well as enable internationally mandated legal arrangements to protect those whose human rights are violated. However difficult, however unstructured, however controversy ridden, the United Nations created that space and opportunity in Durban, South Africa. It was not a "chaotic" conference, as some suggested. It was in fact focused; it focused on the enslaved and on injustice across gender, class, caste, race, ethnicity, location, history, and so forth. The porosity in the ideology of protest, of critique of the state, of calls for justice added another rich flavor to the spirit and strength of the nongovernmental organization forum at the WCAR.

The characteristics and the discussions at the conference highlighted the issue of discrimination, how it is based on prejudice and mind-sets, unreasonable but embedded.

Discrimination based on color, on sex—that is, on birthmarks, marks that cannot be washed out—invited this prejudiced view, this discrimination across regions, class, gender, politics, across all divides and identities. It could be suggested that the conference revealed the ugliness of the human species, what it can do to the Other—a disheartening revelation.

The air at the venue was one of conflict, conflict between peoples within countries, clearly addressed to a given adversary, mostly expressed as information but often also in hateful language and finger-pointing. This explicitness added a kind of clarity and power to the event, usually missing in other such conferences about women, population, poverty, or children. Narratives spoke of lives of fear, from their childhoods spent as thieves and polluters, bodies to be used and thrown aside and kept outside systems of justice and security under one pretext or another—of peoples being deprived of rights not only to land and knowledge but also their bodies, especially for the women.

As one seasoned UN conference traveler said, this was a refreshing conference, bringing hope to the UN as an instrument for facilitating justice and drawing attention to the universality of humans and human rights. Another attendee, a feminist from South Asia, said that this conference can repoliticize the feminist movement, since the women were usually within a racially discriminated group and spoke of experiences of racism, thus emphasizing the ugliest face of discrimination. As the people were mostly those who were at the bottom of the ladder of social exclusion and stigma, there was a kind of class focus, thus highlighting the fact that the rights framework has to be embedded in economic issues such as poverty. This seemed another very important lesson, and it was impressive to see that the only luminary who addressed this directly was President Thabo Mbeki of South Africa (Mbeki 2001).

India had an extraordinary and powerful buildup to the conference, and the experience brings out the problems of human rights struggles as well as those of identity, social classification, and intersection. While earlier WCAR was being seen by India as a conference not of much value to any except the descendants of African slaves, now African Americans, and therefore basically an issue for Africa and the United States, the Dalits of India grasped the conference as an opportunity to internationalize their historical experience of discrimination. They formed coalitions across their usual divides of location, language, social strata, and politics and made an attempt to get caste recognized as race so that the mandates coming out of the conference could also apply to them, who had been discriminated because of birth marks, namely caste, an inherited marker.

The conflict between the government and the Dalit organizations became the most lively debate in the country, giving for the first time large public spaces for the Dalits to reveal, discuss, and describe their situation (Ilaiah 2001; Thorat 2001; Louis 2001; Visvanathan 2001a, 2001b). Across the country, the public and media response showed the sympathy that Indian civil society had for the Dalits—and recognition for the abominable practices that the Dalits endured, a redeeming feature in contrast to the government's position, a vindication of some of the qualities of Indian democracy, a vigilant and bold press.

The suggestion that found some acceptance by the official agencies was the fact that there was discrimination of the worst kind, that the Indian constitution's guarantees against discrimination based on caste were not operating on the ground—that there were violations of human rights. But this was not a relevant agenda for this particular conference. The government argued that ideas such as reparations for slavery, for the expropriation of land and other natural resources from the indigenous people of the Americas and of Australia, were the main agenda of this meeting, and it is better that countries such as India act as bystanders, basically supporting this struggle by the people of African and indigenous origin battling against white supremacy. This attitude that the WCAR was about white and black—and not a conference for the developing countries or ex-colonial countries who faced enslavement and exploitation as nations, not marked peoples, and whose current inner conflicts and macroproblems came from other sources (some social but mostly economic)—was widespread among what for shorthand could be called the Group 77 countries. Within the UN the countries that emerged from colonization—often called the underdeveloped or developing countries—have grouped themselves as a voting bloc, especially on economic issues, and are identified as the Group 77, or G77, countries, in contrast to the G7 or G8 countries, the rich countries. Thus the customary North–South divide emerged here, too.

In the meantime, some Indian feminists saw the conference as an opportunity to link sexism to racism, arguing that while racism had reached heights in terms of being recognized as an important political issue, sexism as a politics and as a mind-set was not a recognized high-profile issue (Jain 2000). The women's question, seen as an inequality and discrimination issue linked to patriarchal values in spite of its many conferences and lobbies, had not been recognized yet as an *ism.*

Prior to the Durban conference, I had written an article in the national daily in India saying:

> In response to racism, "the other," namely the enslaved, had to build a strong mass-based platform where the identity had to be on a single pole. Any attempt to highlight pluralism—a multiplicity of characteristics such as male–female, rich–poor, urban–rural, educated–uneducated, Christian–non-Christian—would not have enabled the black consciousness movement to bring together the kind of courage and sacrifice that pushed back and undid the White regime in South Africa. The more the oppressor pressed his attitude, the more the oppressed recognized his weakness and absurdity. It was this non-slave mentality, the self-confidence of the blacks, their pride and knowledge that the adversary was creating myths, shrouding himself in a glass cage, that finally brought together the black consciousness and the anti-racism movement, eroding the self-confidence of the white minority.
>
> The women's movement it seemed had much to learn from this strategy. A United Nations World Race Conference is being planned and this is an opportunity to take interest in women's struggle and accommodate the women's rights movement in the struggle against racism. Simultaneously, it is a chance for the women's movement to ask for a space in the World Race Conference, to learn from the anti-racist language and adapt the lessons to be applied to their own movement. (Jain 2000)

The Dalit mobilization—their systematic efforts both at home and at the conference—not only drew attention to the phenomena of caste-derived violence and prejudice but also revealed the space available in the Indian democratic system for such mobilization and expression. The dissonance with the government generated so much public debate, opinion building, and an interesting (mostly in support of the Dalit case) chiding of the government for its stand. Getting public opinion engaged in these issues educated the citizens; it even influenced judgments from the judiciary and put checks on police and officials. Its effects, thus, were far-reaching within a country, and with India having such a lively media, this became a rich harvest for the implementation of justice.

Notwithstanding the fact that even within blackness or Dalitness, women faced almost all the elements of violation, exclusion, demeaning values that the larger marking illustrated, when the idea of raising the sexism issue was proposed to Dalit women in India before they left for Durban, when they were going to the preparatory conferences, they hinted that they would not like to bring up the issue. The reason given was that their mobilization and lobbying at the preparatory conferences and with the human rights committees were for the recognition of the case of caste on a level with that of race. Any gendered differentiation would mute that larger struggle. Such a view is well understood by black women in white-dominated countries, who also faced the earlier class-before-gender dialogues with the Marxists and other worker organizations (Eagleton 1996; Kandal 1995).

Another set of questions to a proposal that women could unite as women comes in a personal communication from Barbara Phillips, a civil rights lawyer and practitioner, in response to a thesis I was offering for debate in a lecture at the University of Maryland entitled "Valuing Women—Signals from the Ground" (Jain 2001). In that lecture, I said that "reviewing the various struggles or collective public actions suggests that women find opportunity as well as gains only when they organize as women." Put another way, they have to organize themselves as women within other forms of social stratification and political formations in order to survive, to find a "get out" in the space.

Barbara Phillips asks,

> Is it desirable to forge this primary identity as "Woman"? What are the implications for other aspects of identity? Must we be "Women" first? If so, then what does each woman enter in the category of "second," "third"? Is this primary identity preferable to an "intersectional" identity? Does this primary identity break the bonds as well as the "chains" of cultural context?
>
> If the primary identity of "Woman" is desirable, what are the enabling conditions for its emergence? To take a crude example, during the era of lawful slavery in the United States, surely there was no possibility of primary identity as "woman" for the slave-owning woman and the slave woman.

She continues and considers what I would call a perspective or an ideology as a more meaningful basis for unity than woman because of the history, in this case, of racial oppression:

> I would like to examine the function of identity as a force for social movement solidarity. Can we explore the function of "physical characteristic"

identity as compared to "belief in a vision of justice" characteristic? Was the solidarity among South African Blacks forged upon "physical characteristic" identity or a transformative "belief in a vision of justice"? Is this inquiry even appropriately "either/or"; perhaps it is a matter of some primary characteristic identity that merges or plows the soil through shared experience for the receptiveness to a transformative vision of a just society.

If we think about group identity, what might the characteristics of identity look like from within the group as compared to how the characteristics of identity look from outside the group? Within a minority community such as African Americans, what identities exist internally that are relatively invisible to those who look "at" that community from the outside?

Is a socially dominant group freed from concerns about multiple identities because of its dominance? Are its complexities "invisible"? For example, white women in the U.S. seem never to think of themselves as having a "race." They are "women." Racial designation is used almost exclusively to point to the particularity of "Black women" or "minority women." So that multiple identities are only "visible" in subordinated groups?

These questions would match the questions of Dalit women in India and equally confront any attempt to forge identity on the basis of woman. But since August 2002, other headlines have appeared in the sky. Unfortunately, the full impact of the Durban homecoming and the typology of identity had a resounding shock with the language, posture, and policies followed by the United States, post–September 11, 2001. The classifications are now on the basis of "civilizations," a mask for division across religions. Racial profiling is clearly condemned in the plan of action, which

> urges States to design, implement and enforce effective measures to eliminate the phenomenon popularly known as "racial profiling" and comprising the practice of police and other law enforcement officers relying, to any degree, on race, colour, descent or national or ethnic origin as the basis for subjecting persons to investigatory activities or for determining whether an individual is engaged in criminal activity. (Declaration of the World Conference 2001)

According to the U.S. Patriot Act of 2002, racial profiling is now targeted at persons from Arab countries or Islamic groups.

As for the homecoming of those who were basically at the nongovernmental organization forum—for example, the Dalits from India—it was an empowering experience. Despite the resistance of the Indian government, they had internationalized their issue. But even more significant, they had built up networks on the way, both within the country and outside of it. They had shared strategies of struggle with others in the world. Learning that they were not alone was healing and challenging. The Dalits made natural allies with the Palestinians and the Romas at Durban. At home they had become more visible as individuals, as organizations, as divided lobbies. With the new confidence, they were ready to make allies with, for example the Indian women's movement, which has been known to be strongly biased toward the most deprived—a voice for the poor. For example, the Dalits were confronting a similar dissonance with the Indian state that the Indian women's movement had faced when they tried to internationalize some of the violations of human rights that they were facing. There were other such experiences that the Indian women's movement had already strategized over, and this could be of use to the newly emerging internationalists. Many aspects of the Dalit problematique—for example, that expressed by Gopal Guru (Guru 2002) on the caste hierarchies pervading social science research—could be mirrored by the feminist problematique.[1] These dialogues and alliances are possible as a result of the buildup of the Dalit movement toward Durban and the conference itself.

However, as the demarcation of society and politics shifts from social and economic categories to religious and cultural categories, there is an anxiety among people such as me and Amartya Sen (2001) at this reinvoking of old categories. It takes the world back to the days of the Crusaders of medieval times—to the Dark Ages, when bigotry was the limit to which the human imagination could go. Since then, not only the Enlightenment in the West but also the intellectual expression of societies in the South and the East had grown beyond or extended the boundary of imagination to other categories of stratification and division, such as class, ethnicity, caste, gender, occupation. Nations identified themselves not as Christian and pagan but as being newly liberated and colonial. Religion as conqueror was eroded in the twentieth century, and there was a sharp fall in attendance in churches, temples, and mosques worldwide. However, many of us suggest that there is a slide back.

Amartya Sen, in a lecture entitled "Exclusion and Inclusion," says,

> This issue has become particularly important in the context of the present political crisis and confrontation, *with its ramifications becoming clearer since September 11*, though the roots of the problem go back much further. . . . By categorising the population of the world into those belonging to "the Islamic world," "the Christian world," "the Hindu world," "the Buddhist world," etc., the divisive power of classificatory priority is implicitly used to place people firmly inside a unique set of rigid boxes. Other divisions (say, between the rich and the poor, between members of different classes and occupations, between people of different politics, between distinct nationalities and residential locations, between language groups, etc.)

are all submerged by this allegedly pre-eminent way of seeing the differences between people. . . . [Such boxing] . . . is potentially a great ethical
and political hazard, with far-reaching consequences on human rights.
(2001; emphasis mine)

He then continues, "I would argue that the main hope of harmony in the contemporary world lies in the plurality of our identities, which cut across each
other and works against sharp divisions around one single hardened line of im-
penetrable division."

September 11 has changed all the coordinates of the international systems
of justice and eroded the United Nations process, if not demeaned and humil-
iated it. Intolerance has reached its peaks but due to not race but religion, as
seen recently in Gujarat, India, "where from February 27, 2002 onwards, a
communal frenzy of unbelievable ferocity, brutality and hatred ripped Gujarat
apart. The carnage went on for over two months and simmers under the ve-
neer of calm even today."

I would like to suggest that in response to this new powerdom and the
new categorization, or the emergence of the "new but old" identities, the
buildup of resistance is coming back to economics, to the inequalities that are
being generated in the midst of palpable knowing of the Other.

At the Asian Social Forum (Hyderabad, India, January 2003), a gathering of
fourteen thousand persons identified the adversary as the "empire"—reinvoking
the imperialism of earlier eras. There was an encouraging vitality in the way the
numerous identities, such as Dalits, displaced persons, and unorganized workers,
were able to share a common space, to understand and collectively decide to find
alternatives to the current political and economic regimes and the theories that
back them up (Jain 2003). This could be seen as a defining moment for the "empire to strike back."

At the World Social Forum in Pôrte Alegre, Brazil, that followed the
Asian Social Forum, Arundhati Roy (2003) had this to say:

The disparity between the rich and the poor grows, the fight to corner resources is intensifying. To push through their "sweetheart deals," to corpo-
ratize the crops we grow, the water we drink, the air we breathe, and the
dreams we dream, corporate globalization needs an international confederation of loyal, corrupt, authoritarian governments in poorer countries to
push through unpopular reforms and quell the mutinies.

    Corporate Globalization—or shall we call it by its name? Imperialism—
needs a press that pretends to be free. It needs courts that pretend to dispense justice.

    Meanwhile, the countries of the North harden their borders and stock-
pile weapons of mass destruction. After all they have to make sure that it's
only money, goods, patents and services that are globalized. Not the free

movement of people. Not a respect for human rights. Not international treaties on racial discrimination or chemical and nuclear weapons or greenhouse gas emissions or climate change, or—God forbid—justice. So this, all this, is "empire." This loyal confederation, this obscene accumulation of power, this greatly increased distance between those who make the decisions and those who have to suffer them.

This phenomenon of the new powerdom seems to suggest that some of the old classifications, such as inequality and poverty, need to be reinvoked, that intolerance based on race would need to give space to intolerance emerging from disparities. The intolerance of economic distances, coupled with distances in control over self and the environment—that is, the distances in power, the anger over the new hegemony—is concentrated among the excluded and the economically and politically deprived as that different from the socially stigmatized.

Thus, identity would not only need to go back to the nonsocial categories—that is, to the economically poor, to class—but also to approaches to removing of discrimination. There are modes and models for eliminating distance and thereby eliminating the phenomena of intolerance. One exemplar that comes to mind is Gandhi and his modes of eliminating those differences that lead to violence. Gandhi's ethic was actually to efface difference through absorption of the Other. Symbolic gestures were used with great effect. Inequality, discrimination were his main "target."

For example, to overcome the distance between class—namely, deprivation and some minimal consumer satisfaction—he dressed as a poor man, making two identities into one, and he would only live like a poor man both to experience it, in order to identify himself with the poor, and to generate a motivation in the poor and in others to remove poverty. To overcome the stigma of untouchability related to scavenging, he cleaned night soil from pit latrines and took the bodily stigma of night-soil cleaning to identify himself with this "dirty" task and to draw attention to the injustice.

To enable women to attack the stereotyping of roles that stigmatizes and subordinates women, he transposed roles in the ashrams. Women would come to his marches and his public, peaceful boycotts, and men were asked to weave, sew, and cook. Women were advised to cease to be an ornament for men to enjoy and, if necessary, to boycott sexual advances in order to resist male supremacy.

There is an idea here: it is perhaps the only strategy, namely, the identification with the poor, with which a united stand could in fact eradicate poverty. There is morality, but there are also hardcore politics and attention to economics. It seems that a mental effort is required to efface multiple identities, as is a politics to remove the discrimination against the poor.

NOTE

1. "Social science practice in India has harboured a cultural hierarchy dividing it into a vast, inferior mass of academics who pursue empirical social science and a privileged few who are considered the theoretical pundits with reflective capacity which makes them intellectually superior to the former. To use a familiar analogy, Indian social science represents a pernicious divide between theoretical brahmins and empirical shudras" (Guru 2002).

REFERENCES

Declaration of the World Conference against Racism, Racial Discrimination, Xenophobia, and Related Intolerance. 2001. Preamble (para. 72), Durban, South Africa.
Eagleton, Terry. 1996. *The illusions of postmodernism.* London: Blackwell.
Guru, Gopal. 2002. How egalitarian are the social sciences in India? *Economic and Political Weekly* 37, no. 51 (December 14): 5003–9.
Huntington, Samuel P. 1996. *The clash of civilizations and the remaking of world order.* New York: Simon & Schuster.
Ilaiah, Kancha. 2001. The buffalo's unholy milk. *Outlook* (New Delhi), August 20, www.sikhe.com/gsdno/articles/essay/The%20Buffalo%27s%20Unholy%20Milk%20%20OutLookIndia_com.htm, accessed March 29, 2005.
Jain, Devaki. 1996. Removing discrimination and poverty: The importance of exemplars. Third convocation address at the University of Tirunelveli, India, British Council India.
———. 2000. Gender inequity as racism. *Hindu* (Chennai), September 23, 10.
———. 2001. Cultural diversity and universal norms: Valuing women—signals from the ground. Speech at University of Maryland, June 1.
———. 2002a. For whom the bell tolls: Democracy and development in South Asia. *Cambridge Review of International Affairs* 15, no. 2 (July): 299–310.
———. 2002b. He had a vision for his village. *Hindu* (Chennai), May 13, 11.
———. 2003. The empire strikes back. *Economic and Political Weekly*, January 11, 99–100.
Kandal, Terry. 1995. Gender, race, and ethnicity: Let's not forget class. *Race, Gender, and Class* 2 (2): 139–62.
Louis, Prakash. 2001. Casteism is more horrendous than racism: Durban and Dalit discourse. Unpublished paper, Indian Social Institute, New Delhi.
Mbeki, Thabo. 2001. We must combine to defeat consequences of slavery, colonialism and racism. Address at the opening of the World Conference against Racism in Durban, South Africa, August 31, www.un.org/WCAR/pressreleases/rd-d7.htm, accessed March 29, 2005.
Patel, Alaknanda. 2002. Gujarat violence: A personal diary. *Economic and Political Weekly*, December 14, 4985–86.
Roy, Arundhati. 2002. Not again. *Guardian* (London), September 27, www.guardian .co.uk/print/0,3858,4509735-103680,00.html, accessed March 29, 2005.

————. 2003. Confronting empire. Speech delivered at the World Social Forum, Pôrto Alegre, Brazil, January.

Said, Edward. 2003. Eve of catastrophe: The helpless Arab world. *Deccan Herald* (Bangalore), February 1.

Sen, Amartya. 2001. Exclusion and inclusion. Address at a South Asians for Human Rights (SAHR) Convention, New Delhi.

Thorat, Sukhdeo. 2001. Caste, race, and United Nation's perspective on discrimination: Coping with emerging challenges from Asia. Presentation given at "Beyond Durban: Caste and Race Dialogues," Durban, South Africa, October 5.

Visvanathan, Shiv. 2001a. Durban and Dalit discourse. *Economic and Political Weekly*, August 18, 3123–27.

————. 2001b. The race for caste: Prolegomena to the Durban conference. *Economic and Political Weekly*, July 7, 2512–16.

II

GENDERED COMMUNITIES IN CRISIS AND STRUGGLE

2

Metaphors of Race and Caste-Based Discriminations against Dalits and Dalit Women in India

Subhadra Mitra Channa

In the seventies, when as a young scholar I first began my research work, my choice of field area raised quite a few eyebrows. "Why Dhobis?" many people asked. At that time I did not realize the implications of that question, not also the fact that after me, no one else from the Department of Anthropology at Delhi University had ever worked within an untouchable community. I realized it quite recently when I was standing outside my house, and my neighbor, who was living on the first floor, was trying to throw the keys upstairs to his wife. Our cleaning lady, who belongs to the sweeper caste and is considered immensely untouchable, offered to throw the key up.

"No, no, you do not touch it," the woman upstairs reacted rather violently. The cleaning woman stepped back, and her face looked as if she had been slapped. One could see the humiliation as well as the pain. "So they think I am an *achut* [untouchable]," she muttered, but walked away quietly. I do not know how many times she must have faced such humiliation, notwithstanding that it was during the year 2001 in the city of Delhi and in an urban middle-class neighborhood where most of the intelligentsia lives.

In the seventies when I was working among the Dhobis,[1] in a far more traditional neighborhood of Delhi, similar situations had become imprinted in my mind (Channa 1985). I belong to a liberal family, where caste has never been mentioned overtly, and I was not fully conversant with the full extent of the practice of "untouchability," although as an Indian and a Hindu, I knew that it existed. I did not realize the implication when some of my informants told me that they had tried to open a tea shop but that it did not run. "People would not accept our tea; they kept saying *Dhobi ki chai* [tea of the Dhobi]." At that time I was naïve enough to ask why. But soon the harsh realities of discrimination became clear to me.

The first aspect of discrimination in all areas, urban and rural, is geographical segregation. Everywhere in both village and city, even today, the low castes are segregated and huddled together. The Dhobi, who were part of the old historical city of Delhi and were residing there from the time the Walled City[2] was built, were cramped into small one-room tenements built around a central courtyard and cut off from the main city areas by a narrow entrance that marked the beginning of the Dhobi Katra, as they were referred to. The narrowness of the entrances, coupled with the fact that they were always situated away from the main roads and market areas, made it impossible for any one to wander into them by chance. Such geographical segregation was matched by social segregation as well. In the seventies, the children of the Dhobis had started going to school and even to college, but the stories of their humiliation were manifold.

"The children in our class do not treat us as equals; they call us scheduled caste and avoid us." The teachers were no different. One mother complained to me as to how her son was repeatedly thrown out of the class by the teacher who kept saying that he could never learn anything because he was a Dhobi.

A young boy once shyly confided in me that he was in love with a Brahmin girl who lived nearby. "It is an impossible dream. A person of my caste cannot even think of marrying a girl of a higher caste. Even my mother would never accept a daughter-in-law who did not know how to iron clothes. Nevertheless I look at her from a distance and love her in my heart."

In later life, while doing fieldwork in rural areas of Northern India such as Rajasthan (Channa 1995) and Garhwal (Channa 2000), I saw the same phenomenon repeated again and again. Invariably the low castes would be placed in the most inhospitable and infertile part of the village. They would be occupying marshy lands or arid, rocky, unproductive land and would be situated far away from the sources of drinking water. In fact the harshest cruelty to them was in the matter of restricting their access to drinking water. No untouchable was allowed to touch the sources of water directly, and untouchable women would sit near the wells or streams and wait patiently for hours until the high-caste women would fill their empty vessels with water for them. The high-caste women who did so took care at the same time not to touch the polluting, low-caste bodies. In very few places and only where there was a sizable population of low castes, such as in the villages near Agra, populated by the low-caste Chamars (traditional leatherworkers), the untouchables had their own well or source of water.

While I was working in a village in Haryana in the nineties, I came across some water taps, a sign of modernity in village India (Channa 1997). The state had provided these taps for the untouchables in the village, as they were not allowed to draw water from the wells. But I was also told that no untouchable had the courage to touch these taps and that only women of the high castes were using them. The untouchable women would still sit beside the taps meant for them, waiting for their vessels to be filled. A high-caste person told me that "the government can provide taps for the untouchables, but it can not give them the courage to use them."

When India became an independent democracy, the framers of the Indian constitution banned "untouchability" and made its practice a cognizable offense. Almost fifty years down the line, in spite of a fair number of untouchables having become political leaders and holding responsible jobs, their position has undergone little change. They may have gained economically, but the social stigma as well as the "psychocultural assaults" (Smedley 1993; cf. Harrison 1998, 621) remains. Even today, whenever I go to any village in any part of India, with a few regions exempted,[3] I have no difficulty in identifying the Dalits. One can see their poor residential quarters; the lack of resources, such as fertile land and water; the general lack of prosperity; and their shabby appearance as distinct markers of their caste status. Even in the resettlement colonies of the ousteds, such as those of the Tehri dam in Uttaranchal in Northern India, the newly formed villages also had the untouchables segregated and given the poorest and the smallest portions of the land. Whenever the state gives land, under land-redistribution schemes, the untouchables almost always get the land that no one else wants.

In the religious sphere, the Hindu pantheon contains many gods and goddesses, hierarchically arranged. The lower-order deities are always seen as being associated with the untouchables. They are also believed to have the same characteristics as the untouchables. Thus, people fear them for being "unpredictable, malevolent, spiteful, dirty and dangerous." The higher-order deities, belonging to the high castes, are seen as being benevolent, magnanimous, immensely powerful with a generalized all-pervasive sacredness. The lower-order deities, like the untouchables, have control over small portions of the universe, mostly diseases and specific misfortunes such as snake bites and cholera (Parish 1997, 36). The sacred status of the lower-order deities is also much diluted, and they are seen as having more of nuisance value and evil nature. Thus, one comes to the Durkheimian (Durkheim 1965) conclusion that the sacred cosmology of the Hindus metaphorically reflects the social order and that the hierarchy of gods parallels the hierarchy of human beings.

In this chapter, I do not want to go into either the history of untouchability or the textual and scholastic aspects of it. I simply want to show how a system of oppression survives in subtle and covert forms and has its roots deeply entrenched even when apparently uprooted and done away with in legislation and overt social norms. Even when the educated elite and the intelligentsia overtly deny that they are casteist, they are in no way different from their counterparts of white dominant groups in the West, who deny the fact of racism while, as documented by scholars, the fact of race persists in many different hues (Harrison 1995).

As Chris Shore (1997, 133) has shown in his work on Europe, metaphors used in daily speech are a powerful medium of "subjectification" in the Foucauldian sense, where the people are conditioned almost unconsciously to internalize certain values and beliefs that serve to reproduce those very hierarchies that produce them (Bourdieu 1990). Thus, the metaphors of caste, or *jati* (the Indian term for the numerous endogamous communities into which Indian society is divided), are all in terms of their inherent characteristics, which makes intermixing synonymous with incompatibility. Thus the psychobiological (Miles 1989, 32–40) justification used for the continuity of race is reproduced in caste except that the caste system, having survived over centuries, has perfected the system of self-reproduction in a much more comprehensive manner than even race. Thus, those at the bottom of the ladder have also internalized the values to the extent that they would frown on intermixture, and the caste identities have become synonymous with human identity to the extent that most Indians cannot think of themselves as being apart from their castes. This inherent sense of identity could be one of the reasons why this system has persisted.

A caste group is also a community, and the horizontal solidarity of this community comes in handy as a support group. Traditionally, such support groups were only operative at the social level, but now they have become integrated into the democratic process as much of the work on caste and politics indicates. Thus, caste reproduces itself by adapting to the needs of the new social order and justifies its existence in terms of providing identity and group values and by becoming a positive political force. It is the political potential of caste that has kept it alive and given it a new lease on life in modern India. At the World Conference against Racism,[4] this aspect of caste was most apparent where the label of "untouchablity" had united a group politically and coordinated them into action. The term *Dalit* is itself a product of this political consciousness.

Caste further provides the necessary inequalities to keep the political and economic system going, "a strategy to maintain labor discipline," and in this way a parallel has been drawn between caste and race (Milner 1994, 91). Thus, even today most of the demeaning work in Indian cities and villages are done by the untouchables. The monopolistic advantage mentioned by E. R. Leach (1960, 6)[5] is nothing but a way to tie down groups to socially undesirable tasks. The West realized that racism was an aftermath of the abolition of slavery; in India, casteism in its present form may be viewed as being an aftermath of the constitutional abolition of the caste system and the introduction of a secular democratic form of governance. The scholars of the traditional caste system, for example Oliver C. Cox (1944–1945), differentiated between caste and race by saying that caste was "part of a coherent social system based on inequality" while race was an anomaly in a society built on the concepts of equality. The present-day Indian society is overtly committed to the same principles of equality and human rights as are their Western counterparts. But caste remains in its insidious form in India as race does in the West. Both are operative at the subversive level to maintain morally unacceptable but politically and economically justified forms of inequality.

CASTE AND RACE

Many scholars of Indian society have debated the similarity between caste and race in analytical terms, aptly summarized by Louis Dumont (1961). On the face of it, most scholars of the Indian caste system are of the opinion that caste and race are inherently incomparable as they are rooted in two entirely separate ideological systems. One of the moot points of departure is that race is based on morphological differentiation (overt similarity) while caste is based on concepts of inner purity and pollution not overtly linked to morphology. While to a large extent it might be true that the skin color of a Brahmin or a Shudra makes no difference to status, yet metaphorically the notions of appearance are not absent from caste values. Thus, good-looking persons of low caste are often referred to as being "not like Shudras," and a dark-complexioned Brahmin may be disparagingly referred to as being "like a Shudra." However, if appearance does not make a difference to the status accorded, then what about racial classification? Is it morphological? If it were so, would light-skinned Asians such as Imran Khan be considered black (Werbner 1997)? I think most scholars on race would agree that race is not about color at all; otherwise, why would the Irish and the Polish be discriminated against racially? The color that makes the American WASP the whitest of all races is the same that makes the Brahmin the most superior in the Varna hierarchy. Thus, as J. Baker Miller (1978; cf. Crowley and Himmelweit 1992, 19) understands it, the inequalities come first, and the differences follow. Moreover, even though there may not be overt physical differences between persons of different caste groups, a high degree of visibility was imposed on the lower castes by assigning to them a particularly demeaning dress code. In places where the caste system was most oppressive, such as in South India, men were forbidden to wear shoes, clean clothes, and good fabrics, and women were forbidden to wear a bodice and jewelry. Thus genetically nonexistent differences were socially created and imposed culturally. As Robert Deliege (1997, 31) describes, the ability to dress according to their own liking was a primary restorer of the dignity of the Dalits.

The Indian caste system recognizes that color is metaphoric. The term *Varna* literally means "color," but the four Varnas are arranged not according to color of skin but according to *guna* (quality), of which three types are recognized as being associated with three colors: white, red, and black, with *sattvic, rajasic,* and *tamasic,* respectively.[6] Does the ideology of race differ significantly from this point of view when some qualities are attributed to people on the basis of their "genetics"?

Even though race is not based on the concepts of ritual purity and pollution, the rigidity with which "purity" of blood is maintained makes it no less sacred than the concepts of caste purity and pollution. The intersection of race and caste lies in the "pollution" passed down to the progeny in case of a tainted marriage. Thus, in both cases, it is the progeny who stand to lose more than the parents who commit the "offense." In both cases, the generational aspect makes the biological a reality. "Mixed" blood is abhorred, as it is symbolic of transgression of rights of the group over its women. In *The Laws of Manu* (Tambiah 1973), the origin of numerous other caste, or *jati*, groups from the original four Varnas, is traced from intermarriage between the Varnas. The more the "mixing," the greater the downward mobility. However, the prescription for upward mobility or the restoration of caste status was the repeated marriage, over the generations, in exactly one's own caste status (202).

Both caste and race are patriarchal in that the males of the group use the women as boundary markers, where the power of the men to keep their women protected from "pollution" is the key to the purity/power of their group and is directly related to dominance. *The Laws of Manu,* the guidebook for maintaining social norms, gives the men of highest status the widest range of access to women. Thus, men of the higher Varnas can have access to women of all Varnas lower than them. It means that the Brahmin can access all women, while the Shudra is confined to women only of his stratum, which also means that since men of the higher Varnas can all access his women folk, he may be left with none, with the most undesirable, or with the ones "passed down."

Since Hindu society traditionally permitted polygyny, a Brahmin could have women of the lower Varnas as his secondary wives or concubines, with their children having consequently fewer rights on the property and status of the father. When the status of the mother was well below that of the father, then the children formed a new *jati.*

S. J. Tambiah (1973) has given the mathematical rules by which new *jatis* were churned out by the key principle of classification, where mixtures give rise to new categories. However, the caste status of the child suffered most when a woman married below her level, for the rules were exactly opposite for her. While a woman of lower caste could have sexual or conjugal relations with men of caste higher than her own, the opposite was socially and morally abhorrent. Thus, a high-caste woman was confined to be the consort of only men of her own caste. The progeny of a Brahmin woman and a Shudra man was thus the lowest of all mortals, the *chandala*, condemned to live off carrion and perform the duties of burning dead bodies. Without the scriptural sanctions of caste, race also worked in more or less the same fashion, where the overt power of some races allowed their men to have free access to women of the dominated races while at the same time it restricted the access of men of the inferior race to women of the superior race and often with most dire consequences. In all cases, the power is symbolized in the confinement of one's own women and in the exploitation of other women.

In India, this kind of situation, perpetrated over the centuries, has led to some communities of low-caste men being reduced to pimping their women as a full-time occupation, such as the *nats* of Rajasthan. Pauline Kolenda (1987) has shown how widows of the *churha* caste are sold off forcibly by their own men.

It has also led to several defensive mechanisms on the part of women of the lower caste to uphold their own honor. Low-caste women in the North Indian region of Haryana told me that they never allowed the young daughter or the daughters-in-law to go out of the house for fetching water or fodder. In this part of the country, it is the task of women to fetch fodder, fuel, and water from some distance from the house.[7] However, while I saw young girls, both married and unmarried of the dominant caste, going everywhere for these tasks, the young women of the low castes observed far greater restrictions in their movements. "The high-caste [men] will protect their own women. Who in the village has courage even to raise their eyes at the women of high castes, but who will protect our daughters? The high-caste men will exploit them at the first opportunity. Therefore we have to take care of our own *izzat* [honor]," I was told by a low-caste woman of middle age. But such precautions used to be meaningless in the times before legislatures were made to protect the interests of the low castes. Even today, such legal protections are sterile if not backed by political clout. By and large, the attitudes of the high-caste men toward the low-caste women has not changed, for they are modeled on certain stereotypes reminiscent of the racial metaphors of black women (Gilman 1985).

Further, the rules of exclusion have always tended to push more and more persons out of the privileged categories, thus always maintaining the exclusive group as a minority. Thus, even the slightest breach of caste norms was enough to push people down the ladder. However, it was more often than not the downgrading of class that led to a downgrading of caste as well (Shyamlal 1997). The norms of personal hygiene and food taboos made it impossible for the very poor to stick to these terms. Thus, as Shyamlal has recorded, history shows many instances in which because of famine, conquest, or poverty, persons of high caste were forced to eat forbidden foods and perform lowly tasks for sheer survival. Such persons or groups invariably went down the caste hierarchy. Thus, although scholars of Indian society (e.g., Dumont 1970) are not willing to concede that economic status plays a significant role in caste hierarchy, they are being too idealistic at the ground level, and as shown by M. N. Srinivas (1991) and others, economic status and power play significant roles in determining the hierarchy of castes. Also, the normative order always works in ways to ensure that the top layer is small in number and powerful.

CASTE, RACE, AND GENDER

Whether caste or race is the basis of oppression, one mode of oppression is the creating of two models of womanhood: one of the dominant group and one of the oppressed. Both work for the domination of women but in different ways. While the high-caste women suffered isolation and immobility, being confined to their homes, the low-caste women suffered from a stereotyping that made them into diametric opposites of the high-caste "goddess," a woman seen as the epitome of chastity and virtue. Hindu society, unlike Christian society, worships its women but only as chaste, nonsexual beings. The highest honor given to a woman is that of a mother, and the most respected category of woman is a widow. Indian men find it difficult to adjust the image of a sexually active woman with one whom they can respect. Thus, all women who rise high in social esteem are either widows of high caste (e.g., Indira Gandhi)—which equates them with ascetics, as they are expected to live a life of renunciation—or women who for some other reasons are living a life of asceticism. A woman of a low caste could never aspire to the model of an ascetic or woman of virtue. In India, the same patriarchy that forbade women of higher castes to expose their bodies or even their faces, that condemned them to remain confined to the space within the house, and that forced them to find glory in renunciation or even death (*sati*) forbade these very practices to the women of the lower castes (Channa 1998).

Thus, the bodies of both high-caste and low-caste women were inscribed with the patriarchal values of the men of high caste. The women of high caste had to preserve their bodies in pure state, reducing its sexuality by fasting and by rigorous physical confinement. The body of a woman was the exclusive property of her husband, and after his death she lost all rights to adorn it or even to keep it with care. She had to reify it by starvation and lack of any kind of decoration. Shaving one's hair desexualized a widow. A high-caste man ensured that even after his death the body of his woman would remain his exclusive property. The most extreme form of it was her glorification by burning her on her husband's funeral pyre. The bodies of low-caste women were on the other hand treated as common property. The low-caste women such as the Dhobi women were not allowed to wear the nose ring that among the high-caste women in Northern India was a symbol of virginity before marriage and of chastity after marriage. The low-caste women were allowed no such symbol, for they were not seen as being worthy of having any virtue.

Thus, the moral order of virtuous women and compliant women was legitimized on "claims of tradition," which as Victoria Ana Goddard (2000, 7) points out, are nothing but "the protection of existing hierarchies and values." The metaphors of virtue such as *sati* were reserved only for women of high caste. Thus, while *sati* (women who had actually burnt themselves on the funeral pyre of their husbands) were worshipped for posterity as "goddesses," only the queens and women of ruling families had the privilege of becoming *sati*. If a woman of low caste professed such virtues, she would become the subject of ridicule by both the high castes and the low castes. Thus, the model of a low-caste woman led to creation of a sexual object of forbidden desire. The high-caste women were expected by their own men to be virtuous to the extent of being sexually passive. Even today, most men do not expect their wives to be excessively sexual. Most Indian men maintain double standards by which they look for sexual titillation outside of marriage and quite often secretively, for excessive sexuality is seen as being a base quality befitting men only of the low strata. Even for men of high castes, the desirable standards are of sexual restraint. However, if at all they wanted to satisfy their baser instincts, they were expected to look toward the low-caste women and not to their own wives.

Such sexual metaphors of lewdness and hypersexuality, as applied to persons of low caste, are no different from those applied to persons of the dark races. Thus darkness or blackness becomes a metaphor for inner darkness or moral degradation. Good-looking Dhobi children often came back from school complaining that the teacher had told them that they "did not look like Dhobis." "Does one have to be dark and ugly to look like a Dhobi?" The stereotype for a man of low caste is that he is always dark looking, and that of a woman of low caste is that she is also dark looking but well endowed physically and usually sexually attractive.

Thus, many of the metaphors used in speech employ the labels of the low castes to depict uncouth and nonnormative behavior. Thus, "Do not behave like a Chamar" is a common form of saying "Do not misbehave." A woman dressed in nonacceptable aesthetic standards may be referred to as being dressed like a *bhangan* (sweepress), and a dark and ugly woman is often described as being a *churhi* (very low caste). All terms for low castes are synonymous with abuse much like that deriving from the term *nigger*.

The laws of the land forbid the use of abusive language toward persons of the low caste. Thus, it would be a cognizable offense under the Indian penal code to call a Chamar a Chamar. But the people of high castes keep the ideological denigration alive by using these terms among themselves and making them synonymous with what they consider the low castes to be.

POSITIVE DISCRIMINATION AND LABELING

The constitution of India was prepared in 1947, when India became an independent country, and it made special provisions for the hitherto marginalized populations of the country, listing them definitively as scheduled tribes and scheduled castes (Bhagwan Das 1996), with the latter predominantly including those considered untouchable. It was recognized that centuries of oppression would have left them with little resources, both material and psychological, to come up to the level of the rest of the population. The facilities included reservation of seats in institutes of higher education and government jobs. However, very little input was given at the formative period, such as good educational inputs at the primary level. Thus, those who were at the bottom of the class hierarchy had hardly any resources that would bring them up to the level of being capable of claiming reservation for such high-level facilities. While I was doing my fieldwork among the Dhobis in the seventies, a large number of Dhobi children were going to school and even to college. Their main complaint against this form of positive discrimination was that it was discrimination in a different garb. "They label us and then put us in a corner." "Throughout our educational life, we carry the stigma of 'scheduled caste.'" In fact, in the speech of contemporary people, the term *scheduled caste* carries with it the same connotation of disgust and contempt as the words *Dom* and *Chamar* in earlier times. Thus, the label derives its meaning from the people with whom it is associated. As long as the people suffer from discrimination, any word used for them will carry the same derogatory meaning, no matter what the literal meaning of the term is. Thus, Mahatma Gandhi had used the term *harijan* instead of *achut* for the untouchables. Although *harijan* means literally "children of god," after being used for the untouchables, it became a synonym for "untouchable" and was being used as such until the untouchables themselves rejected it, preferring instead the politically charged term *Dalit* (Fernandes 1996), which means "downtrodden."

The manner in which the privileges granted to the untouchables are dispensed to them makes it more a practice synonymous with the *daan* that was given to them traditionally. The concept of *daan* carries with it not only a power differential of the giver and the receiver in the idiom of caste but also the stigma of purity and impurity. Thus, in traditional *daan*, the high-caste giver divests himself or herself of impurity through the gift given to the low caste

(Raheja 1989), who absorbs it within his own already impure state. The benefits given to the low castes under various schemes of the government have taken on almost the same symbolism of *daan*, where the authorities, most of them high caste, give away these privileges not as a matter of right to the low caste but in the idiom of *daan*. Low castes at the receiving end are made to feel inferior, with the giver being morally superior. This is manifest in the condescending attitude of most government officials and even school and college authorities in their dealing with the lower castes. Thus, most untouchables said that they were made to "feel like beggars."

Moreover, even when they occupy prestigious positions, they are stigmatized, and various labels are used for them. For example, the term *quota doctors* is widely prevalent for those who have entered the medical profession through the reservation quotas.

Thus, speech, as Michel Foucault (1980) puts it, is a powerful medium of discourse. As long as the discourse of inequality based on caste remains, all forms verbal reformation in referring to the low castes will only be recast in the idiom of contempt and ridicule. The power of the elite to convert speech into oppression is proportional only to the extent of the oppression. Thus, the term *Dalit* has now become synonymous with the emergent power of the low castes in the political arena. It is also a symbol of their protest against oppression. When people want to turn the discourse toward the power acquisition by the untouchables, they use the term *Dalit*. This also symbolizes the emergence of an untouchable selfhood. This is the first term the untouchables have evolved for themselves in contrast to the earlier process of being labeled from above. It is thus symbolic of their developing consciousness.

DALIT WOMEN AND SELFHOOD

The discourse on Dalit women has often referred to their being doubly discriminated against and highly marginalized. For example, according to the Charter of Dalit Human Rights—put forward by the National Campaign on Dalit Human Rights in India, an organization fighting for the abolition of untouchability—states "We recognize that Dalit women have three-fold discrimination. They are discriminated against because they are women (gender), because they are Dalits (caste), and because they are Dalit women by their own men folk (gender and caste)" (Asian Human Rights Commission 1999). I find this sort of rhetorical labeling objectionable in the sense that it takes away from the Dalit women any agency and selfhood that they may possess. If we describe them as being thrice oppressed, then we are making them only objects of our *daan* or pity and not taking cognizance of their strengths and muting whatever voices they may have.

In my work on the untouchables, I have found that the women in these communities have more agency and are stronger than their counterparts in the higher castes. One of the major theoretical premises in the debates on gender inequality has been the public–private dichotomy—introduced by M. Rosaldo (1974), extensively used by other scholars, but critiqued by recent scholars as being "ethnocentric"—and the need felt to dispense with such rigid dichotomies in favor of anthropologically constructed situational conceptualizations (Goddard 2000, 17).

The untouchables had traditionally been entrusted with most of the services and productive activities, such as scavenging, sweeping, washing of clothes, pottery, iron smithy, cutting hair, and so forth. All these activities were performed as household enterprises, with the women participating equally. In some cases, such as in the case of the scavengers, there may have been no division of labor, and in others, such as that among the Dhobi and barbers, there may have been a division of labor but not one involving a separation of men or women from the arena of work. The work was performed on the domestic front and treated as a domestic service, even by the high castes receiving the service. The productive unit was always the household (Channa 1985, 1989). Thus, kinship relations were predominant in the work situation, and the women worked along with the men in what may be called a "household-based work situation." The women's space often extended beyond the four walls of the house, when they were required to go out for their work. Thus, Dhobi women would stand at the street corners ironing clothes, would visit the household to deliver washed clothes, and would go the banks of the river to help their men thrash out the clothes in the river water. The women also had the control of the household economy, which was not significantly different from the productive economy. They bought all the requirements for washing clothes, which was their livelihood, along with their subsistence requirements.

Most important, the relationship between husband and wife and between men and women in general was far more symmetrical than the ones found among the high castes. Lower-caste men and women were bound by feelings of "shared oppression" (Lorde 1992, 50), sentiments not felt by men of higher castes. The men of the dominant group had models for both their own women and their "other" women that were not shared by the men of the marginalized groups. I have never come across any man from the low castes who believed that his woman was morally degraded or sexually unrestrained. On the contrary, most men treated their wives as equals, and the relationship was symmetrical to the extent that a low-caste man would not be averse to helping his wife out with domestic work. The women treated the men as equals, and I often heard a Dhobi woman address her husband with the familiar *tu* instead of the respectful *aap*, used by high-caste women. Such sharing of roles has been reported by other scholars who have worked among the lower castes (Searle-Chatterjee 1981).

THE NARRATIVES OF CONTESTED SPACE

Labels such as *dominated, subjugated,* and *marginalized,* in my opinion, tell only half the story. They create pictures in our minds of shapeless, huddled, muted figures. I believe that too much emphasis on exploitation is a view from the top. Looking from the bottom up, one sees a different picture. There is dissent, resentment, as well as counternarratives that run in directions contrary to the ones created from the top. At the World Conference against Racism (WCAR), the Dalits demonstrated that "the oppressed are not totally powerless. They always discover spaces to assert themselves, they always have more 'power' than what is ascribed to them by the oppressors" (Franco and Parmar 1996, 83). They also refuted once and for all the debate as to whether they themselves are party to their own oppression, a debate carried on by many scholars on the caste system.

The most significant aspect that came forth in view of the political action of the Dalits was their capacity for organization and positive action. It is well known that the categories of "untouchable" or "scheduled caste" were creations of different regimes, the former by the British and the latter by the Indian government. Before that, for centuries Dalits had no common identity and were just hierarchized, scattered communities isolated in their oppression and suffering, not identifying with others in similar plight. More than anything else, this may have been one of the prime reasons why they did not rebel against their situation. The labeling, even the one external to them, has definitely given them a political identity by which to assert themselves. Today, as the Dalits, they are a powerful community, one large enough to act as a pressure group in a democracy.

During the conference in Durban, their leaders told me that they had been preparing themselves for this event for three years. Even at the venue they demonstrated extraordinary discipline and eagerness to make the maximum impact. Even while the delegates were waiting outside to enter for participation in the opening ceremony, a man dressed in colorful traditional attire began a song and dance while drummers took up the beat. The effect was that as desired: everyone turned around to take a look. This high-visibility and dramatic visual impact in the forms of jackets, headbands, and drumming made the Dalits a highly recognizable and visible part of the proceedings. This, from a sociological as well as a symbolic point of view, was an announcement by the Dalits that they were now both visible and audible. From a people who had borne the burden of silence and invisibility for centuries, it was a great achievement. The presence of Dalit women in large numbers at the conference and their prominent leadership of the proceedings support my argument that the space granted to Dalit women in their own community far exceeds that occupied by women of higher castes. The men and women who represented the Dalits at the conference were perhaps not representative of all Dalit communities in India. It was heartening to see poor and uneducated Dalits being escorted to the venue by their more-educated and better-placed counterparts. The Dalit leaders had certainly made an effort not to limit themselves to the more privileged members of their communities. The representation was certainly symbolic of the emerging Dalit power in India.

ACHIEVEMENTS AT THE WCAR

Although paragraphs 84–88 of the NGO Forum Declaration are a true description of the indignities faced by the Dalits in contemporary times, and even though the declaration has taken a clear stand in recognizing caste as a form of discrimination (para. 52), it is disheartening to note that the official declaration of the WCAR makes no separate mention of the Dalits and does not recognize caste as a form of discrimination that is still persistent. Except for a general recognition covering all forms of discrimination, such as that in paragraphs 10, 26, and 28, which mainly deal with the violation of human rights, and particularly that of paragraph 28, which mentions the words *group, collectivity,* and *community,* there is nothing significant to support the Dalit cause in this document.

The official state representatives at the conference were probably influenced by the Indian government's staunch stand against the inclusion of the Dalits in the WCAR declaration and the mention of caste as a form of discrimination still existing in India.

It is true that the Indian government has, from the time of the framing of the Indian constitution, disowned the idea of caste and that all Indians have constitutionally granted equal rights. It is also true that to make up for centuries of oppression, a number of benefits under positive discriminatory practices have been granted. But as I have argued in this chapter and as has been recognized by the NGO Forum Declaration, it is not the state but civil society that perpetuates the atrocities, and the state maintains its approval of such by its silence. The state's refusal to recognize the continued oppression of Dalits is a pointer toward its lack of real commitment to the cause of the Dalits.

There is also an intellectualist and possibly patriotic point of view of Indian scholars that objects to the West's justification of colonization on the basis of the "uncivilized" practices such as caste. Andre Beteille (1983) and others like him have been bitter critics of what they consider to be the colonial attitude toward Indian society. But while I would fully agree with this point of view, I am also of the opinion that the Indian intellectual should not lose sight of the ground-level realities. They should join hands with like-minded Western scholars and expose the similarities in the forms of discriminations such as race and caste. I would also fully agree with Beteille that Indian society is no better or worse than Western society and that both have equal degrees of discrimination as well as egalitarian ideologies. As he has written, "Surely, in the early years of this century the hierarchical symbols of the British Raj in India were just as extravagant as those of caste" (53).

At the WCAR, the point to be driven home was not that caste is a unique form of discrimination to be found only in India but that there were enough similarities and intersections between caste and race for them to be taken up at the same platform.

NOTES

1. The low castes are also designated as being service castes, as they traditionally provide many services to the higher castes. The Dhobis are the caste assigned to the washing of clothes. However, their work does not involve only the cleaning of clothes but the ritual absorption of pollution from these dirty clothes, especially from the clothes of menstruating women and those of women postdelivery. The ritually impure status of this caste group thus derives from the association with bodily impurities. The women of this group cut nails and assist in childbirth, again highly impure activities.

2. The Walled City of Delhi was built by the Moghul emperor Shah Jehan in the sixteenth century. It was enclosed by seven gates and a running wall. Some parts of the wall and the gates still remain. The city of New Delhi is adjunct to this old city, both of which form contemporary Delhi. The old city is now a hub of commercial activity, but some of the traditional aura remains, as do some of the old structures. The Dhobi Katras, however, are almost gone, and most of the Dhobis settled in new parts of the city.

3. Although in every part of India that is Hindu people practice untouchability in some form or the other, the harshness of segregation varies from place to place, being least noticeable in regions such as Bengal and Punjab and most conspicuous in the southern and western parts.

4. The World Conference against Racism, held in Durban in September 2001, where the Dalit had made their presence felt as a pressure group.

5. Some scholars of the caste system have seen the traditional occupations such as those providing monopolistic advantages to the groups, as those who are assigned to these tasks are the only ones who can do them. In times of economic change, such monopoly may have its advantage, as described by Owen Lynch (1969) in his study of the Jatavs of Agra, who became rich when shoe making became an industry and high castes

would have nothing to with this polluting occupation. However, in later periods, with the development of the leather industry, many high-caste businessmen entered it, but the actual processing of leather is still done by the low castes. I have studied a similar situation for the Dhobis and the laundry business (see Channa 1985).

6. The *sattvic* qualities associated with the color white represent purity and involve the taboo of eating forbidden or stale foods, drinking liquor, engaging in violence, and so forth; it epitomizes restraint. The *rajasic* qualities, associated with the color red, represent a rich lifestyle; eating meat (that of approved qualities), drinking liquor, gambling, and living an ostentatious lifestyle are permitted. The *tamasic* qualities are represented by the color black and represent a degraded lifestyle that permits eating stale and impure foods, carrion, and forbidden meats; drinking liquor; and living in poverty and filth. Usually, the Brahmins are enjoined to live a sattvic life; the Kshatriyas, a rajasic life; and the Shudras, a tamasic life. The fourth category of the vashyas falls somewhere between the sattvic and the rajasic. Its members usually live a rich life, wearing ornaments and possessing wealth but eating vegetarian food and not drinking liquor.

7. Even today, few villages in India have a piped water supply. It is the task of women to walk to the nearest natural source of water, such as a well or stream, and fetch water for drinking and domestic use. Men never fetch water in any part of the country.

REFERENCES

Aggarwal, Surabhi. 1990. Violence against women. *Eastern Anthropologist* 43 (2): 169–86.

Asian Human Rights Commission. 1999. A charter of Dalit human rights. *Human Rights Solidarity* 9 (3).

Beteille, Andre. 1983 Homo hierarchicus, homo equalis. In *The idea of natural inequality and other essays*, 33–54. Delhi, India: Oxford University Press.

Bhagwan Das. 1996. Reservations today and tomorrow. In *The emerging Dalit identity: The reassertion of the subalterns*, ed. Walter Fernandes. New Delhi, India: Indian Social Institute.

Bourdieu, Pierre. 1990. *The logic of practice*. Cambridge: Polity Press.

Channa, Subhadra Mitra. 1985. *Tradition and rationality in economic behaviour*. New Delhi, India: Cosmo.

———. 1989. Change and adaptive process in a traditional occupationary group in an urban setting. *South Asian Social Scientist* 5 (2): 21–32.

———. 1992. Changing gender relations of a traditional occupationary caste group in urban India. *Eastern Anthropologist* 45:321–41.

———. 1995. Indian peasantry: Some analytical issues. In *Peasants in India History*, ed. V. K. Thakur. Ranchi, India: Janaki Prakashan.

———. 1997. Gender and social space in a Haryana village. *Indian Journal of Gender Studies* 4 (1): 21–34.

———. 1998. Violence as practice: The sociology of power relations. In *Gender and violence*, ed. Abha Avasthi. Lucknow, India.

———. 2000. Caste: Pragmatism or ideology. Unpublished lecture delivered as an Ambedkar Lecture at University of Calcutta.

Cox, Oliver C. 1944–1945. Race and caste, a distinction. *American Journal of Sociology* 50:306–8.

Crowley, Helen, and Susan Himmelweit. 1992. Discrimination, subordination, and difference: Feminist perspectives. In *Knowing women: Feminism and knowledge*, ed. Helen Crowley and Susan Himmelweit. London: Polity Press.

Deliege, Robert. 1997. The world of the "untouchables": Pariyars of Tamil Nadu. Delhi: Oxford University Press.

Dumont, Louis. 1961. Caste, racism, and "stratification": Reflections of a social anthropologist. *Contributions to Indian Sociology* (5): 20–43.

———. 1970. *Homo hierarchicus*. English ed. Repr., Chicago: University of Chicago Press, 1980.

Durkheim, Emile. 1965. *The elementary forms of religious life*. English trans. New York: Free Press.

Fernandes, Walter. 1996. Introduction. In *The emerging Dalit identity*, ed. Walter Fernandes. New Delhi, India: Indian Social Institute.

Foucault, Michel. 1980. *Power/knowledge*. Ed. and trans. Colin Gordon. New York: Pantheon Books.

Franco, F., and Vijay Parmar. 1996. Dalit organisations: Reconstituting reality. In *The emerging Dalit identity*, ed. Fernandes. New Delhi: Indian Social Institute

Gilman, Sander L. 1985. Black bodies, white bodies: Towards an iconography of female sexuality in late nineteenth century art, medicine, and literature. In *"Race," Writing, and Difference*, ed. Henry Louis Gates Jr. Chicago: University of Chicago Press.

Ginwalla, Persis, and Suguna Ramanathan. 1996. Dalit women as receivers and modifiers of discourse. In *The emerging Dalit identity*, ed. Fernandes. New Delhi, India: Indian Social Institute.

Goddard, Victoria Ana. 2000. Introduction. In *Gender, agency, and change*, ed. Victoria Ana Goddard. London: Routledge.

Hansen, Karen Tranberg. 2000. Gender and difference: Youth, bodies and clothing. In *Gender, agency, and change*, ed. Goddard. London: Routledge.

Harrison, Faye V. 1995. The persistent power of "race" in the cultural and political economy of racism. *Annual Review of Anthropology* 24:47–74.

———. 1997. The gendered politics and violence of structural adjustment: A view from Jamaica. In *Situated lives: Gender and culture in everyday life*, ed. Louise Lamphere et al., 451–66. New York, Routledge.

———. 1998. Introduction: Expanding the discourse on "race." *American Anthropologist* 100 (3): 609–31.

Kolenda, Pauline. 1987. Widowhood among untouchable Churhas. In *Regional differences in family structure in India*, ed. Pauline Kolenda. Jaipur, India: Rawat.

Leach, E. R. 1960. Introduction: What should we mean by caste? In *Aspects of caste in South India, Ceylon, and north-west Pakistan*, ed. E. R. Leach. Cambridge: Cambridge University Press.

Lorde, Audre. 1992. Age, race, class and sex: Women redefining difference. In *Knowing women*, ed. Crowley and Himmelweit, 47–57. Cambridge: Cambridge University Press.

Lynch, Owen. 1969. The politics of untouchability: Social mobility and social change in a city in India. Tucson: University of Arizona Press.

Miles, Robert. 1989. *Racism*. London: Routledge.

Miller, J. Baker. 1978. *Towards a new psychology of women*. Harmondsworth, Eng.: Penguin.

Milner, Murray, Jr. 1994. *Status and sacredness*. New York: Oxford University Press.

Parish, Steven, M. 1997. *Hierarchy and its discontents: Culture and the politics of consciousness in caste society*. Delhi, India: Oxford University Press.

Raheja, Gloria Goodwin. 1989. *The poison in the gift*. Chicago: University of Chicago Press.

Rosaldo, M. 1974. Woman, culture and society: A theoretical overview. In *Woman, culture, and society*, ed. M. Rosaldo and L. Lamphere. Stanford, Calif.: Stanford University Press.

Searle-Chatterjee, Mary. 1981. *Reversible sex-roles: The special case of the Benares sweepers*. Oxford: Pergamon Press.

Shore, Chris. 1997. Metaphors of Europe: Integration and the politics of language. In *Anthropology and cultural studies*, ed. Stephen Nugent and Chris Shore. London: Pluto Press.

Shyamlal. 1997. *From higher caste to lower caste*. Jaipur, India: Rawat.

Smedley, Audrey. 1993. *Race in North America: Origin and evolution of a worldview*. Boulder, Colo.: Westview.

Srinivas, M. N. 1991. India: Social structure. Delhi: Hindustan Publishing.

Tambiah, S. J. 1973. From Varna to caste through mixed unions. In *The character of kinship*, ed. Jack Goody. London: Cambridge University Press.

Werbner, Prina. 1997. "The lion of Lahore": Anthropology, cultural performance, and Imran Khan. In *Anthropology and cultural studies*, ed. Stephen Nugent and Chris Shore. London: Pluto Press.

• 3 •

Margins of Democracy:
Aboriginal Australians and Inequality

J. Maria Pedersen

$\mathcal{I}$ am an Australian Aboriginal woman from the remote Kimberley region of Western Australia, and I am confronted daily with the legacy of all that colonization implies. As a woman and a mother, I am challenged by perceptions that seek to diminish my capacity to contribute to society. As an Aboriginal woman and a single parent, I am even further challenged to overcome these "additional conditions" that have the potential to seriously disadvantage my family.

Living in remote areas such as the Kimberley region has a tendency to encourage an acceptance of the constraints of oppression. The tyranny of distance creates socially, economically, and politically isolated communities that often do not recognize discrimination as being a divisive and destructive entity. I believed that the World Conference against Racism would be a means to break the culture of silence, to seek allies in the struggle for recognition of human rights for all people, and to establish proactive networks in the fight against global marginalization.

There is an increasing number of our strong women who see our roles as improving the future for our children and breaking down some of the barriers that potentially impinge on the lives that our children and grandchildren will lead. Like many Aboriginal Australians, I was not born a citizen of my country but became one as a consequence of the 1944 Native Citizenship Act. It must be understood that if one's parents were "citizens," this did not automatically confer citizenship to children. My father obtained his citizenship in 1948 and applied for my sisters and me to be added to his citizenship papers in 1964. I am constantly reminded of the inequalities and inequities in our society, as I have personally experienced the direct effects and practices of racism.

I am one of many women who are attempting to challenge the oppressive social constructs that continue into the twenty-first century, to have our rights to full citizenship validated, and to maintain our cultural and social dignity. We do this by presenting indigenous perspectives of who we are and about our own lives, by questioning the ways Europeans have identified and stereotyped Aboriginal people, and by asserting our rights as legitimate citizens of this country. As the sole and primary caregivers of our children, as mothers, grandmothers, aunts, and sisters, we have watched our young people be discriminated against because of their race; we have shared stories of abuse and intimidation by nonindigenous people in positions of authority or power; we have despaired that life will not be better for our children and grandchildren; but we have never given in to the perceptions that we are lesser human beings or that we deserve to be oppressed. We come from histories of strong women who protected their families in times of severe disadvantage, and we have learned to meet those who would oppress us, on our own terms.

Social injustice in our communities threatens to overwhelm the positives in our lives, but we have learned to employ those aspects of the European culture that will assist us in our struggles for recognition and for self-determination. Strength from our families, our culture, and our histories has instilled the capacity to challenge the methodologies used to further silence our oppressed people. Rather than accept the stereotypical perceptions of inferiority, subservience, and weakness imposed on us, we have acquired those skills that will empower us to challenge the inequalities of our world in the language and the ways of the dominant culture.

THE MARGINS OF DEMOCRACY: ABORIGINAL AUSTRALIANS AND INEQUALITY

Equality in a democratic society suggests that there is the same distribution, to all citizens, of positive social resources that have the same degree of quality and quantity in operation or effect. It is evident from the poverty and disadvantage that exist in developed countries such as Australia that this does not occur. Those living in the margins of any society and being confronted daily with hunger, inadequate housing, reduced health, and minimal educational and employment prospects do not fit the liberalist assumptions of a level playing field for all and typically operate under survival conditions. These marginalized citizens cannot employ their existing resources to acquire and accumulate material possessions and wealth; instead, their resources are exhausted in the day-to-day struggle to maintain a life of poverty and disadvantage.

Australia's history since 1788 has resulted in a legacy of social inequality that continues to resonate throughout the Australian Aboriginal community. This social exclusion is evident in the presence of disproportionate amounts of negative social values, such as the poverty, crime, and imprisonment (Sidanius and Pratto, 1999) confronting Aboriginal Australians in the twenty-first century. Race has been described as the most recognizable, important, and enduring collective identity that groups possess (Helms 1994); it can equally be seen that race then becomes the factor that identifies a group and contributes to that group's collective disadvantage more than any other single factor.

The colonization process began the initial deconstruction of the Aboriginal identity within the European psyche, through social and cultural alienation. Australia was proclaimed *terra nullius* and therefore could be claimed as crown land for the British Empire. Not only did the Europeans consider that the Aboriginal inhabitants did not productively utilize the country and therefore had no enduring links to the land, but they also considered these people to be little more than local wildlife. Little thought was given to the Aboriginal inhabitants who had occupied the land for hundreds of generations. *Terra nullius* attempted to invalidate the history, the lives, the very existence of the Aboriginal population, thus setting up an unequal balance of power for generations of Aboriginal Australians.

Many Australians are still coming to terms with the reality of an Australian history that is a brutal reminder of how this nation was created and the treatment meted out to the Aboriginal inhabitants (Austen 1998; Elder 1998). There are significant sectors of the community who seek to diminish these experiences and minimize the impact they had on the Aboriginal population; thus, inequality has been an overriding condition in the lives of Aboriginal people since 1788. Aboriginal people continue to conduct their lives in the shadow of all that citizenship and equality imply. Many Aboriginal Australians are challenging the perception that all Australians should be treated "equally," as it suggests that *all* Australian citizens currently enjoy equality and equitable access to appropriate resources. Such ambassadors for Aboriginal Australians are speaking out about the ways in which Aboriginal people were, and still are, subjected to the processes of dehumanization and alienation.

The dehumanization of Aboriginal people began as cultural ignorance and social dominance, and it was perpetuated by the theories of social Darwinism. Therefore, those of mixed blood were seen to be marginally better than their native mothers and could be assimilated into white society. However, the "degrees of Aboriginal blood" the children possessed determined the degree of perceived negative traits inherited from their native mothers. The imported British ideologies meant that the colonists and the subsequent Australian society would always view Aborigines as being inferior, training them for lower-order manual laboring jobs. The rigid class structure and social hierarchies of British society typically meant attempting to train them "to have some idea of the respective relations of Master and Servant" and bringing them into "habits of order and subordination" (Reynolds 2000). This set the scene for a history of inequality in all facets of Aboriginal life that continues into the new millennium. Alienation included separation from land, culture, and heritage; from family and kin; and ultimately from practices that recognized the humanity of the individual. Those of mixed race were consequently being seen as a "race of outsiders, . . . with no place in the community," with some referring to half-castes as a "blight on the community" (Beresford and Omaji 1998).

This led to the introduction of quantum blood types (Helms 1994), such as half-castes, quadroons, and octoroons. In effect, they were considered little more than savages or animals and were treated as such. Of the ways colonists have constructed the identities of Aboriginal peoples, L. T. Smith (1999) quotes a First Nation Canadian woman: a "female horse, a female Native, but everyone else gets to be called a man or a woman." The inequalities of British colonization had their foundations in the imported ideologies of a male-dominated, class-oriented Eurocentric social structure. Australia had become a colony of the British Empire, and the rules governing the colony were in line with the colonialist views of creating and maintaining social order.

Colonization meant that Aboriginal people came under the direction and control of the British Empire and, as such, were British subjects when it came to matters of the law. However, they were not legally defined as being citizens of Australia; thus, they were denied the legal, social, and economic rights that the European citizens enjoyed as a matter as course. This was largely due to the assumptions that the Aboriginal Australians were a simple, childlike race, lacking in the morals and the intellectual capacity that Europeans possessed. It can be seen that the Europeans arrived in Australia with preconceived ideas of how human beings behaved; thus, Aboriginal people were considered little more than animals that could be bred out.

The various legislations of colonial Australia may have been initially set up with philanthropic ideologies to protect Aborigines; however, the haphazard nature of such policies led to inconsistencies in how they were administered (Berndt and Berndt 1988). This administration of the policies was typically carried out by untrained, undisciplined, and, in so many cases, racist individuals driven primarily by self-interest. The policy of protection was supposedly carried out "for their [Aboriginal Australians'] own good." Those children who had some European blood were considered better than their Aboriginal mothers; in addition, the Roth Inquiry of 1904 (Western Australia) found that, if left to their own devices, Aboriginal girls would become promiscuous and the young men would turn to criminal behavior—two traits determined to be genetic predispositions.

The 1905 Aborigines Act (Western Australia) placed all Aboriginal people under the guardianship of the state. It became illegal for non-Aboriginals to cohabit or consort with natives—typically this law referred to Aboriginal women—and the state had automatic custody of Aboriginal children. Thus, the separation of children from their mothers, under the quantum blood theory, led to generations of "stolen children." The assimilation policy of the mid-1950s set in motion practices designed to absorb the half-caste population into the white population. The decision makers firmly believed that the blacks would die out if left to their own devices and with the absorption of the "coloreds." Thus, Aboriginality would gradually die out, becoming nothing more than an anecdotal reminder of a hidden past. Despite this attempted absorption into white society, Aborigines were and still are confronted with the lack of integration into, and of access to, the opportunities and values of mainstream Australia. Beresford and Omaji (1996) comment on the complex social forces that continue to marginalize Aboriginal youth, noting that "the forces driving these experiences lie in the deeper issues of racism, historical oppression and dispossession which have a cumulative effect upon generations of Aborigines in Western Australia." Inherent racism has become entrenched in the psyche of the Australian public, and this continues the marginalization and inequality experienced by Aboriginal Australians. The 1905 Aborigines Act (Western Australia) was passed because lawmakers believed that Aborigines had to be controlled and guided in order to prevent the inherently biological deficits of criminality and immorality from dominating their behavior.

The police were the agency instructed to enforce and administer this act, and this has led to generations of disproportionate contact with the legal system and the negative effects of racism. The historic relationship between Aboriginal people and law enforcement has resulted in a negative mentality that permeates the police culture. There is still the perception that all Aboriginal youth have criminal tendencies and that young Aboriginal females have an inclination toward promiscuity and loose morals (Haebich 1992). While it is quite encouraging to know and work with police officers who are actively involved in trying to make a difference in the interaction between the law and the community, the social indicators for Aboriginal Australians are clear examples of how insidious value judgments continuously affect the lives of Aboriginal Australians.

Instances of arrest and the resultant police records for Aboriginal Australians reduce the employment prospects of individuals and consequently reduce the economic status of families who may have lost the sole breadwinner in the family (B. Hunter 1999). The introduction of mandatory sentencing laws in some states in Australia can only be seen as a racist policy designed to further affect Aboriginal people (Jonas 2000), as evidenced by the following social indicators: first, Aboriginal juveniles aged ten to fourteen years are twenty-five times more likely to be arrested and charged by police (Aboriginal Justice

Council 1999); second, young Kimberley Aboriginal people are eighteen times more likely to be held in detention than other Australian youth, setting a pattern for future contact with police and the courts (Council for Aboriginal Reconciliation 1997); and, third, Aboriginal women are fourteen times more likely to be arrested by police than non-Aboriginal women (Blagg 2000).

It can be seen that Aboriginal people have more frequent contact with the legal system, which is even more notable considering that they make up approximately 3 percent of the population of Western Australia (Human Rights and Equal Opportunity Commission [HREOC] n.d.) and approximately 2 percent of the national population (Western Australian Department of Training 1997). The Council for Aboriginal Reconciliation (1995) found that "indigenous people, particularly young men, face arrest and imprisonment at such a high rate compared to the Australian average as to have no rational justification."

The education system is another way that firmly established the unequal playing field for Aboriginal Australians. Of great significance is the fact that Aboriginal history is not formally acknowledged as being part of the curriculum in all Australian schools. Aboriginal children are still being taught that Captain James Cook was the first man to "discover" Australia. This is despite scientific evidence that indicates Aboriginal communities were established and functioned with the mechanisms of social order for thousands of years. This dismissal of Aboriginal history immediately has the effect of relegating it to the realm of the unimportant and the insignificant. R. Kidd, in her publication *Black Lives, Government Lies* (2000), speaks of "the depth, the deliberateness and the desolation of this exclusion [of Aboriginal Australians]" that leaves non-Aboriginal Australians feeling horrified and incredulous.

It is a matter of history that in 1905 the Australian government was given the mandate to educate Aboriginal Australians. In the twenty-first century, Aboriginal children are still failing to achieve according to European standards. For example, a study by the Human Rights and Equal Opportunity Commission, *National Inquiry into Rural and Remote Education* (2000), found that over one-third of Aboriginal students between the ages of fifteen and twenty-four had not completed their tenth year of school. This is in a society that has compulsory schooling for all children up to the age of fifteen years, a society that legally allows the police to pick up these young people if they are seen out of school. Subsequently, the retention rate of Aboriginal students to year twelve is approximately one-half the rate for other students (HREOC 2000). There appears to be a failure to recognize that Aboriginal ways of learning and knowing about one's world are different from Western learning methodologies. These differences can be apparent in how things are valued, in how Aboriginal Australians work individually and collectively, and in what is considered important in life (Western Australian Department of Training 1997).

To add further to these inequalities, in 2000 the Australian government brought about changes to allowances for Abstudy, which is a study support program for Aboriginal people. In 1999 the Aboriginal and Torres Strait Islander Commission (1999) provided a report on the proposed changes. This report found that the reductions in financial assistance, the more stringent criteria to access this program, and the removal of benefits originally included as special measures to allow Aboriginal people access to the benefits of educational institutions would disadvantage the majority of Aboriginal tertiary students, with sole parents being the most disadvantaged. Women returning to study constituted approximately one-half of all tertiary and further education populations. Figures from 1998 show that about 15,760 Abstudy recipients would be disadvantaged and that approximately nine hundred students would be advantaged. It can be seen that the government has diminished the effectiveness of this study support program. The pattern of learning for many Aboriginal women is that they return to study after raising families, so it can be seen that these changes attempt

> to force Indigenous Australians into a pattern of further study most suited to non-indigenous middle-class Australians, and reduces the financial support for those Indigenous community members most ready and most equipped to contribute to their community's economic, social and political determination. (Aboriginal and Torres Strait Islander Commission 1999)

Educational prospects can be linked to the health of the family, with subsequent health issues having a significant role in the way that Aboriginal people operate in their world. It is essential that spiritual health also be recognized as being fundamental to physical and psychological health. The European idea of what was best for Aboriginal children led to the "stolen generations" (HREOC 1997; Haebich 2000), the practice of removing those Aboriginal children of mixed blood, a practice that overlooked the holistic well-being resulting from living within the security of families that love their children. "Black children could be treated as chattels, were exchanged between friends, relatives and neighbours and were occasionally sold for profit" (Reynolds 2000). With the separation of these forced removals came the unresolved loss and grief that are now linked to psychological problems (B. Hunter 1999).

Traditional Aboriginal life had periods when food was not as plentiful but when the diets sustained communities. European appropriation of land led to the removal from traditional hunting grounds and from other sources of food and traditional medicines (Berndt and Berndt 1988). Health problems that disproportionately affect Aboriginal Australians include diabetes, circulatory and respiratory disorders, cancer, and injuries (B. Hunter 1999). The instances of abuse and misuse that Aboriginal children experienced through removal to institutions continue to affect the health of families as well. Substance abuse and risk-taking behavior have become the means used by many in an attempt to make sense of their fragmented world. The result is often repeated instances of family violence (E. M. Hunter 1991). It should also be noted that since colonization, physical violence was regularly used to "tame" the natives; it was the only language they were considered to understand (Reynolds 2000). Tragically, youth suicide has become a frequent fact in the lives of Aboriginal Australians. For example, the suicide rate for young Kimberley Aboriginal people is more than twelve times the national average (*Choose Life Report* 1999), and homicide is the leading cause of death among young Kimberley Aboriginal women between the ages of fifteen and twenty-four years (Kimberley Aboriginal Medical Services Council 2000).

The setting up of ration depots and institutions signaled the beginnings of the Aboriginal industry, in which funds originally intended to provide food and clothing for Aboriginal workers or depots were diverted for profit or for use in other areas. Aboriginal people were charged high prices at station canteens and stores; food was substandard; and in some instances, some supplies did not even arrive. In government accounting, typically "health and nutrition [for Aborigines] were always subverted to the financial bottom line" (Kidd 2000).

These living conditions resulted in poor health that affected the ways people had their children, raised their children, worked, and lived out their lives. The inappropriate and new diets on which Aboriginal people were expected to survive led to the manifestation of deficiencies in vitamins, minerals, and the like, with the resulting lethargy leading to the perceptions that Aboriginal people are lazy. Aborigines were always linked by race, and as such their mode of behavior was considered to be part of the "collective." This could arguably have led Commissioner H. D. Moseley to believe that "half-castes were disinclined to work"; they were "loafers" and were naturally possessed of "begging habits" (Beresford and Omaji 1998). These perceptions also overlook the malaise that must have manifested in the psyche of an abused, misused, dispossessed, and traumatized people.

From positions of privilege and power, Europeans have continued to deconstruct and redefine the identities of Aboriginal people. It could be argued that these changes were and continue to be "manipulated for policy purposes" (Chesterman and Galligan 1997). This typically allows the continued distribution of fewer positive social resources to those people considered racially inferior through "exclusionary regimes [that] have denied Aborigines the rights of citizenship" (Chesterman and Galligan 1997).

In some sectors of Australian society, there is a misconception regarding "the privileges Aboriginals enjoy over other Australians" (Chesterman and Galligan 1997), and this further adds to negative perceptions of Aboriginal people. Racial discrimination acts, equal opportunity legislations, and legal recognition of indigenous rights can arguably be seen as theoretical victories yet to be proven in the field of practicalities.

Many Aboriginal people continue to live in the social, political, and economic margins of contemporary Australian society. Dr. Boyd Hunter (1999), of the Centre for Aboriginal Economic Policy Research, found that "Indigenous people's living standards are both qualitatively and quantitatively different from that of other poor and rich Australians." In effect, Australian Aboriginal people continue to experience controlled and discriminatory access to positive social resources. While many Aboriginal Australians have become immersed in the reality of being oppressed (Freire 1972), non-Aboriginal people have become submerged in the societal assumptions of superiority and power.

Aboriginal Australians continue to live as second-class citizens in their own country. The ideologies of reconciliation need to be embraced in the home and demonstrated by all individuals and institutions under the guidance of receptive and proactive political parties. Only then will all Australians have equitable access to positive social resources, rather than minority groups being excluded from such access because of their differences.

REFERENCES

Aboriginal and Torres Strait Islander Commission. 1999. *Analysis of the proposed changes to Abstudy on indigenous students.* Canberra, Austral: Aboriginal and Torres Strait Islander Commission.

Aboriginal Justice Council. 1999. *Our mob, our justice: Keeping the vision alive.* Perth, Western Austral.: Aboriginal Justice Council Secretariat.

Austen, T. 1998. *A cry in the wind: Conflict in Western Australia, 1829–1929.* Darlington, Western Austral.: Darlington.

Beresford, Q., and P. Omaji. 1996. *Rites of passage.* Fremantle, Austral.: Fremantle Arts Centre Press.

———. 1998. *Our state of mind.* Fremantle, Austral.: Fremantle Arts Centre Press.

Berndt, R. M., and C. H. Berndt. 1988. *The world of the first Australians.* 5th ed. Canberra, Austral.: Aboriginal Studies Press.

Blagg, H. 2000. *Crisis intervention in Aboriginal family violence.* Perth: Crime Research Centre University of Western Australia.

Chesterman, J., and B. Galligan. 1997. *Citizens without rights: Aborigines and Australian citizenship.* Melbourne: Cambridge University Press.

Choose life report. 1999. Broome, Western Austral.: Kimberley Aboriginal Medical Services Council.

Council for Aboriginal Reconciliation. 1995. *Going forward: Social justice for the first Australians.* Canberra: Australian Government Publishing Service.

———. 1997. *The path to reconciliation: Issues for a people's movement.* Canberra: Australian Government Publishing Services.

Elder, B. 1998. *Blood on the wattle: Massacres and maltreatment of Aboriginal Australians since 1788.* Sydney: New Holland.

Freire, P. 1972. *Pedagogy of the oppressed.* Ringwood, Austral.: Penguin.

Haebich, A. 1992. *For their own good: Aborigines and government in the southwest of Western Australia, 1900–1940.* 2nd ed. Perth: University of Western Australia Press.

———. 2000. *Broken circles: Fragmenting Aboriginal families, 1800–2000.* Fremantle, Austral.: Fremantle Arts Centre Press.

Helms, J. E. 1994. The conceptualization of racial identity and other "racial" constructs. In *Human diversity: Perspectives on people in context,* ed. E. J. Trickett, R. J. Watts, and D. Birman. San Francisco: Josey-Bass.

Human Rights and Equal Opportunity Commission. 1997. *National inquiry into the separation of Aboriginal and Torres Strait Islander children from their families: Bringing them home.* Sydney: Human Rights and Equal Opportunity Commission.

———. 2000. *Recommendations: National inquiry into rural and remote education.* Sydney: Human Rights and Equal Opportunity Commission.

———. n.d. *Statistic: Aboriginal and Torres Strait Islander peoples.* Available at www.hreoc.gov.au/social_justice/statistics/index.html (accessed March 3, 2000).

Hunter, B. 1999. *Three nations, not one: Indigenous and other Australia poverty.* Canberra: Australian National University, Centre for Aboriginal Economic Policy Research.

Hunter, E. M. 1991. The intercultural and socio-historical context of Aboriginal personal violence in remote Australia. *Australian Psychologist* 14 (2): 89–98.

Jonas, W. 2000. *Statement on mandatory sentencing.* Available at www.hreoc.gov.au/1social_justice/speeches/j8_7_16.html (accessed March 3, 2000).

Kidd, R. 2000. *Black lives, government lies.* Sydney: University of New South Wales Press.

Kimberley Aboriginal Medical Services Council. 2000. *Issues for Aboriginal controlled health services in the Kimberley.* Available at www.hcn.net.au/kamsc/hlthstat.htm (accessed November 8, 2000).

Reynolds, H. 2000. *Black pioneers: How Aboriginal and Islander people helped build Australia.* 2nd ed. Ringwood, Victoria, Austral.: Penguin.

Sidanius, J., and F. Pratto. 1999. *Social dominance: An intergroup theory of social hierarchy and oppression,* chaps. 1–3. Cambridge: Cambridge University Press.

Smith, L. T. 1999. *Decolonizing methodologies: Research and indigenous peoples.* Dunedin, New Zealand: University of Otago Press.

Western Australian Department of Training. 1997. *Just enough to tease us.* Perth: Australian National Training Authority.

Desperately Seeking Justice: Women of Color in Springfield, Missouri, and Their Quest for Civil and Human Rights

Cheryl Fischer

It was a historic event when more than sixteen thousand people from around the world gathered for the United Nations' World Conference against Racism, Racial Discrimination, Xenophobia, and Related Forms of Intolerance (WCAR), held from August 27 through September 7, 2001, in Durban, South Africa. I was one of those participants, an African American woman and human rights activist who has been living in the Ozarks on and off for nearly a quarter of a century. For those unfamiliar with the United States, the Ozarks is primarily a rural area in Missouri predominately populated by European Americans, an area composed of rocky hills, streams, and terrain that is generally unsuitable to most lucrative agricultural endeavors. Despite being located near the geographic center of the nation, the Ozarks has a history of isolation, in part because of its distance from major urban centers and the lack of widespread economic opportunity. Although I live in the Ozarks, I was raised in southern Louisiana during the 1950s and 1960s, a time of segregation and revolutionary change in regard to American civil rights. I have always felt deeply about the importance of social and economic justice, and in accord with Harrison (1995, 2000, 2002), I contend that it is imperative that justice be delivered to those who suffer most, those who are most underserved. In the Ozarks, those whom I describe are African Americans and other people of color. Although in this chapter I describe my experiences working with individuals struggling to achieve justice in the Ozarks, my interests and experiences are not limited to this area. I have observed the struggles of the Uighurs and ethnic minorities while studying and teaching in China; I have studied the struggles of Ainu, Okinawans, and ethnic Koreans in Japan, as an intern working with the International Movement against Discrimination and Racism; I have observed the struggles of Roma, Africans, and Arabs during visits to Europe. I attended the

WCAR as a delegate interested in learning more about these struggles, as one who hoped that the exchange of ideas and experiences would facilitate the transition toward a civil society in all of our communities.

One of the last presentations at the WCAR in Durban was entitled "Connecting the Disconnected." The panelists who participated in this presentation suggested strategies for keeping the world's people informed about post-WCAR activities, and they outlined possibilities through which victims of racism could obtain assistance from the UN system offices, such as the recently established post-WCAR Anti-discrimination Unit (ADU) of the United Nations High Commission on Human Rights. Ensuring that underserved people benefit from the ADU and other offices will be a monumental task to be shared by the people themselves: community activists, advocates, public intellectuals, and radical educators; the civil rights / human rights nongovernmental organizations, community-based organizations, and civil society organizations; governmental civil rights offices and agencies as well as the various branches of the UN system, especially the ADU.[1] Ascertaining the particular needs of women of color, those often bypassed by the feminist movement, deserves special attention, especially in areas where minority percentages are low. Successfully connecting these women with the post-Durban process and assisting their search for solutions to their problems will be a true test of the implementation, effectiveness, and durability of the WCAR's program of action.[2] Keeping the WCAR's goals in mind, I outline in this chapter some of the racial problems against which women of color struggle in Springfield, Missouri, the third-largest city in Missouri and the Ozarks' major metropolitan area.[3]

As feminism is still in the process of being defined, newer definitions must assume more nonessentialist meanings with regard to various aspects of feminism. Some feminist scholars have generally thought that women should concentrate on themselves to the exclusion of all others (e.g., Friedan 2001; Steinem 1995). Historically, women have had to think of husbands/significant others, children, grandchildren, extended family, and clans to the detriment of their own happiness, personal development, mental stability, peace of mind, and other pursuits. While some feminists have the luxury of considering only themselves and their individual aspirations, many women, including feminists of color (owing to the nature of continuing racism based on race, color, and national origin) must additionally consider the oppression, abuse, and exclusion of male relatives and significant others (cf. Harrison 1997; Hill Collins 1990; hooks 2000; McClaurin 2001). Therefore, feminist scholars must expand their concepts to include feminist concerns heretofore rarely examined in the academy and the community. Until recently, feminist studies seemed to focus on urban dwellers, academicians, professionals, workers, and intellectuals. Women in small cities, semirural towns, rural areas, and areas where people of color are a low percentage have rarely had their voices heard in ongoing activist and feminist discourses. To formulate plans of action for the future, all women from all backgrounds and geographical areas and their specific concerns must be included. Injustice anywhere threatens justice everywhere.

While it is important for women of color to focus on themselves for their own enrichment, the women I know and work with often need to focus on certain issues that the males in their families encounter, as local and national civil rights and human rights organizations—for whatever reasons—have failed. Most civil/human rights organizations in the United States focus on issues in "inner cities" rather than on those of small cities, semirural towns, and rural areas. As a result, for example, almost the entire country knows about the deaths of Ahmadou Diallo, Patrick Dorismond, and the brutal sodomizing of Abner Louima, thanks to the intercession of the National Action Network and other civil rights organizations. In contrast, most Americans, including the major actors of the national civil rights groups, have no knowledge of the hanging deaths (or lynchings) of Lenwood Shawn Howard in Buffalo, Missouri (in 1994), or Leonard Gakinya in Springfield, Missouri (in 2002). The women of color who file complaints with activists of color in Springfield are desperately seeking recognition of and solutions to the racial abuse from which they and their loved ones suffer. As citizens of the United States, they would like the U.S. civil rights organizations to be aware of these issues. As citizens of the world, they would like the UN system offices, in particular the ADU, to regard their concerns as being equally important to the similar concerns that those offices investigate in other parts of the world.

A BIT OF SPRINGFIELD'S RACIAL HISTORY

According to R. I. Holcombe's *History of Greene County, Missouri, 1883* (1883) African Americans in Springfield, Missouri, constituted roughly 20 percent of the population in 1876. Proportionately, this percentage exceeded those of St. Louis, Missouri (6 percent African American in 1880), and Kansas City, Missouri (14 percent African American in 1880; Department of Interior Census Office 1883). According to local researchers and members of the African American community, the African American population was faring relatively well around 1900; the largest grocery store was African American–owned as was the largest funeral parlor (Bennett 1970; Decatur 1981, 1982; Stewart-Stafford 1996; Young 1998). Moreover, African Americans were active in civic functions, including membership on the city council and school board and participation in the local Republican Party, which at that time was Abraham Lincoln's party and the party with which African Americans were aligned. On

Easter weekend in April 1906, a lynching in which three innocent young African American men accused of having sexually molested a European American woman occurred on the town square (Bennett 1970; *Springfield Republican* 1906; Decatur 1981, 1982; Stewart-Stafford 1996; Young 1998). The young men were hanged from a replica of the Statue of Liberty, set afire while they were still barely alive, and then had their charred remains dismembered as some of the six thousand–strong lynch mob took body parts as souvenirs. As the mob turned to find other African American victims, word of the heinous event spread to most in the African American community, and many fled Springfield, never to return. Some were able to get shelter in the basements and cellars of sympathetic European Americans, but from that time on, the African American population percentage dwindled until it reached 2 percent, where it hovers today.

CURRENT GENERAL INFORMATION: INCOME, HEALTH, AND EDUCATION

Statistical reports for African Americans in Springfield have usually been dismal. According to the City of Springfield's own *Consolidated Plan: Fiscal Year 2000–2004* (2000), roughly 4.7 percent of African Americans live in dilapidated housing compared to roughly 0.5 percent for European Americans and zero percent for Asian, Hispanic, and Native Americans. Approximately 35 percent of African Americans live in substandard housing (44). Moreover, roughly 51 percent of African Americans earn $20,000 or less annually, which indicates that many African Americans in Springfield are near poverty. Also according to this document, only 12 percent of African Americans earn between $30,000 and $60,000, and zero percent earn over $60,000 (45). New census data, however, indicate that the poverty rate may be lower. According to census data, in 1999, 30 percent (1,348 out of the total African American population of 4,437) of African Americans had income below the poverty level (U.S. Bureau of the Census 2003). However, the corresponding statistics for European Americans in 1999 was 11 percent (32,123 out of the total European American population of 292,930). Moreover, the recent census indicates that the per capita income for European Americans in 1999 was $19,036, whereas for African Americans it was $11,847. The same data source indicates that in 1999, 68 percent (1,824 out of 2,666) of African American males worked at any given time compared to a higher percentage for European American males of 79 percent (91,264 out of 114,863) (U.S. Bureau of the Census 2003). [4]

Inadequate health care often results from African Americans' lack of access to adequate income. For example, the infant mortality rate for African

Americans in Greene County is 26.0 per 1,000 live births (Truchard 2002). This figure is almost double that of the rate reported for African Americans in the sixty largest U.S. cities: 13.9 per 1,000 live births. When compared to the rate of 6.9 per 1,000 live births for European Americans in Greene County, these numbers underscore an even greater tragedy. The HIV/AIDS rate is a problem as well in that although African Americans locally are roughly 2 percent of the population, they comprise at least 6 percent to 10 percent of the HIV/AIDS cases.[5]

The Springfield Public School system lacks diversity among its professional and nonprofessional staff. Approximately twenty-three teachers and administrators are of African descent out of a total of about seventeen hundred teachers and administrators.[6] The security department of Springfield Public Schools has had no African Americans as school security guards for the past three years.[7] A new policy, one for which no one will claim responsibility in initiating, demands that all security personnel have three years of police experience. Such a policy excludes African Americans, as perhaps only one may have ever graduated from the police academy of the Springfield Police Department, and the two African American officers who are currently serving on the force may not be interested in becoming school security officers.

The dropout rate is also a problem. Eighteen percent of African American high school students drop out of Springfield Public Schools, which is higher than all other ethnic/racial groups.[8] Peer assistance and review documents from the Kansas City Office for Civil Rights of the U.S. Department of Education that Springfield Public Schools signed in 1996 and 1998 to prevent racial discrimination within the school system have never been fully implemented and therefore have seemingly had no effects on stemming the tide of dropouts or ameliorating other racial problems.

PROBLEMS IN THE GREENE COUNTY DIVISION OF FAMILY SERVICES

African American families have complained about racism from social workers and supervisors in the Greene County Division of Family Services (DFS).[9] Most recently, a biracial two-year-old of African descent, Dominic James, was shaken to death by his European American foster father who, some have claimed, has ties to area hate groups in Southwest Missouri, an area that is home to at least thirteen white supremacy groups mainly of the Christian Identity ilk (Bauer 2002; Sylvester 1999). Although the foster father has been charged with second-degree murder and is now serving a fifteen-year sentence for Dominic's death, Sidney James, Dominic's father, is dissatisfied and plans to continue fighting the

Division of Family Services in 2005. The social work supervisor involved in Dominic's case has been accused of racism by other African American parents who have filed complaints with the Office for Civil Rights of the U.S. Department of Health and Human Services (HHS).[10] Other African American children placed in foster care have experienced many problems, including being abused by European American foster parents and being given antipsychotic drugs without having been seen by physicians. Examples of abuse include the following: one African American girl having her hair cut because the European American parent did not know how to take care of it; African American children being made to listen to racial slurs and jokes from their foster family members; African American children being called names by foster family members; African American children being forced to go to churches with which they and their families were unaffiliated (e.g., the Mormon church); and more.[11]

African American parents have also complained about the Juvenile Justice Center in Springfield. None of the parents whose children have been placed in foster care have seen their children's juvenile records, including court records. Moreover, they have never even seen their own records, which are kept by the justice center.[12] Censoring parents from their and their children's own records prevents them from knowing whether or not the records are accurate. The parents have also complained that they have never been informed of their rights by DFS or justice center workers. Moreover, they believe that their due process rights and those of their children have been denied. One parent complained that the juvenile judge never listened to her side but, rather, rubber-stamped the testimony of DFS case workers and social work supervisors.

Other problems exist as well. Although African Americans form 2.3 percent of the population, some people think that possibly 15 percent to 25 percent of the children and youth in foster care are of African descent.[13] So far, DFS and even the Office for Civil Rights (HHS) have not informed concerned parents and activists here of their rights to get statistics and other information about children of color in the foster care system. One young woman who was placed in foster care at the age of thirteen is almost nineteen years old. She overdosed on drugs twice while in the care of DFS. Her parents, whose parental rights were never terminated and who still pay child support to the child support enforcement office, asked the DFS and the Office for Civil Rights (HHS) to have their daughter transferred to a place where she could get psychological help after her second overdose. Neither office responded to the parents' request.[14]

EMPLOYMENT

African Americans experience racial discrimination when trying to get hired for jobs, and they also endure racially hostile environments while being employed. An African American man who worked at the Southwest Power Administration in Springfield for nine years kept a diary of the racial discrimination he experienced (e.g., nooses in his work space, having the word *nigger* used in his presence).[15] He finally decided to move to another state. African American postal workers and their European American supporters tried to bring a class action suit against the U.S. Postal Service in Springfield after having endured looking at many hangman nooses and "nigger face" balloons and experiencing other racist abuse. In November 1999, they retained Louis Gilden of St. Louis, a litigator in the famous *McDonald-Douglas v. Greene* case. Gilden died in December 2000, however, and his partner, Charles Oldham, took the case. Currently, Mr. Oldham is handling each plaintiff one by one, as the case has been refused class-action status. The postal workers believe that the St. Louis Equal Employment Opportunity Commission (EEOC) has been remiss in assisting them (Young 2002). Another African American man who suffered employment discrimination was only able to get help from the district EEOC office in St. Louis after my spouse and I inundated both the St. Louis and the Washington, D.C., EEOC offices with letters, faxes, e-mail messages, and many telephone calls about his case. That man, who is the only African American (out of three hundred) working for Tuthill Pneumatics, describes a litany of abuse, including having a dead cat placed in his truck as well as the words *nigger* and *monkey* and the pejorative phrase "Even a seven-year-old Mississippi nigger would know . . ." frequently used in his presence. Further, his projects were maliciously tinkered with so that they would fail quality control and he would be discredited and have to work extra hours fixing them.[16] Although the St. Louis EEOC did find probable cause in his case, that office is not going to court on his behalf as other regional EEOC offices have done for seemingly similarly situated victims (EEOC 2002). In yet another case, an African American food service manager for the Greene County jail was brutally beaten by a European American jail lieutenant after the two had argued about the amount of food available for a given meal.[17] The lieutenant reportedly slammed the food service manager several times against a concrete pillar causing him to suffer a dislocated shoulder and bruised bone for which he had to receive hospital attention and therapy. The food service worker was fired, but no charges were brought against the lieutenant. Moreover, the food service worker could find no attorney willing to take his case. Incidents similar to the aforementioned ones continue to occur in Springfield and surrounding areas.

PROBLEMS WITH THE POLICE

African and Hispanic Americans in Springfield endure racial profiling, abuse, and harassment from police just as they do elsewhere in this country. Recent data reveal that police search the African Americans they stop at a rate that is nearly triple that of European Americans—a rate that is higher than any of Missouri's other major cities (Wilson 2001). A compounding problem is that in Springfield there is no recourse for victims as civil/human rights groups are ineffective and the local American Civil Liberties Union (ACLU) is apathetic.[18] Nevertheless, many African Americans continue to complain about police harassment, profiling, and abuse. For example, young African and Hispanic American males not only have their photos taken by the police but are also systematically stopped and searched without probable cause. Furthermore, the mother of one young African American college student who is an education major states that local police have told her son they will make sure he gets a felony record and never has a teaching job in Greene County. Another example of one of the abuses perpetrated by the police is to wait years after an incident has occurred to start criminal proceedings against an accused person. In this sense, those accused do not get tried in a timely manner, and their right to a speedy trial is violated.

Citizens report that the Springfield police refer to African Americans from outside Springfield as "blow-ins" and make concerted efforts to rid Springfield of their presence.[19] At one time, it was rumored that the Springfield Police Department kept a book with pictures of African American "suspects" called the "Rogues' Gallery," which was basically a police guide to those who must be watched or picked up on occasion. Older African Americans have stated that they fear leaving their homes after dark to avoid potential harassment in being stopped by Springfield officers. African American males have stated that they are ready to leave Springfield because of the hostile treatment they have received from Springfield officers. One African American man told me that after he complained to the European American police chief about police harassment, soon he had a visit from two European American police officers who threatened to take him to jail if he ever complained to the chief again. While harassment increases as socioeconomic class decreases, even professional level people are affected. An African American program director was recently heard complaining about being frequently stopped by Springfield officers and falsely accused of petty traffic violations when he spoke at a forum sponsored by a local university.

JUDICIAL SYSTEM/JUSTICE DEPARTMENT ISSUES

Activists often hear African Americans say that lawyers in Springfield do not take civil rights cases. All of the lawyers in town are European Americans; the only resident African American lawyer left in February 2002, after having stayed less than two and a half years in Springfield. African Americans here not only have problems getting attorneys to take civil rights cases but also suffer from having to pay exorbitant fees—$10,000 to $15,000 up front—to criminal attorneys to take criminal cases.[20] African Americans are not more disposed to committing crimes in this area but are disproportionately criminalized. Moreover, certain people in the European American community promote the image that African Americans are responsible for the majority of the local crimes. Certain rich and powerful European Americans have allegedly stated to newly arrived European Americans that Springfield is a good place to live because few African Americans live here, thereby making the city a "white man's paradise."[21]

Perhaps the statements uttered by Thomas McGuire, a long-time judge of the Thirty-first Judiciary who is now retired, epitomizes the attitudes of local legal professionals.[22] These statements appear in a writ of habeas corpus for Jermaine Perry written by Kansas City criminal defense attorney Sean O'Brien of the Public Interest Litigation Clinic. In one case, the judge said to the parents of a youth accused of murdering his grandfather that "those two are just breeding little niggers that killed the best nigger in town." After sentencing an African American man, the judge stepped into chambers and said, in regards to the man, "Hitler couldn't have been all wrong." When an African American friend of the judge's bailiff walked to the courtroom and tapped on the door glass to get the bailiff's attention, the judge later asked, "What did that nigger want?" Reportedly, every Friday the judge would go to lunch at a particular restaurant and would always come back with a new stock of what he called "nigger jokes." The judge would then spend all Friday afternoon "hearing routine motions and relaying these jokes to various attorneys that came into the courtroom" (O'Brien 2001).

The local judiciary also seems reluctant to prosecute and convict racist skinheads. In December 1997, an African-descent man was brutally beaten by three European American skinheads (Shurley 1999a). He had to get care for his bruises at a local hospital. Two of the skinheads were arrested, but they eventually received sentences of five years' unsupervised probation (Shurley 1999b). On June 17, 2001, an African American man was beaten and stabbed three times in a Denny's restaurant by skinheads; he was reportedly stabbed by one of several skinheads who were sporting shaved heads, "Aryan Nation" T-shirts, swastikas, and white supremacist tattoos (Strait 2001). Although there were several witnesses and the U.S. Department of Justice (DOJ) was involved in the investigation, no one has been arrested as of this writing. Moreover, neither the DOJ representative nor the U.S. attorney in Springfield will respond to my phone calls, e-mail messages, and letters written to them requesting updates of the incidents.

Incidents also occur that alert concerned citizens and activists to the problems in the local county jail. In August 2001, four African American inmates in the Greene County jail complained that two European American jail guards urinated on them while they were playing basketball (Bauer 2001). The inmates contacted local activists requesting assistance, but the jail officials would not let the activists (including myself) meet with the inmates. The Kuumba Human Rights Focus Group filed a complaint with the Special Litigation Section of the Office of Civil Rights of the U. S. Department of Justice requesting that the jail be investigated, as that complaint was not the first complaint of abuse received from inmates of color and also because at least ten inmates have died in the jail in the past ten years. The Special Litigation Section responded in May 2003, only after activists asked the U.S. Commission on Civil Rights to look into the matter. During the Clinton administration, activists did get responses from some representatives of the DOJ. Since roughly March 2001, activists have not heard from anyone in the DOJ and, more significantly, from no representatives in either the Coordination and Review Section (CRS) of the DOJ's Civil Rights Division or the DOJ's Special Litigation Section.

In addition, local activists have consistently asked representatives from the CRS to hold a community forum in Springfield to explain its role and purposes and to describe citizens' rights in reference to racism experienced from the police department, local jails and prisons, and the local judiciary, including the Juvenile Justice Center. The CRS could additionally be helpful to underserved communities of color by providing information about Title VI of the 1964 Civil Rights Act. According to Title VI, any entity that receives federal funds cannot discriminate on the basis of race, color, or national origin. Springfield activists seem to have uncovered many Title VI violations in Springfield, yet the CRS, which monitors Title VI implementation, has not shown an interest in investigating Springfield's lack of compliance.

THE CONFEDERATE FLAG

The Confederate flag has for decades been a prominently displayed object in Southwest Missouri. In April 2002, a large Confederate flag was drawn near the grounds of Neosho High School in Neosho, Missouri, which is located about forty miles southwest of Springfield (Majeske Robinson 2002). The flag was part of the Neosho High School seniors' tradition of leaving expressions and artwork on a street adjacent to the school's campus before they graduated. An African American colleague of mine who lives in Willard, Missouri, which is about ten miles to the northwest of Springfield, spotted a large Confederate flag being displayed in a small parade for Willard High School on May 15, 2002.[23] Both Neosho High School and Willard High School are public schools, which receive federal funds through the U.S. Department of Education. On June 2, 2002, activists witnessed the Sons of the Confederacy hold a Confederate praise ceremony in the national veterans' cemetery in Springfield (O'Dell 2002). Three extremely large Confederate flags were erected in the "Confederate part" of the cemetery, and small Confederate flags had been placed at the graves of all Confederate soldiers. Although a colleague and I contacted the office for veterans' cemeteries at the Veterans Administration in Washington, D.C., we still have not received a response explaining exactly which statute or executive order allows a Confederate flag to fly in a federally funded veterans' cemetery. The flying of the Confederate flag in schools and cemeteries that receive federal funds may be a violation of Title VI of the 1964 Civil Rights Act.

RECENT PROBLEMS, OR THE RACIST BEAT GOES ON . . .

The details of Dominic James's death are explained earlier. In addition, an incident occurred in early July 2002 in which an African American youth, a recent high school graduate, was reportedly brutally beaten with a baseball bat by three European American youth. The African American youth, who was hospitalized, lost his college soccer scholarship and, for a while, walked with a limp. Activists who struggled to get an incident report of the crime discovered that the African American victim was labeled "white," which may prevent the incident from being investigated as a hate crime.[24] Another incident, which involved African American, Mexican American, and European American youth, occurred in early September 2002. All of the youth were attending a party where a young Mexican American male was fatally shot in the head, allegedly by someone using a nine-millimeter gun. Although none of the African Americans had a nine-millimeter gun, only African American youths were arrested, and bail was initially set for $500,000 each, despite the fact that any evidence linking them as the perpetrators was flimsy. Recently, so-called forensic experts picked by the prosecutors have said that the death could have been caused by other kinds of guns. Eventually, the young African American males' bonds were lowered to $100,000, and all six of the youth have been bailed out at great expense and newly incurred debt to parents and other relatives. The county prosecutor is asking for the death penalty or life imprisonment with no possibility of parole for the young men, almost all of whom are between eighteen and twenty-two years of age, based on little and confusing evidence. The young men may eventually go free but not without serious emotional and financial costs to them, their parents, and their relatives.

THE SPRINGFIELD RACIAL SCENE

Race relations in Springfield are strange and strained. The powers-that-be have made sure that a social order exists in which people of color do not relate to one another but rather to the white power oligarchy. Such a pattern can be described as the wagon-wheel paradigm in which each group of color represents a spoke on the wheel and the European American male-dominant patriarchal power center is represented by the hub. Driving certain groups of people—mainly African-descent people—away from the city through racial profiling has been one way to ensure Springfield's whiteness and position as the sixth-whitest city in the United States (*Springfield News-Leader* 2001). Indeed, Rosemary Stewart-Stafford, a Springfield researcher-activist, notes that Springfield may possibly be the whitest city in the United States in that it is not located next to or near a major diverse, multicultural urban area (at least two of the whiter cities in the list—Independence, Missouri, and Livonia, Michigan—are located next to Kansas City, Missouri, and Detroit, Michigan, respectively). Profiling and harassment serve to increase the discomfort levels of the populations of color, in particular those of African descent, and helps to maintain that population at lower levels. In fact, according to the 2000 census, all groups of color in Springfield have the same proportionate representation in the state of Missouri except African Americans—Hispanic Americans are 1.8 percent in Springfield and 2.1 percent in the state of Missouri; Asian Americans are 1.1 percent in Springfield and 1.1 percent in the state; Native Americans are 0.7 percent in Springfield and 0.4 percent in the state. African-Americans, on the other hand, are 2.3 percent in Springfield and 11 percent in the state.

Keeping groups of color apart is another way of ensuring white power. For example, in the early eighties, a Vietnamese priest asked a Protestant minister who headed the local council of churches about helping Ethiopian refugees resettle in Springfield in the way that the city had opened its arms to Southeast Asian refugees. The minister replied that resettling Ethiopians "wouldn't work here."[25] In a similar vein, a Vietnamese high school student once related a problem that a Vietnamese refugee student encountered when he made friends with an African American student at his high school. The Vietnamese guy's European American male friends told him they would have nothing to do with him until he stopped associating with the African American.[26] One rarely sees in Springfield either Asian Americans associating with African Americans or Native Americans associating with Hispanic Americans, not even at the local universities. The various civil rights groups for people of color—the NAACP, the League of United Latin American Citizens, and the American Indian Center—have rarely come together to evaluate and assess the similar problems encountered by the people they serve. The only time people of color seem to assemble is at the request of a European American organization. Even then, the representatives from the groups of color rarely have anything to say to one another. When well-meaning European Americans start race relations discussion groups, very little interaction occurs among people of color. For example, when the Coalition for Change in Springfield's Climate started a series of discussions in fall 1997, European Americans (mainly a representative from the local state university, Southwest Missouri State University) took over the leadership. When the European American "leader" left Springfield, the coalition fizzled and evaporated. To my knowledge, no representative from the civil rights or community-of-color organizations tried to continue the efforts. In fall 1999, a series of race relations discussions took place over an eight-week period. After the discussions concluded, no follow-up occurred even though many participants asked for such follow-up. One speculation for such lack of follow-up is that the powers-that-be in Springfield, Missouri, host discussions when they are on the "hot seat" and are being scrutinized from outside (a meeting of the regional United States Commission on Civil Rights in Springfield spearheaded the Coalition for Change in Springfield's Climate). Once the scrutiny no longer exists, the coalitions and discussion groups fade away leaving the racial conditions in Springfield no better and possibly worse than before, as African-descent people tend to bear the retaliatory brunt for having exposed the racism to "outsiders."

THE WOMEN OF COLOR

Not much has been written on the history of women in Springfield, Greene County, Missouri. Even less has been written concerning women of color, even though African American women were among the first settlers and inhabitants in Southwest Missouri, ever since the time when this area was part of Francophone Louisiana. African American, African-descent Hispanic American, and African American–identified European American women in Springfield, Missouri, generally seem to survive in a state of crisis. For the women I know and work with, major concerns include providing for themselves and their families through being employed and earning decent incomes, finding adequate and affordable housing, educating themselves and their children, seeking business development opportunities through local lending institutions, and having good access to transportation and medical care. In this sense, the women are the leaders of their households. Concerns about housing, employment, health needs, education, and the abuse of African American males in the judicial system are of prime importance to them and may be given equal weight to concerns about rape, gender-based low wages, and other traditional feminist issues. Rights issues of women in the private sphere have not occupied the time of many women with whom the activists have engaged. Instead, the problems of the public sphere toward them and their families as people of color have been constant preoccupations. Of course, these women are concerned about the freedom to go wherever they want, maintaining their bodily integrity and respect, being able to work outside the home, and more. Nevertheless, they have been primarily concerned about the well-being of family and friends, including significant males. Moreover, both women and men of color generally talk about and commiserate over incidents of racial profiling, unfair judicial practices in the local courts, and their family members' being warehoused in jails and prisons. Therefore, the intersectionality of the problems demands that concerns not be limited to one specific gender. Women of color here are the emotional agents for their children (including—and especially for—male children) who are targeted by police. An example of women of color elsewhere zealously fighting for their sons has been shown in the case of the Central Park jogger, where five African American and Hispanic (Puerto Rican) American youth were falsely accused of rape and brutal assault on an affluent female jogger. The women of color who maintained the innocence of the young men were greatly at odds with the European American feminists who demanded the most severe punishment for those whose innocence was finally revealed (Maull 2002).

The concerns of women of color with regard to their male relatives and significant others include the following: keeping them from becoming high school dropouts; protecting them from the abuse, harassment, and profiling of law enforcement officers; keeping them out of the jails and prisons of the criminal justice system and away from other kinds of abuses and problems; as well as ensuring that they stay alive. The women have a special concern with male youth in that middle-aged and older men seem to have adapted survival strategies in handling the aforementioned concerns. Problems affecting the male youth start when they are in the elementary grades in a school system where less than 1 percent of the teachers are of African descent and almost 6 percent of the students are of African descent (Chase 2001). By the time the sons are preteens and teens, they have been suspended from school many times. Some are even expelled for spurious reasons. Appealing for help from the local NAACP has been done in vain in that the organization often has neither the will nor the resources to solve problems. Furthermore, the local ACLU is disinterested and has never assisted people of color who are concerned about the biased actions in the local schools or rampant racial profiling and police harassment and abuse directed toward people of African descent in this area. The fact that the sons of women of color have difficulty becoming educated, acquiring jobs and/or job training, and often experience abuse from the law enforcement and judicial system means that these women must spend less of their leisure doing things for themselves, such as engaging in their own self-development.

A significant number of the women have husbands and sons who have been in and out of the criminal justice system. The relationship between the police and the African American community has rendered it so that the African American males are often reluctant to freely go wherever they wish around the city. These women also see their male children, who are extensions of themselves, being arrested in their development early in life. Moreover, they see male partners cut down in their prime and prevented from fulfilling roles, such as being supportive for families. They do not have the luxury of well-heeled white feminists, who have no worries about racial profiling and can devote time to the "I." Therefore, the racial concerns of women of color and European American women with offspring of color are often overlooked in the gender debate. Woman of color here cannot go on with their lives and self-fulfillment with the assaults from the public sphere against their children (including male children) and other significant males in their lives. The current zealous support given to the plight of Afghan women should be the kind of support that all oppressed victims get, no matter what part of the world they are from. The rest of the chapter highlights the issues faced by four African American women, two Puerto Rican women, and three European American women who fear for their children's lives as well as lament their inability to get help from any source in solving the problems.

Their Concerns and Issues

The women portrayed in this piece are women I have been in contact with for five to twenty years.[27] All of them live in Springfield, Missouri, and all are either women of color or European American women who have families (husbands, boyfriends, significant others, and children) of color. For purposes of this chapter, I call the African American women Ms. Robinson, Ms. Walker, Ms. Johnson, and Ms. Prince. I call the Puerto Rican women Ms. Perez and Ms. Gonzalez. Some information is provided by two European American mothers and a European American grandmother of African-descent biracial children who are friends of the African American and Puerto Rican women and who share the same concerns. I call these women Ms. Landsford, Ms. Casely, and Ms. Ford.

Ms. Robinson has suffered much, as she is one of the African American postal workers who has endured abuse in the racially hostile workplace environment in the main U.S. Postal Service (USPS) in Springfield.[28] In addition to the personal trauma she has experienced, Ms. Robinson has seen her sons, grandsons, and other young males of color followed and harassed by police. She additionally believes that attacks on African American males in Springfield is so common that she expresses fears for her eight grandsons. Ms. Robinson reacted strongly to the October 2, 2002, hanging death of Leonard Gakinya and to the related attempts of other near-lynchings. According to Ms. Robinson, in 1991, an African American youth attended an all-European American high school party. As the young European American males proceeded to get drunk, they attempted to hang the African American youth. Ms. Robinson stated that the young man had rope burns on his neck for weeks after the incident. The young man's parents intended to press charges but changed their minds when the parents of the European American youth prevailed on them not to do so. Ms. Robinson also relates that the son of one of her colleagues, an African American man who worked at the USPS in Springfield, was almost lynched in 1998 in Republic, Missouri, a small town approximately ten miles west of Springfield. The postal worker had filed numerous complaints of discrimination against the USPS. One day after he returned to his home in Republic, he found that European American males had tried to lynch his son. The postal worker immediately sent his son to live with his grandmother in Indiana. Soon after, the postal worker and the rest of his family moved from Springfield. Ms. Robinson stated that when the African American postal workers tried to bring a class action suit of discrimination against the USPS, the postal worker in Indiana sent an eleven-page statement about the racism he had encountered at the USPS and included the account of his son's attempted lynching. Although Ms. Robinson does not currently have any male members of her family involved with the local judicial system or being racially attacked, she knows that her luck could change.

Ms. Walker has experienced much pain from Springfield institutions, including having her four grandchildren placed in foster care based on pretexts and having her son arrested for trivial reasons. Some of the incidents outlined in the aforementioned section on the Division of Family Services were some of the experiences that Ms. Walker's grandchildren had. Her son has ended up in jail based on old warrants already satisfied. In one situation, Ms. Walker's son, who has a disability, was bailed out of jail by family members. The court judge refused to grant him a public defender, stating that if the young man could be bailed out of jail, he could pay for a private attorney, although there is no state statute explicitly stating that such a policy exists. The fact that the family used its rent money to bail the young man out of jail was of no concern to the judge. Ms. Walker lamented that the kind of treatment her son received through the local judiciary affected her negatively in elevating her hypertension and increasing stress.

Ms. Johnson currently works in a factory, even though she previously worked as a secretary in San Francisco. She says that she grew up in Springfield and left, but after returning to Springfield, she has not been able to obtain employment commensurate with her work experience. Her male companion is now serving time in federal prison for alleged conspiracy to sell crack cocaine. Ms. Johnson, who has tirelessly worked for his release, has discovered many problems in how his case was handled. She filed a complaint about the ineffective counsel of her companion's lawyer and won. Moreover, she has read enough to learn that her companion should not be serving a twenty-seven-year prison term for what he has been accused of. Ms. Johnson laments that times have been hard for her and her daughter as they have had to do without her companion's income and support.

Ms. Prince is a factory worker and has recently remarried. Her main concerns are her sons, who experience police harassment and go in and out of the local judiciary. Ms. Prince's oldest son is serving a ten-year prison sentence. He had been found in the company of other African American men who had allegedly stolen car parts. Because he refused to talk about the others to the police—Ms. Prince contends he really did not know that the others were involved in petty crimes—he received a harsh sentence instead of probation. Even though Ms. Prince's son has been a model prisoner, each time he comes up for parole, the state parole board denies it. Ms. Prince's second son has been fairly successful in that he is currently a college senior majoring in education. Nevertheless, he is currently experiencing harassment from the local police. Ms. Prince relates that every time the police stop him, her second son calls her on his cellular phone, and Ms. Prince goes to wherever he is. The second son has related that the police taunt him and tell him they will make sure he gets a "felony record" and will never get a teaching job in Springfield. Ms. Prince's third and youngest son has been harassed by the police for years. In 1997, I would accompany the third son to court. At least three times when the third son went to court, his public defender would not appear. The third son's connection with the local judiciary started in 1996 when as a high school student he and a few other African American and African-descent Hispanic American youth helped a young European American female classmate move from her home to an apartment because she alleged that she and her parents were not getting along. During the process of the moving, some firearms "came up missing." The third son told his mother that the young female gave the firearms to the young men for helping her move. Many months later, after the young female had made amends with her parents, she allegedly told the county prosecutors that she had not asked the young men of color for help in moving. All firearms were returned to the father of the young female, but he pressed charges against the young men. The third son served jail time for the "theft" of the firearms. After he was released from prison, he was put on probation. One of the terms of his probation was to get a forty-hour-a-week job. He could only get a job working thirty hours a week. That was enough for his probation officer to recommend that he be returned to prison, where he is currently. Ms. Prince communicated to me that she believes that putting young African American males in jails and prisons is done purposely in Springfield.

Ms. Perez is Puerto Rican, originally from New York City. She is a single mother and grandmother whose ex-husband is African American. She has consistently been concerned about her youngest son and his brutal encounters with Springfield police officers. Ms. Perez's theory about her son's brutalization is that police have a certain code of behavior. She theorizes that the local police would like to get at her ex-husband, who is a retired police officer from New York. Since the code of behavior will not allow them to get at her ex-husband, the local police have attacked her youngest son instead. In one of the youngest son's encounters with the local police, he was beaten until he vomited. His girlfriend noticed the vomit on him after she picked him up from the police station. The youngest son has also been accused of having committed crimes in places where he would not have been. Ms. Perez stated that one night the police came to her house without a warrant looking for her son. In the process of arresting her son, the police officers also arrested Ms. Perez for questioning them about why they were at her home without a warrant. Even though Ms. Perez and her son's girlfriend were at least fifteen feet away from the officers, they were accused of "obstructing an officer" and were taken to jail along with her son. During that encounter, the police officers searched Ms. Perez's car but found nothing illegal. Nevertheless, the police towed Ms. Perez's car away. Although she only earned $1.50 an hour in wages, Ms. Perez had to pay $45 to get her car back, $250 to get her son out of jail, and $100 each for her and her son's girlfriend to get out of jail.

Ms. Perez stated that she felt her rights as a mother had been taken away. She said that she had the right to know what was happening to her son. Others members of the family have been stopped by the police who either make comments or ask them questions about Ms. Perez's youngest son. One officer stopped Ms. Perez's son-in-law (married to her oldest daughter) allegedly for an "expired tag." The officer got the son-in-law into the police car and started naming all of Ms. Perez's family members. The officer said that he knew the father (Ms. Perez's ex-husband): "Wasn't he a police officer?" The officer continued, "We got the privilege of knowing [the name of the youngest son]," then he gave the youngest son's nickname. "We know the mother. We know [nickname's] girlfriend. We know your wife, [nickname's] sister." In another incident, where a police officer stopped Ms. Perez's oldest daughter as she was going to work, the daughter said she asked the officer why she was being stopped. She knew she had not been speeding, and her tags were fine. According to the sister, the officer replied, "I just wanted to stop you to see if you were [nickname's] sister." The sister replied, "Unless you want to stop me for a ticket or expired tags or a warrant, I'm late for work and I got to go." The daughter left, and the officer did not pursue her.

Ms. Gonzalez is the mother of one of the six young African-descent men accused of murdering a Mexican American. Her family moved to Springfield from Puerto Rico approximately twenty-five years ago, when she was a child. She remarked that European Americans in Springfield accepted the light-skinned members of her family but rejected them when they realized that other family members looked phenotypically African. She stated that their troubles began when they were perceived as being African American more so than Hispanic American. Ms. Gonzalez corroborates the stories of the other women about the police. She states that the police often take photos of young African American and African-descent Hispanic American men as they go about their daily lives, no matter whether they are washing their cars in the driveways of their homes or sitting on their porches. She named certain police officers—also named by others—who seem to frequently harass African Americans.

Ms. Landsford has two grown children of partial African descent. She has complained about how abusively her children were treated in the Springfield Public Schools when they attended, especially how teachers and administrators reacted to her son. When her son was in middle school, he was called to the principal's office for a minor problem. The European American male principal asked the young man to have his mother call the principal that evening. When the young man responded that his dad would call the principal, the principal allegedly retorted, "Oh, you have a father?" After the same young man finished high school, it took him two years before he could find a decent job. He once told me that out of about fifty young African American males he knew in Springfield, none of them had jobs. The young man has also been harassed by the Springfield police. In summer 2001, Ms. Landsford told me that her son had been stopped about twenty-three times in a two-month period by one particular officer of the Springfield Police Department.

Ms. Casely has lived in Springfield all of her life. She has three children, all of whom are part African descent. Ms. Casely has complained that she can find an apartment with no problem, yet once the landlord or landlady realizes that she is the mother of "mixed" children, complaints start to get lodged against her until the family is forced to move. Ms. Casely has also complained that similar incidents have occurred while she was employed. As long as bosses and coworkers do not know her children are mixed, her evaluations are high. Yet, when they ask to see pictures of her children and if she shows the pictures to them, eventually she starts to get negative evaluations and is let go from her job. Hence, for

Ms. Casely, being connected to the world of people of color has negatively affected her finding suitable housing and suitable employment.

Ms. Ford, a grandmother, complained often about the negative treatment of her granddaughter, an African-descent young lady who was often stopped by the Springfield police. In fact, Ms. Ford mentioned that her granddaughter's photo had been snapped by a police officer of the Springfield Police Department and appeared in the infamous book of "offenders" of color called the "Rogues' Gallery." Ms. Ford's granddaughter refused to accept a four-year scholarship to a local private university after she graduated from high school because she was so fed up with the racist treatment she had received in Springfield (Stewart-Stafford 1999). She now lives in Kansas City, Missouri. Ms. Ford has complained to local officials and legislators about the horrid treatment of African-descent youth in particular, but she has never had any satisfactory responses.[29]

NO JUSTICE . . . ?

Activists of color in Springfield have done much to try to bring justice to the area. A small committed group intensified its efforts in fall of 1996 after the passage of the Missouri Safe Schools Act. They knew that students of color in the public schools would be targeted more so than European American students. The activists also started paying attention to other issues, including those of health care, housing, social services, employment, and law enforcement and the judicial system. They, moreover, decided to see what could be done to get the federal government's civil rights offices involved in scrutinizing civil rights issues in Springfield. After months of contacting the U.S. Commission on Civil Rights by telephone, e-mail, fax, and postal mail, the activists were able to get the Missouri Advisory Committee to the Office of Civil Rights to hold a town hall meeting in Springfield, August 1997. Two years later, the report *Race Relations in Springfield* was published.[30] Although it was not as far-reaching as the activists had hoped it would be, the information contained within it was a first effort to begin to get the government to document racial problems in Springfield. Eventually, the activists were instrumental in getting representatives from the regional Office of Civil Rights of the U.S. Department of Education, the regional Department of Labor's Office of Federal Contract Compliance Programs, the Community Relations Section of the St. Louis Federal Reserve Bank, as well as the director of the state of Missouri's Workforce Development Office and others to come hold talks in Springfield to educate people of color about the offices and how they could assist citizens. Some of the visits were successful, but others yielded few results. The representatives seemed to fear coming to Springfield, and many would make excuses about why they did not need to come. Sometimes they would not even let Springfield activists know about civil rights meetings in other parts of the state. For example, on April 24, 2000, I learned that the regional U.S. Commission on Civil Rights was holding a two-state (Kansas and Missouri) hearing on racial profiling and hate crimes, by accidentally stumbling across that information through the Internet. When I telephoned a representative at the regional office, the person stuttered and stammered in surprise, wondering how I had found out about the meeting. When I actually appeared at the meeting on April 27, 2000, I thought that representatives from the U.S. Commission on Civil Rights tended to ignore me. In addition to civil rights activists and representatives from civil rights organizations attending the meeting, law enforcement officers from major cities in Kansas and Missouri were there. I noticed that a police officer from the Springfield Police Department was scheduled to give a report about racial profiling and hate crimes in Springfield but never appeared. He had not even sent a report to be read, as one absent law enforcement officer from Kansas had done. No one at the police department has satisfactorily explained why the officer never appeared as scheduled.

In contacting government civil rights offices during the past seven years, activists have learned about many government programs that could benefit people of color. Local elected officials and leaders, however, do very little community outreach and public notification to inform people of color, in particular African Americans, about these programs. Therefore, local activists believe that they get no help from the government civil rights offices, which are mandated to protect and enforce civil rights and should ensure that local leaders comply with Title VI and other civil rights laws. An African American female postal employee stated that in 1996 she bought five hundred 8-1/2-by-11-inch envelopes and started sending information about the racist treatment of African American postal workers at the main USPS in Springfield to major civil rights organizations and to federal government offices for civil rights and similar appropriate agencies. She recently stated that she has forty remaining envelopes but that she has had no responses from those agencies.[31] This woman is now on leave from the post office, as she could no longer tolerate the post office's stressful environment. She states that she is traumatized and exhausted and that the civil rights organizations have not made their presences felt. In the end, she has lost total faith in the civil rights systems, both governmental and nongovernmental. Civil rights offices seem designed to assist already-powerful institutions to know the civil rights laws and their updates. Therefore, clever attorneys who represent these institutions can evade or get around certain laws successfully. Parents, students, and community members are not aware of such laws. For example, an attorney from the Office of Civil Rights of the U.S. Department of Education may present information on special education laws as an update for educators and school administrators. The same attorney will not provide the same information to parents of special-education students—a disproportionately high percentage of whom are African American—despite parents' reported written requests for information and assistance.

Despite the disappointments and hardships, some activists in the Ozarks are determined to continue to educate themselves about how they can assist the underserved in this area. To try to seek resolutions to problems, they are going to regional and national conferences—such as the Emory University Conference on Lynching and Racial Violence in America, the Congressional Black Caucus Annual Legislative Conference, and the National Consortium for Racial and Ethnic Fairness in the Courts. Moreover, they are educating themselves on fundraising and other development strategies. They look forward to networking with other activists nationally and internationally in order to exchange ideas regarding how to lighten the burdens and expenses associated with dismantling racism.

Most so-called civil rights organizations in the United States seem loath to tackle the kind of racism that occurs in Springfield and Southwest Missouri. Contrary to what many people from other parts of the world seem to believe, U.S. nongovernmental organizations, including the dominant civil rights organizations, *do not* handle all of the problems of racism in the United States. One of the problems is that major civil rights organizations are concentrated mainly on the East and West coasts and in major metropolitan areas, and their representatives rarely get to the "outback" to see what is happening. To effectively monitor what is happening in each part of the country, civil rights organizers will have to step in the shoes of Walter White, Ida B. Wells Barnett, Thurgood Marshall, Fannie Lou Hamer, Martin Luther King Jr., and others who fearlessly traveled across the nation to ensure justice and equality for the downtrodden.

In addition, both the governmental civil rights offices and the civil rights nongovernmental organizations need to be more effective in solving civil rights issues. Referring local complainants to local offices—an offshoot of "states' rights"—to resolve complaints of racism is not working, as many in those offices share the same sentiments as the perpetrators of racism. The civil rights nongovernmental organizations must ensure that the federal government expands the effectiveness and increases the budget for its civil rights offices. More important, making sure that the staff persons in those offices are seriously concerned and informed about civil rights and are willing to dismantle racism and racist practices will be a key to civil rights successes.

HUMAN RIGHTS INSTITUTIONS; THEIR PROMISES AND PROBLEMS

Although the United Nations High Commission on Human Rights has good intentions, not much can be done to dismantle racism around the world by a commission with only two offices—the main one in Geneva, Switzerland, and a branch office in New York. The recent post-WCAR Anti-discrimination Unit (ADU) set up at the Geneva office seems too inadequate to monitor the numerous acts of racism committed worldwide. ADU offices should be established in every country with a United Nations membership. An additional problem is that historically the UN system offices have seemed reluctant to criticize the United States, and it appears that only on rare occasions have special rapporteurs investigated systemic racism in the United States (Mihlar 1998). In addition, being able to meet face-to-face with representatives from the ADU will be crucial if the goals of the WCAR are to be implemented. If local activists and women of color could ask questions of ADU staff members, they would be the following: How will racism be monitored in a country such as the United States, a country that walked out of the WCAR in Durban and that refuses to acknowledge that racism is a problem? How will the United States be held accountable for even the small provisions in Durban's program of action? What could activists tell the family and friends of the young African American stabbed by skinheads in June 2001, the four African American inmates urinated on by European American jailers, the relatives of hanging victims Lenwood Shawn Howard and Leonard Gakinya, and other racially abused people about any hope of an international body's willingness to help them find relief? Much has been declared, but so much remains to be fully implemented.

Finally, what follow-up plans exist for the post-WCAR organizations and secretariats? Will future conferences be teleconferenced so that they can become global events accessible to all? Will small groups that work daily to dismantle racism have the same opportunity to become accredited with the United Nations Economic and Social Council and other UN agencies similar to the large so-called civil rights and human rights groups heavily subsidized by foundations? Most important, when these poor, small civil society organizations send complaints to the ADU, will that office respond? Getting the appropriate offices in the UN system to monitor human rights issues and compliance in the United States would be a boon to helping eliminate racism in underserved areas.

CONCLUSION

Women and families of color in Springfield are desperately looking for solutions to the problems that keep them bound in shackles. Most of the women interviewed and documented always thought the Mississippi paradigm of civil rights activism and enforcement would be in effect even into the twenty-first century. In that sense, many beleaguered African Americans still expect civil rights groups to be the cavalry coming to rescue the weary settlers broken down by civil rights violations, private and public. In addition to blacks and latinos being underserved, the racism in Springfield and Southwest Missouri has been severely underdocumented. A corrective step would be for social scientists to document the racism and its deleterious effects on local people of color. Such documentation would assist activists, advocates, and radical educators as they continue to attempt to cut and plough through the dense thicket of institutionalized local racism.

Keeping the movement initiated by the WCAR will be an important task. Women of color in Springfield and Southwest Missouri belong to the weakest links on the human rights chain, links that must be strengthened. Underserved areas need attention and help. The following ideas suggest concrete ways underserved people can be helped:

- Underserved people need lawyers and/or second- and third-year law students who are willing to monitor and document problems in the local legal system as well as assist local residents with litigation. Most of all, this group needs lawyers who are not afraid to tackle inbred, "old boy" political and judicial systems.
- They need investigators from the offices for civil rights of governmental departments such as education, transportation, commerce, justice, health and human services, housing and urban development, and labor to enforce Title VI of the Civil Rights Act. This law prohibits discrimination, denial of benefits, and prevention of participation in federally funded programs on the basis of race, color, or national origin. This title has rarely, if ever, been enforced in Springfield, Missouri. Moreover, the community outreach and public notification that recipients of such funds should provide to potential beneficiaries does not take place in the community. In addition, they need investigators from civil rights offices of agencies such as the Small Business Administration, the Minority Business Development Agency, the Office of Federal Contract Compliance Programs, the Equal Employment Opportunity Commission, the United States Commission on Civil Rights, and others to adequately investigate discrimination complaints.
- They would like assistance from the private civil rights/human rights/civil liberties organizations such as the National Urban League, the NAACP, the Leadership Conference on Civil Rights, the ACLU, and others. These groups could hold town hall meetings to ascertain people's concerns.
- They would like the Progressive Congressional Caucus, the Black Congressional Caucus, and the Hispanic Congressional Caucus to hold town hall meetings here (and in other underserved places) so that members of these caucuses can listen to people firsthand and learn their concerns.

- They want legal literacy. When civil rights legislation was first enacted, many people of color assumed that honest, caring people would staff the offices and seriously work to eliminate discrimination. After decades of very little improvement in regards to the elimination of racism (and other forms of intolerance), they now understand that they will not realize civil rights/human rights/civil liberties until they are educated about them. Groups such as the NAACP, the ACLU, and others could accomplish much by having educational divisions that do nothing else but educate underserved communities around the country about their rights.
- Finally, if all of the above does not materialize, they would like to start a campaign to get Article 14 of the International Convention on the Elimination of All Forms of Racial Discrimination ratified—that is, the article dealing with people's right to file complaints directly with the United Nations.[32]

The goals listed here are achievable. Getting our sisters and brothers from around the globe to participate will be the most significant step. More amazing, though, will be efforts to engage our bewildered sisters and brothers in the states to start collaborating in these endeavors. If penniless activists can accomplish some of these objectives with no help at all, surely those with abundant resources and finances can successfully complete the job.

NOTES

1. Although in the United States the definitions of nongovernmental organizations, community-based organizations, and civil society organizations can lead to nonmutually exclusive taxonomies, in general, nongovernmental organizations are nongovernmental, nonprofit entities that have a superordinate national structure in addition to local chapters (e.g., NAACP); community-based organizations are nongovernmental, nonprofit entities that are organized in specific locations and not directly affiliated with or subordinate to larger national structures (e.g., Kuumba Human Rights Focus Group of Springfield, Missouri); civil society organizations are defined more in terms of the organization's mission—they are entities that attempt to empower individuals to promote their social, economic, and cultural interests for mutual benefit (e.g., the Reunion Club of Springfield, an organizational board that mobilizes citizens around the common cause of an annual Park Day festival, an event that focuses on recreation, entertainment, socializing with friends/relatives, as well as community improvement).

2. The full text of WCAR's program of action can be found at www.racism.gov.za/substance/confdoc/index.html.

3. Springfield, Missouri, is the hometown of former U.S. attorney general John Ashcroft, and it is where he "cut his political teeth." Many of us believe that those in power in the Ozarks share his political agenda.

4. Some Springfield activists have questioned whether or not the 2000 census accurately reflects the actual number of African Americans (implying that the numbers concerning income that are presented here underestimate the true disparities), as only one full-time African American clerical worker and one part-time African American recruiter worked at the Springfield census office, compared to fourteen full-time Hispanic American census workers. Having worked with the Springfield office of the Census Bureau during the collection of these data, I maintain that it is doubtful any African American enumerators were employed.

5. Jim House, education director, AIDS Project of the Ozarks, personal communication, March 24, 2003.

6. Human Resources Office, Springfield Public Schools, telephone interview, Springfield, Missouri, February 5, 2003.

7. Phyllis Chase, deputy superintendent, Springfield Public Schools, community meeting, Springfield, Missouri, February 2001.

8. Community meeting on local public schools' concerns, Mt. Olive Baptist Church, Springfield, Missouri, September 26, 2001.

9. Sidney James, Eleanor Brown, and others, personal communication.

10. James, Brown, and others, personal communication.

11. James, Brown, and others, personal communication.

12. James, Brown, and others, personal communication.

13. Kenya Kimbrough, activist in Columbia, Missouri, interview by author, February 12, 2003.

14. James, Brown, and others, personal communication.

15. James, Brown, and others, personal communication.

16. David Carr and others, personal communications with the author.

17. Personal communications with the author.

18. Gay Reevy, personal communication.

19. Community meeting with representatives from the Springfield Police Department, Springfield, Missouri, September 25, 2002.

20. Personal communication.

21. Personal communication.

22. The Thirty-first Judiciary encompasses Greene County, where Springfield is located.

23. Arthur Hodge, personal communication.

24. Personal communication.

25. Personal communication.

26. Personal communication.

27. The information reported in this section was collected through many years of participant observation as a community activist and as a personal advocate of the people whose lived experiences of injustice are described.

28. See the Employment section of this chapter on page 82.

29. My daughter reports similar experiences regarding her complaints to elected officials. In 1995, state senator Jet Banks told my daughter to move if she did not wish to endure the racial abuse and terror that she suffered in the Ozarks, because the elected officials "do not have enough resources to help people who live in areas where there is not a high concentration of African Americans."

30. See Missouri Advisory Committee to the United States Commission on Civil Rights, *Race Relations in Springfield, Missouri* (United States Commission on Civil Rights, 1999).

31. Personal communication.

32. For more information about International Convention on the Elimination of All Forms of Racial Discrimination and Article 14, see www.unesco.org/human_rights/dcc.htm.

REFERENCES

Bauer, Laura. 2001. Two charged in urination assault. *Springfield News-Leader*, August 2, 1A.

———. 2002. DFS and the death of Dominic James. *Springfield News-Leader*, www.springfieldnews-leader.com/webextra/dfs.dominic/timeline112702.html (accessed January 28, 2003).

Bennett, Jane. 1970. "A lot of good colored people left" in 1906. *Springfield News-Leader and Press*, July 8, 1.

Chase, Phyllis. 2001. Assistant superintendent, Springfield Public Schools, interview.

Consolidated plan: Fiscal year 2000–2004. 2000. Springfield, Mo.: City of Springfield, Department of Planning and Development.

Decatur, William. 1981. Interview by author, Springfield, Missouri.

———. 1982. Interview by author, Springfield, Missouri.

Department of Interior Census Office. 1883. *Tenth census of the United States: 1880*. Vol. 1, *Population*, 421. Washington, D.C.: U.S. Government Printing Office.

Equal Employment Opportunity Commission. 2002. *EEOC settles racial harassment suit for $1.8 million against Apollo Colors of Illinois: African-American workers subjected to hangman's nooses, racist slurs and graffiti*, www.eeoc.gov/press/3-27-02.html (accessed March 27, 2002).

Friedan, Betty. 2001. *The feminine mystique*. New York: W. W. Norton.

Harrison, Faye V. 1995. The persistent power of "race" in the cultural and political economy of racism. *Annual Review of Anthropology* 24:47–74.

———. 1997. The gendered politics and violence of structural adjustment: A view from Jamaica. *Situated lives: Gender and culture in everyday life*, ed. Louise Lamphere, 451–68. New York: Routledge.

———. 2000. Facing racism and the moral responsibility of human rights knowledge. In *Ethics and Anthropology*, special issue of the *Annals of the New York Academy of Sciences* 925:45–69.

———. 2002. Global apartheid, foreign policy, and human rights. *Souls* 4 (3): 48–68.

Hill Collins, Patricia. 1990. *Black feminist thought: Knowledge, consciousness, and the politics of empowerment*. Boston: Unwin Hyman.

Holcombe, R. I. 1883. *History of Greene County, Missouri, 1883*, http://thelibrary.springfield.missouri.org/lochist/history/holcombe/grch31pt1.html (accessed May 22, 2003).

hooks, bell. 2000. Feminism: A movement to end sexist oppression. *Readings for diversity and social justice: An anthology on racism, sexism, anti-Semitism, heterosexism, classism, and ableism*, ed. Maurianne Adams et al., 238–40. New York: Routledge.

Majeske Robinson, Diane. 2002. Confederate flag creates stir in Neosho. *Springfield News-Leader*, May 10, 1A, 9A.

Maull, Samuel. 2002. *Judge vacates convictions in Central Park jogger case*, www.lexisone.com/news/ap/ap121902c.html (accessed February 15, 2003).

McClaurin, Irma. 2001. *Black feminist anthropology: Theory, politics, praxis, and poetics*. New Brunswick, N.J.: Rutgers University Press.

Mihlar, Farah. 1998. *UN official seeks reforms in U.S. prisons*, December 18, www.mapinc.org/drugnews/v98.na04.html (accessed March 27, 2003).

O'Brien, Sean. 2001. "Perry v. Kemna: Claim number 3, writ of habeus corpus for Jermaine Perry." (Case no. 01-3129-CV-S-1), United States District Court for the Western District of Missouri, March 16, 2001.

O'Dell, Kathleen. 2002. Ceremony pays homage to ancestors. *Springfield News-Leader*, June 3, 1B, 5B.

Shurley, Traci. 1999a. Punishment offers chance to change ways: Kenneth R. Booth pleaded guilty to ethnic intimidation after 1997 attack. *Springfield News-Leader*, June 12, 1B.

———. 1999b Intimidation case brings probation: Wayne Kelly's sentence stems from assault on an African-American man. *Springfield News-Leader*, September 18, 1B, 6B.

Springfield News-Leader. 1998. Man charged with ethnic intimidation: Kenneth R. Booth Jr. was originally charged with assault in 1997 case. December 9, 1B.

Springfield News-Leader. 2001. Springfield 6th on list of whitest U.S. cities. August 13, 1A.

Springfield Republican. 1906. Greene County lynchings. April 16, 3.

Steinem, Gloria. 1995. *Moving beyond words: Age, rage, sex, power, money, muscles; Breaking the boundaries of gender*. Reprint ed. New York: Touchstone.

Stewart-Stafford, Rosemary. 1996–2003. Conversations and interviews by author, Springfield, Missouri.

Strait, Jefferson. 2001. U.S. agency studies stabbing at Denny's. *Springfield News-Leader*, June 22, 1A.

Sylvester, Ron. 1999. Hate groups find homes in heartland. *Springfield News-Leader*, July 12, 1A, 4A.

Truchard, Liam. 2002. Death rates set off alarm: Black infants in county die at nearly four times rate of whites. *Springfield News-Leader*, April 19, 1A.

U.S. Bureau of the Census. 2003. *Data on Springfield, Missouri*, http://factfinder.census.gov/servlet/DTTable?_ts=70812625036 (accessed May 7, 2003).

Wilson, Angela. 2001. Local searches of blacks disproportionate. *Springfield News-Leader*, June 2, 1A, 8A.

Young, Gladys. 1998. Conversations with author, Springfield, Missouri.

———. 2002. Conversations with author, Springfield, Missouri.

· 5 ·

Welfare Reform, Racism, and Single Motherhood in the Americas

Helen I. Safa

*W*elfare reform has reopened the debate on single mothers in the United States. Female-headed households and particularly black single mothers are attacked as the primary symbol of the welfare state and a key factor in the formation of a permanent underclass (e.g., Abramovitz 1988). They are seen as examples of family disorganization and a breakdown of family values and are held responsible for rising rates of poverty, juvenile delinquency, and crime. This stigma culminated in the 1996 passage of the Personal Responsibility and Work Opportunity Act, which effectively ended AFDC (Aid to Families with Dependent Children) and gave women a five-year period to get off welfare and find a job. Financial incentives were also given to states to encourage single mothers to marry. As this legislation was up for renewal in 2002, the debate on its effects has again heated up. The Bush administration asked that $350 million be taken out of the welfare budget to promote marriage among welfare recipients, and his new welfare chief, Wade Horn, has suggested giving married couples preferential treatment in public benefits with limited spots (*Gainesville Sun*, September 24, 2002, 9A).

This chapter is designed to demonstrate the flaws in the government's welfare reform policy. I suggest that neither forcing single mothers to seek paid employment nor requiring them to marry will stem the growth in single motherhood, which has been phenomenal since the 1960s. The government's argument is based on the popular assumption that public welfare is primarily responsible for this growth, failing to take into account other factors that favored the increase in numbers of single mothers, such as male unemployment. It is also based on the flawed assumption that single mothers are inherently deviant or pathological because they do not conform to the two-parent nuclear family in which the conjugal bond is deemed primary. The government's assumption is that the family is centered on marriage or the conjugal bond, while I argue that in many urban low-income households in the United States, particularly in the African American and Latino communities, conjugal bonds are weak and unstable in comparison to consanguineous relationships between a mother, her children, and her female kin (Safa 1999a). Here I draw on my own research among female industrial workers in the Hispanic Caribbean (Safa 1995), where I have demonstrated that conjugal bonds have been weakened through a history of slavery, consensual unions, and particularly a deterioration in the man's ability to fulfill his role as economic provider. Similar arguments can be made for the growth of numbers of single mothers in the African American community in the United States, as I demonstrate here.

Before proceeding further, a few definitions are in order. Not all single mothers are unwed mothers; they may also be separated, divorced, or widowed, who until the 1930s, constituted the majority of female household heads. At the same time, not all single mothers are heads of household, who take full responsibility for their children and other members. This distinction is important because until the 1950s, most single mothers in the United States lived within an extended household and not independently as female heads. Welfare appears to be an important factor contributing to independent female heads of household and therefore added to their visibility and growth. Single mothers living as subfamilies with their children in extended households were usually not counted as female heads but as members of the household headed by their parents or other relatives. Therefore, the apparent increase in female heads of household starting in the 1960s may reflect in part this change in household composition from subfamilies to independent female-headed households, rather than simply an increase in their actual number. But in the eyes of public opinion, it turned welfare away from deserving widows to undeserving, "immoral" single mothers.

THE IMPORTANCE OF MARRIAGE IN THE UNITED STATES

Nancy Cott's history (2000) of marriage in the United States helps us to understand the enormous significance of the conjugal bond in American life since colonial times. Couched originally in Christian religious terms, marriage came to symbolize freedom, the right of consent, and the basis of civilization. Marriage was considered a civil right restricted basically to white men, since blacks could not marry, while white women were considered subordinate to their husbands in the marital contract, which made the couple one legal person. The husband's role as provider ensured his supremacy in marriage while the wife remained a dependent who owed her husband complete sexual fidelity and who lacked a legal persona (she could not own property, keep her own wages, vote, serve on juries, etc.). Though the terms of the marriage contract were made more flexible as women entered the labor force in the twentieth century, men continued for a long time to be considered the primary wage earners, and their position at the head of the household conferred on them full citizenship.

A brief history of marriage, motherhood, and female employment among African Americas from slavery to the present demonstrates that family structure evolved quite differently in the white and black subcultures. As Cott (2000) demonstrates, in the United States, a nuclear family based on a male breadwinner and dependent housewife was held up as the model and enshrined in social policy, including the welfare state. However, as in the Caribbean, few black families could adhere to this model because high female employment coupled with male economic instability contributed to the growth of single mothers. I argue that deviance from the nuclear family norm helped to marginalize black single mothers and stigmatize them as being immoral and unrespectable, a tendency that persists to this day and is manifest in the current attack on single mothers through welfare reform in the United States. Failure to conform to white middle-class American values was seen as "family disorganization" and became another basis for racism and exclusion of African Americans from the social polity.

African Americans were not the only group that was marginalized because they failed to conform to the nuclear family norm. Cott (2002) shows that native Americans, communitarians (such as the Oneida community in upstate New York), Mormons, Asians, and European migrants in the early twentieth century were labeled deviants and subjected to intense Americanization campaigns to teach them the value of the nuclear family norm. Marriage among ex-slaves became a prime requisite for civilizing the African American population, who under slavery were not permitted to marry.

THE HISTORICAL EVOLUTION OF CONJUGAL NORMS IN THE AFRICAN AMERICAN HOUSEHOLD

Several factors contributed to the weak conjugal bond in many African American families in the United States, including slavery and a high rate of female employment. Slaves had virtually no rights, including the right to marry, and the master was able to sell individual family members. Children took the status of their mother and were seldom separated from her at an early age. Black men were denied the patriarchal privileges assumed by white men, who often established nonrecognized sexual liaisons with their female slaves, though these were also prohibited. Strong consanguineous bonds between maternal kin and be-tween a mother and her children persisted so that in colonial Virginia "the ex-tended slave family remained the most consistent norm and the most clearly identifiable ideal" (Stevenson 1995, 36). As a result of missionary activity, many unions were legalized in the postemancipation period, but black women as a whole never became dependent housewives (Cott 2000). On the contrary, black women continued to work as wage laborers or alongside their husbands as share-croppers because discrimination in employment and education made it difficult for men to be the sole breadwinners of their families or claim a "family wage," which became an ideal for white workers in the late nineteenth century.

Sexual patterns also differed in the black community. Premarital sex was much higher among blacks than among whites, and women often had children from several sexual liaisons before settling down with one man and sometimes marrying him (Degler 1980). Since slavery, the proportion of female-headed households has always been higher among blacks than among whites, although the two-parent household predominated until 1950 (128–29).

Racial lines also hardened after the Civil War and were used to deny African Americans the full rights of citizenship. Bans on intermarriage or even casual unions with whites were strengthened, not even being rejected by the Supreme Court until 1967. Anyone with even a drop of African American blood was considered black, thereby establishing a bipolar color line that be-came more rigid with the imposition of Jim Crow laws in the 1900s.

Female morality and the "cult of domesticity" in the United States con-tributed to the stigmatization of black women and reinforced the ideal of the nuclear family. Victorian women suspected that economic independence bred sexual licentiousness and poverty, and any form of sex outside marriage was condemned (Brownlee and Brownlee 1976, 30). Women's place within the home was seen as ensuring their moral virtue, but black women continued to be employed, albeit in low-status jobs, primarily as domestics because they were barred from factory and clerical employment. Unwed mothers already constituted a significant segment of black single mothers but were predomi-nantly invisible because they lived largely in extended households rather than heading households of their own.

Among African Americans, as those among European immigrants who entered the United States in great numbers from 1890 to 1920, "marriage suited a man for full citizenship by placing him at the head of the household" (Cott 2000, 133). Marriage and earning an income were considered the two pillars on which citizenship stood, and though women had freedom of consent in the marriage contract, they were not considered equals. For example, a woman in the United States lost her citizenship if she married a foreigner, but a man could confer citizenship on his foreign bride. This rule was not amended until the

1920s, when women obtained the vote, conferring on them greater civil rights than they had held. Though wives now controlled their own property and inheritance, husbands were still obliged to support them because few married women were gainfully employed. During the Great Depression of the 1930s, married women were removed from public-sector jobs, and most benefits such as Social Security went to white working men. Mother's aid was given only to widows, not to unmarried or abandoned mothers (Cott 2000, 117–18). African Americans were devastated by the Depression, and increasing numbers migrated North in search of better job opportunities and less discrimination.

Roosevelt's New Deal to assuage the social ills resulting from the Depression was focused on white working men. The Social Security Act of 1935 from the beginning distinguished between primary entitlement programs, which were designed primarily for white men, and secondary public assistance programs, which were based primarily on need among women and minorities (Gordon 1994). Means and morals tests restricted the number of women eligible for public assistance, especially black women, and were predicated on a moral code controlling women's sexuality. From the late nineteenth century until the 1930s, in all classes, races, and ethnic groups, most female heads of household were widows (Gordon 1994, 19), and public assistance was designed to keep them in the home, maintaining the semblance of a family wage through public patriarchy.

WELFARE AND THE RISE OF FEMALE-HEADED HOUSEHOLDS IN THE UNITED STATES

The debate on the nature of the black family became politicized after the 1965 publication of the Moynihan report (a report authored by Daniel Patrick Moynihan and prepared for the Office of Policy Planning and Research), which, like welfare reform, blamed the social ills of the black community on a pathological family structure dating from slavery. Revisionist historians such as Herbert Gutman (1976) rejected the Moynihan report by arguing that white and black families were quite similar, sharing monogamy, a nuclear family, and distinct gender roles. Unfortunately, it seems that these revisionist historians shared Moynihan's view of single mothers as those disorganized and deviant from the nuclear family norm, and therefore attempted to minimize their existence. My argument, like Brenda Stevenson's (1995), is that single motherhood was important among African Americans but that it should be seen as an alternative to, rather than deviant from, the nuclear family.

The debate on the black family was heightened by demographic changes in the African American community. In the 1960s, African American women's educational and occupational profile improved, supported by civil rights legislation and affirmative action programs. But unemployment was always higher among black women than among white women, who were themselves joining the labor force in greater numbers. Nevertheless, the number of welfare recipients among black single mothers increased dramatically, from 3 million recipients in 1960 to 11.4 million in 1975 (Jones 1995, 306). In contrast to the definition used during the 1930s, single motherhood was now defined in racial terms (Gordon 1994, 34). Several factors contributed to this increase in welfare recipients: deindustrialization, especially in the Northeast, had a devastating effect on black male unemployment; the National Welfare Rights Organization, formed in 1967 on behalf of women welfare recipients, led to an increase in women applicants; and Johnson's war on poverty in the late 1960s, which added Medicaid and food stamps to the welfare allowance, substantially increased stipends, making welfare more attractive. Eligibility requirements for welfare were also relaxed. But the most important factor in the increase in welfare recipients is the precipitous rise in female heads of household, particularly in the black community. Black households headed by women grew from 17.6 percent in 1950 to 28.3 percent in 1970 and to 40.2 percent in 1980. White rates also increased but not at the same rate (Jones 1995, 305–6).

Is the rise in black female heads of household linked to the availability of welfare, as many opponents of public assistance have asserted? This ignores major structural factors contributing to this increase, including an imbalanced sex ratio in the African American community due to the high rate of male mortality and male incarceration in the black inner city (Amott 1990) and the further reduction in the pool of marriageable men through deindustrialization and suburban flight (Wilson 1987). Female employment has always been high in the black community, but as Orlando Patterson (1998) shows, African American women are now outdistancing men in education and employment, contributing to strong marital discord and a high divorce rate in the black middle class. The marriage rate has declined in the overall population since the 1970s but is particularly low among African Americans. Among African Americans, the marriage rate of women aged twenty to twenty-four declined from 55.8 percent in 1970 to 21.6 percent in 1980 (Tucker and Mitchell-Kernan 1995). As of March 1997, 41 percent of African American women and 46 percent of African American men had never married, compared to 21 percent and 27 percent of Euro-American women and men, respectively (Patterson 1998, 57). Again, welfare is mentioned as a precipitating factor, though the real value of AFDC stipends, food stamps, and Medicaid declined during this period (Wilson 1996, 94). Perhaps the major impact of welfare on the rise in female household heads in the black community is to enable the single mother and her children to live alone rather than to live in an extended family (Garfinkel and McLanahan 1986, 58).

Despite the 1960s sexual revolution and the gains women have made in terms of their rights in marriage, I would argue that the model of monogamous marriage and the nuclear family is still hegemonic. Taxation still rewards "normal" families, where the husband is the primary wage earner, despite the enormous rise in women's labor force participation and the consequent rise in two-paycheck families. The family wage has become an illusion, as both adults are required to be gainfully employed in order to support a modest middle-class lifestyle. Cohabitation has become the norm, as the number of unmarried-couple households multiplied almost ten times from 1960 to 1988 (Cott 2000, 203). After 1980, the white women's rate of unmarried childbearing more than doubled, while the black rate increased only 2 percent (Cott 2000, 204). In the 1990s, as a result of both nonmarriage and divorce, among women with children, one-fifth of white families were female headed compared to almost three-fifths of black families and almost one-third of Hispanic families (204).

The increase in the number of single mothers also contributed to the clamor for welfare reform, enshrined in the Personal Responsibility and Work Opportunity Act (PRWOA) of 1996. The act replaced welfare with workfare but also encouraged single mothers to marry. The sanctity of marriage is confirmed in the act's opening statement, which reads, "Marriage is the foundation of a successful society. Marriage is an essential institution of a successful society which promotes the interest of children" (quoted in Cott 2000, 222). The preliminary results of welfare reform will be examined in the conclusion of this chapter. I turn now to a brief analysis of female-headed households in the Caribbean, particularly Puerto Rico, where the U.S. normative policy on marriage has also had an impact.

FEMALE-HEADED
HOUSEHOLDS IN THE HISPANIC CARIBBEAN

The African American single mother living alone with her children differs radically from most low-income female-headed households in the Hispanic Caribbean, whose members depend on the contribution of extended family members to survive (Safa 1995, 1999a, 1999b, 1999c). Female-headed households have been increasing in both Cuba and the Dominican Republic and now number about one-third of all households, but the majority of these are extended and able to raise their income through the contribution of various household members (Safa 1995, 1999c). Extended family members also provide assistance in child care so that young single mothers maintain high labor-force participation rates, essential to their survival because neither country provides public assistance to single mothers (which clearly is not a factor in their continued increase). As in the African American community, subfamilies embedded in larger, extended families are particularly prevalent among young teenage mothers, many of whom become pregnant while still living at home; an analysis of a national household survey taken in the Dominican Republic in 1991 reveals that 70 percent of women heading subfamilies are under thirty years of age; three-fourths are daughters of the head of household; and over half have only one child (Duarte and Tejada Holguín 1995). Marriage rates have always been low among the poor in both Caribbean countries, and the percentage of consensual unions is increasing dramatically (Catasús 1992; Báez 1991).

Consensual unions were also important in Puerto Rico but over the past century of U.S. occupation have almost disappeared. Colonial officials were shocked to find that 50 percent of the marriageable population was living in consensual union in 1898. As part of its "civilizing mission," the United States promoted a new civil code, which made both civil marriage and divorce more accessible (Findlay 1999). Initially, the Puerto Rican poor did not respond, but legal marriage was later reinforced by privileging access to federal transfer payments, such as social security and veterans benefits, to legally married couples, while women in consensual unions had to prove lengthy cohabitation and paternity. Today, consensual unions in Puerto Rico have declined to about 5 percent (Vásquez Calzada 1988). I would argue that legal marriage was also seen as a sign of respectability and "whiteness" and became a means by which Puerto Ricans tried to distance themselves from the racial and cultural inferiority ascribed to them by the United States (Guerra 1998; Thompson 1995). Whether legal marriage ever held this meaning for African Americans remains to be explored (cf. Dominguez 1994).

It seems clear that in Puerto Rico, as in the United States, welfare has made it easier for single mothers to live alone, which has dampened labor force participation and made them more dependent on public assistance (Colón 1997; Burgos and Colberg 1990; Hernández-Angueira 2001). In female-headed Puerto Rican households, 47 percent are dependent on welfare, and 45 percent have no one employed (Colón 1997, 164), although a study of welfare recipients conducted recently suggests that many (as in the United States) have disguised part-time employment in the informal sector (Hernández-Angueira 2001). Extended families are far less prevalent in Puerto Rico than in Cuba or the Dominican Republic, where they reach close to 40 percent and are more numerous in urban than in rural areas. Clearly migration, urbanization, and industrialization in all three countries have modified family forms and gender norms. Among Puerto Rican and Dominican families living in New York City, however, the percentage of female-headed households living in multigenerational households has been increasing since the 1980s, which improves their labor force participation (Department of City Planning 1994; Rosenbaum and Gilbertson 1995).

WELFARE REFORM AND SINGLE MOTHERS

Clearly, the effects of household extension on single mothers and its impact on family well-being and how living arrangements were affected by welfare need more exploration. Carol Stack's older ethnography (1974) of African Americans confirms the existence of a domestic kin group that provides mutual aid and help in child rearing, which Katherine Newman's extensive ethnographic study (1999) of fast-food workers in Harlem maintains is still operative. Newman documents the essential role that welfare mothers play in child care for their working daughters and other relatives in central Harlem, with its high levels of unemployment and low (minimum) wages. In her sample of adult children aged twenty-five to thirty-four, 30 percent were still living at home, pulled together by the family's economic necessity, their own limited economic opportunities, and changing norms regarding marriage, which make it difficult if not impossible for a couple in low-wage work to survive on their own (2001, 772).

Newman's findings contradict those of Orlando Patterson (1998, 150) and William Wilson (1996). Wilson argues that welfare, urban renewal, public housing, the exodus from the inner city of upwardly mobile blacks, the reduced role of black churches, and the growth of crime and high incidences of AIDS and drug addiction have all contributed to the social disintegration of the inner-city ghetto community. Anne Roschelle (1997, 149) suggests that the elaborate social support networks characteristic of poor urban minorities in the United States in the 1960s and 1970s no longer persist. She uses this to explain her surprising finding, based on survey research of a nationally representative sample, that white women are more likely to offer and receive child care support than are minority women, particularly blacks. In a careful study that showed higher rates of return to welfare among African American single mothers than among white single mothers, the critical variable lacking among African Americans was social capital—that is, assistance from kin, boyfriends, and so on—even though human capital and structural variables such as labor market resources were very similar (Edin and Harris 1999). Kathryn Edin and Laura Lein (1997) show that neither working or welfare-reliant single mothers can survive without the assistance that family and men provide. Even boyfriends among working and welfare-reliant single mothers in the United States are expected to contribute or not remain in the household (145). But this is not supported by state policy. Roschelle (1997, 60) notes that before welfare reform, about half of all states had AFDC rules that carried penalties for shared housing arrangements. Newman (2001) also suggests that the "carrying capacity" of social networks may be severely strained under the new PRWOA regulations requiring all welfare recipients to work, thereby disrupting existing child care and other mutual aid arrangements.

The passage of PRWOA has dramatically altered the demographic profile of welfare recipients, as shown by a recent study comparing demographic and other variables among welfare recipients before and three years after the passage of PRWOA (Institute for Women's Policy Research 2002b). While whites constitute the largest share of low-income single-parent households in both periods, the share of white welfare recipients declines from 34 percent to 24 percent; however, the percentage of black welfare recipients remains stable, and the proportion of Hispanic welfare recipients increases dramatically, from 20 percent to 29 percent (4). Blacks and Hispanics now constitute the majority of welfare recipients and are more likely than whites to be living in extended families (Flippen and Tienda 1998). Never-married mothers, who are more numerous in the Hispanic and especially in the black community, exhibit the longest welfare duration (Ellwood and Bane 1994).

Studies by the Institute for Women's Policy Research (2002c) demonstrate that President Bush's marriage proposal is deeply flawed for several reasons: first, marriage does not necessarily end poverty, because men do not necessarily bring in added income, much less support the family; and, second, the majority (64 percent) of single mothers earn incomes above the poverty level, particularly now that single motherhood is no longer confined to the low-income group. Single mothers who work full-time are especially likely to have above-poverty incomes. But this requires affordable child care and transportation, which many welfare reform programs do not currently provide. Educational attainment has also been shown to sharply reduce the poverty rate among women of color, but the proportion of welfare mothers attending college dropped by roughly 17 percent after welfare reform (International Center for Research on Women 2002, 2).

I would argue that the current emphasis in welfare reform policy on legal marriage and paid employment will do little to correct the structural forces documented here as those responsible for the rise in the number of single mothers, particularly male unemployment and the breakdown of the extended family. If household extension proves to be as beneficial to the employment of single mothers and their children's welfare as my Caribbean data suggest, then public support might be given to encourage single mothers to live in multigenerational households or even to cooperate through neighborhood networks in child rearing and other forms of mutual aid. The 1996 PRWOA initiating welfare reform does make it mandatory that teenage mothers reside with their parents and continue to go to school, an issue that stirred considerable concern in feminist circles who saw this as an infringement on the woman's autonomy.

As Rachel Gordon (1999) explains in an article on multigenerational residence and welfare policy, though teenage single mothers now constitute a fraction of welfare recipients, they were singled out in this legislation because adult mothers who had given birth as teenagers were close to a majority of all single female AFDC recipients and were also among the most likely to be long-term recipients. However, according to Gordon (530–31), the majority of teenage single mothers already live in extended arrangements, mostly with their own parent(s). Among the small number (about 5 percent) of teenage mothers who do live alone, AFDC was not found to be a determining factor in leaving home, although higher AFDC benefits did deter mothers living alone at the time of pregnancy from returning home. Older single mothers with larger numbers of children and greater own economic resources are more likely to live alone (531–32). In short, Gordon's research suggests that welfare may not have been as strong a factor in the explosive growth of female-headed households in the 1960s as I suggested earlier. However, further research is needed because she focuses exclusively on young mothers (who are less likely to live alone) and her data are from the 1980s and 1990s, when conditions were quite different from those of the 1960s. Gordon explains how census techniques in the United States prior to the 1980s made the measurement of subfamilies more difficult to discern.

Gordon (1999, 530–38) also reviews the evidence from existing studies on the consequences for young mothers of multigenerational residence. Her findings support my suggestion that extended living arrangements benefit young single mothers in terms of greater economic self-sufficiency and more social support and child care assistance. A considerable number of studies show that across all race and ethnic groups, single mothers living in subfamilies are more likely than mothers living alone to remain in school, find employment, lower their fertility, and not become welfare recipients. Children also benefit, particularly if they are young, while the evidence for teenage high school students is still mixed. Gordon's findings also show that multigenerational residence may slow the development of parental competence in young mothers (536–37), a finding that would concur with my own observations among young single mothers in the Hispanic Caribbean. I agree with Gordon on the need for more study (especially longitudinal and comparative) on the impact of multigenerational residence on single mothers.

The effects of the PRWOA on the economic well-being of children in low-income single-parent families are only beginning to emerge. The share of children living in poverty has fallen, at least as of 2000, due largely to the economic boom of the late 1990s. But a recent study by the Institute for Women's Policy Research (2002a), shows that children in poor single-parent families in 2000, especially the very young, are less likely to receive cash assistance, Medicaid, and food stamps than in 1996. Now that the economy has deteriorated and unemployment has grown, the plight of these poor children may be worse than ever.

CONCLUSION

Rather than focus on legal marriage and paid employment among single mothers, welfare legislation should enable men to fulfill their role as economic provider by raising employment levels and providing more training programs, particularly in the inner city where African Americans and other minorities live. The man's contribution as breadwinner is basic to the meaning of marriage in the low-income household, while for the middle class the respectability of legal marriage may be more important. In the Caribbean household as well as in the African American household, the length and stability of a relationship matters more than legalization, which is often postponed until children are born. However, even in the middle class, the erosion of the male breadwinner role has robbed marriage of its legitimacy, as cohabitation has become more common and accepted (Patterson 1998; Cott 2000).

There is also the danger that a renewed emphasis on legal marriage and the nuclear family will make it appear that only the conjugal bond can uphold "family values," while I maintain that single mothers with the aid of extended kin can provide an adequate alternative. Stressing conformity to American middle-class values undermines tolerance for diversity, which has grown substantially in the United States in the last few decades. Racism and exclusion of African Americans and Latinos may be justified less on skin color or phenotype, a basis now regarded as being politically incorrect, and more on cultural characteristics, such as family "disorganization." As racism based on physical characteristics has been discredited, exclusion based on cultural and social traits has become more common. As the International Center for Research on Women (2002, 1) notes, this approach is not antimarriage, "it is pro-family in the ultimate sense, in that it respects and supports the many faces of America's families."

REFERENCES

Abramovitz, Mimi. 1988. *Regulating the lives of women: Social welfare policy from colonial times to the present.* Boston: South End Press.

Amott, Teresa. 1990. Black women and AFDC: Making entitlement out of necessity. In *Women, the state, and welfare,* ed. Linda Gordon. Madison: University of Wisconsin Press.

Baéz, Clara. 1991. *Mujer y desarrollo en la República Dominicana: 1981–1991.* Santo Domingo, Dominican Republic: Unedited report prepared for the Inter-American Development Bank.

Bolles, A. Lynn. Perspectives on U.S. kinship. In *Cultural diversity in the United States,* ed. Ida Susser and Thomas C. Patterson. New York: Blackwell.

Brownlee, W. Elliot, and Mary M. Brownlee. 1976. *Women in the American economy.* New Haven: Yale University Press.

Burgos, Nilsa, and Eileen Colberg. 1990. *Mujeres solteras con jefatura de familia: Características en el hogar y el trabajo.* Unpublished ms. University of Puerto Rico.

Catasús, Sonia. 1992. La nupcialidad de la década de los ochenta en Cuba. In *La demografía Cubana ante el quinto centenario,* 30–42. Centro de Estudios Demográficos (CEDEM). Havana, Cuba: Editorial de Ciencias Sociales.

Chant, Sylvia. 1997. *Woman-headed households: Diversity and dynamics in the developing world.* New York: St. Martin's Press.

Colón, Alice. 1997. Reestructuración industrial, empleo y pobreza en Puerto Rico y el Atlántico Medio de los Estados Unidos: La situación de las mujeres Puertorriqueñas. *Revista de Ciencias Sociales* (3): 135–88.

Cott, Nancy F. 2000. *Public vows: A history of marriage and the nation.* Cambridge, Mass.: Harvard University Press.

Darity, Wm., Jr., and Samuel Myers Jr. Family structure and the marginalization of black men: Policy implications. In *The decline in marriage among African Americans,* ed. M. Belinda Tucker and Claudia Mitchell-Kernan. New York: Russell Sage Foundation.

Degler, Carl. 1980. *At odds: Women and the family in America from the Revolution to the present.* New York: Oxford University Press.

Department of City Planning, City of New York. 1994. *Puerto Rican New Yorkers in 1990.* New York: Department of City Planning, City of New York.

Dominguez, Virginia R. 1994. *White by definition: Social classification in Creole Louisiana.* New Brunswick, N.J.: Rutgers University Press.

Duarte, Isis, and Ramón Tejeda. 1995. Los Hogares Dominicanos: El Mito de la Familia Ideal y los Tipos de Jefaturas de Hogar. Sto. Domingo, Dominican Republic: Instituto de Estudios de Población y Desarrollo.

Edin, Kathryn, and Kathleen Mullan Harris. 1999. Getting off and staying off: Racial differences in the work route off welfare. In *Latinas and African American women at work,* ed. Irene Brown. New York: Russell Sage.

Edin, Kathryn, and Laura Lein. 1997. *Making ends meet.* New York: Russell Sage Foundation.

Ellwood, David, and Jonathan Crane. 1990. Family change among black Americans? What do we know? *Journal of Economic Perspectives* 4 (4): 65–84.

Ellwood, David, and Mary Jo Bane. 1994. Welfare realities: From rhetoric to reform. Cambridge, Mass.: Harvard University Press.

Findlay, Eileen Suarez. 1999. *Imposing decency: The politics of sexuality and race in Puerto Rico, 1870–1920.* Durham, N.C.: Duke University Press.

Flippen, Chenoa, and Marta Tienda. 1998. *Family structure and economic well-being of black, Hispanic and white pre-retirement adults,* opr.princeton.edu/papers/opr9802.pdf.

Fraser, Nancy, and Linda Gordon. 1994. A geneaology of dependency: Tracing a keyword of the U.S. welfare state. *Signs* 19 (2): 309–36.

Garfinkel, Irwin, and Sara McLanahan. 1986. *Single mothers and their children.* Washington, D.C.: Urban Institute Press.

Godreau, Isar. 2000. La semántica fugitiva: Raza, color y vida cotidiana en Puerto Rico. *Revista de Ciencias Sociales* (9): 52–71.

Gordon, Linda, ed. 1990. *Women, the state, and welfare.* Madison: University of Wisconsin Press.

———. 1994. *Pitied but not entitled: Single mothers and the history of welfare, 1890–1935.* New York: Free Press.

Gordon, Rachel. 1999. Multi-generational coresidence and welfare policy. *Journal of Community Psychology* 27 (5): 525–49.

Gregory, Steven. 1998. *Black corona.* Princeton, N.J.: Princeton University Press.

Guerra, Lillian. 1998. *Popular expression and national identity in Puerto Rico.* Gainesville: University Press of Florida.

Gutman, Herbert. 1976. *The black family in slavery and freedom.* New York: Pantheon Books.

Harden, Blaine. Two-parent families rise after change in welfare laws. *New York Times,* August 12, 2001, national edition, l.

Hernández-Angueira, Luisa. 2001. *Mujeres Puertorriqueñas, "welfare" y globalización.* Hato Rey, Puerto Rico: Publicaciones Puertorriqueñas.

Hill, Robert B., with Andrew Billingsley, Eleanor Engram, Michelene Malson, Roger Rubin, Carol Stack, James Stewart, and James Teele. 1993. *Research on the African American family: A holistic perspective.* Westport, Conn.: Auburn House.

Institute for Women's Policy Research. 2002a. Children in single-parent families living in poverty have fewer supports after welfare reform. By Deanna M. Lyter, Melissa Sills, and Gi-Taik Oh. Research in Brief D451, September, 1–11. Washington, D.C.

———. 2002b. Life after welfare reform: Low-income single parent families, pre- and post-TANF. By Janice Peterson, Xue Song, and Avis Jones-DeWeever. Research in Brief D446, May, 1–6. Washington, D.C.

———. 2002c. Welfare, poverty, and marriage: What does the research say? By Heidi Hartmann and M. K. Tully. Quarterly newsletter, Winter/Spring, 1–4. Washington, D.C.

International Center for Research on Women. 2002. Marriage promotion and low-income communities. By Avis Jones-DeWeever. Research in Brief D450, June, 1–6. Washington, D.C.

Jones, Jacqueline. 1995. *Labor of love, labor of sorrow: Black women, work, and the family from slavery to the present.* Reprint. New York: Vintage Books. Orig. pub. 1985 (New York: Basic Books).

McLanahan, Sara, and Gary Sandefur. 1994. *Growing up with a single parent.* Cambridge, Mass.: Harvard University Press.

Moynihan, Daniel Patrick. 1965. *The Negro family: The case for national action.* Prepared for the Office of Policy Planning and Research of the Department of Labor. Washington, D.C.: U.S. Government Printing Office.

Mullings, Leith. 1997. *On our own terms: Race, class, and gender in the lives on African American women.* New York: Routledge.

Newman, Katherine. 1999. *No shame in my game: The working poor in the inner city.* New York: Knopf/Russell Sage Foundation.

———. 2001. Hard times on 125th Street: Harlem's poor confront welfare reform. *American Anthropologist* 103 (3): 762–78.

Patterson, Orlando. 1998. *Rituals of blood: Consequences of slavery in two American centuries.* New York: Basic Books.

Roediger, David. 1991. *The wages of whiteness: Race and the making of the American working class.* New York: Verso.

Roschelle, Anne. 1997. *No more kin: Exploring race, class and gender in family networks.* Thousand Oaks, Ca.: Sage.

Rosenbaum, Emily, and Greta Gilbertson. 1995. Mother's labor force participation in New York City: A reappraisal of the influence of household extension. *Journal of Marriage and the Family* 57:243–49.

Safa, Helen I. 1995. *The myth of the male breadwinner: Women and industrialization in the Caribbean.* Boulder, Colo.: Westview.

———. 1999a. Female-headed households in the Caribbean: Deviant or alternative form of family organization? *Latino(a) Research Review* 4 (2): 16–26.

———. 1999b. *Women coping with crisis: The social consequences of export-led industrialization in the Dominican Republic.* Agenda paper 36. North-South Center, University of Miami, Florida.

———. 1999c. Free markets and the marriage market: Structural adjustment, gender relations and working conditions among Dominican women workers. *Environment and Planning* 31 (2): 291–304.

Solinger, Rickie. 2000. *Wake up, little Susie: Single pregnancy and race before* Roe v. Wade. New York: Routledge.

Stack, Carol. 1974. *All our kin.* New York: Harper and Row.

Stevenson, Brenda. 1995. Black family structure in colonial and antebellum Virginia: Amending the revisionist perspective. In *The decline in marriage among African Americans,* ed. 1995. M. Belinda Tucker and Claudia Mitchell-Kernan, 27–56. New York: Russell Sage Foundation.

Stoler, Ann. 1989. Making empire respectable: The politics of race and sexual morality in 20th century colonial cultures. *American Ethnologist* 16 (1): 634–60.

Thompson, Lanny. 1995. Nuestra isla y su gente: La construcción del "otro" Puertorriqueño. In *Our islands and their people.* San Juan: Centro de Investigaciones Sociales y Depto. de Historia, Universidad de Puerto Rico.

Tucker, M. Belinda, and Claudia Mitchell-Kernan, eds. 1995. *The decline in marriage among African Americans.* New York: Russell Sage Foundation.

Vásquez Calzada, José. 1988. Tendencias recientes de las uniones consensuales en Puerto Rico. *Revista de Ciencias Sociales* 27 (3–4): 51–66.

Wilson, William Julius. 1987. *The truly disadvantaged: The inner city, the underclass, and public policy.* Chicago: University of Chicago Press.

———. 1996. *When work disappears: The world of the new urban poor.* New York: Vintage Books.

III

SEXUAL MATTERS IN WORK, HEALTH, AND ETHNONATIONAL POLITICS

Structurally Adjusted Intercourse: Exoticized Sex Workers and Anthropological Agency

Melissa D. Hargrove

$\mathcal{H}$uman rights abuses are often framed in reference to catastrophic abuses of power resulting in harm or death; however, there are many forms of human rights abuse that go unnoticed throughout the world, masked by the forces of globalization and tourism. Particular instances occur frequently among women of color and the minority poor in what can be referred to as the "commoditization" of body, identity, and culture. Sexuality, identity, and cultural heritage are being commercialized by tourism sectors in ways that compromise the livelihood, safety, and economic future of women globally. The purpose of this chapter is to examine the myriad ways in which tourism, as a strategy of economic development, constrains women's options for economic survival while compromising their cultural and sexual identity and agency. Neoliberal restructuring policies are pushing women into peripheral and dangerous areas with few or no options. In order to deconstruct the issue effectively, I find that it is necessary to investigate the ways in which structured inequality, race and racism, ethnicity, and gender intersect within the globalization of tourism to produce economic disparity and desperation. Once such intersections are established, it becomes necessary to question the role of anthropology in the ongoing struggles against globalized inequality.

BACKGROUND

For the past several years, I have been conducting anthropological research within the Gullah nation of the United States Southeast. The Gullah represent a link to the earliest enslaved Africans brought to North America to harvest rice and pick cotton under an earlier system of globalization and human rights abuses often referred to as the Transatlantic Slave Trade. From emancipation to the present, the Gullah communities of South Carolina, Georgia, and Florida have been struggling to maintain economic and cultural autonomy against the rising tide of encroachment, spatial segregation, paternalistic racism, and economic development.

Gullah communities are embroiled in a battle against multiple forms of development, known in Gullah folk terms as *destructionment* (Goodwine 1998). Gated-community development, resort development, commercial development, and tourism development have pushed Gullah people to small peripheral pockets of their former homeland. Million-dollar homes and gates of segregation dot a landscape once home to self-sufficient Gullah communities. A tourism industry has developed around the commoditization and exoticization of Gullah identity, culture, and ethnic history. Advertisements and tourism brochures depict Gullah women in particular in ways that invite tourists to "experience" authentic Gullah culture. This type of development transforms the Gullah into an exotic Other while tourism planners, city officials, and entrepreneurs revel in the money to be made and the international exposure, all at the expense of the keepers of this cultural legacy. It is within this context that I became interested in the commoditization of culture and ethnicity, with particular attention to women of color.

This type of exoticization, as an instrument of economic exploitation within development strategy, is being globally broadened to include culture, heritage, ethnicity, gender, and sexuality as a way to market the "tourism experience" of international destinations around the world. Governmental agencies, ministries of tourism and culture, and private global entrepreneurs are using whatever it takes to compete for the tourist dollar. These dilemmas of development translate into a global phenomenon within which the world's women are being drawn into an exploitative system based upon racial, gendered, and class inequalities, which compels their struggle for basic human survival.

STRUCTURAL ADJUSTMENT: "THE FEMALE UNDERSIDE OF GLOBALIZATION"[1]

Enormous increases in the frequency of business travel, as well as increased international leisure tourism, are often cited as forces pulling numerous developing countries into the globalized tourism market (O'Neill 2001). Many such countries, however, have been instead "pushed" toward tourism as a development strategy by international lending agencies (Barry 1984, cited in Cabezas 2002). Consequently, as they entered into programs with lending agencies such as the International Monetary Fund and the World Bank, they were, and remain, unprepared for the multiple human realities that tourism development brings.

Policies mandated by these lending institutions, specifically those known as structural adjustment programs (SAPs), often have devastating effects on the poorest of the poor (Ehrenreich and Hochschild 2002; Gilliam 1998; Kempadoo 1999; Mayorga and Velasquez 1999). SAPs mandate such actions as the devaluation of currency, privatization or cutbacks of social programs such as health care and education (Stivens 2000), and an intensified economic focus on export processing and service industries (Cabezas 2002). With respect to female workers, these steps toward economic globalization often produce gendered inequality in the labor market, as women find their labor devalued and reconstructed as being cheap and expendable (Cabezas 2002; Harrison 1997).

In a world in which billions of people exist in abject poverty, of which 70 percent are women, the brunt of economic chaos is heaped onto female shoulders (as well as symbolically heaped onto other, less-accessible parts of their bodies). Behind the statistics, a majority of these women represent marginalized groups who have been affected by processes of racialization. In many parts of the Caribbean and Latin America, racial identity is dependent on more than simply skin color; however, whiteness occupies a privileged position in the social hierarchy. Blackness, particularly for women, is associated with labor and service, often for the benefit of white or whitened segments of society. Women of the African diaspora, historically and presently, have been economically and sexually exploited by such racialized images.

The developing regions of the Caribbean are a microcosm of this gendered reality. Structural adjustment programs, often coupled with other neoliberal policies of globalization, constrict women's access to the means of satisfying basic human needs such as water, sanitation, health care, and economic autonomy and stability (see Brock and Thistlethwaite 1996; Gilliam 1998). In Caribbean countries choosing tourism as a development agenda, SAPs serve to plunge the majority of the nation's women deeper into economic turmoil, accompanied by decreased social programs, involuntary currency devaluation, rising costs for basic human necessity items, and a lack of options for earning a living wage (Cabezas 1999; Harrison 1997; Mayorga and Velasquez 1999; Mellon 1999).

Under the guidelines of SAPs, infrastructural investments are siphoned away from the interest of the local economies and invested into an infrastructure solely aimed at building a market for the target industry (in this case tourism), therefore prioritizing foreign investment over human well-being (Mellon 1999). Governments, to encourage investment, offer impressive tax cuts for foreign investors in hopes of creating employment for the local population. The unfortunate result, however, is the creation of an economy in which locals have extremely limited economic options. Women are often left to choose between a "culture of servitude," employment as domestic servants, housekeepers, or barmaids in the tourism sector (Faulkenberry et al. 2000), or work within the informal sector. In an attempt to make a living wage, more women are turning to the informal sector for economic survival (Harrison 1991). With an estimated economic impact of over U.S.$20 billion a year, international sex tourism must appear to be a viable option for desperate women in such desperate situations (O'Neill 2001).

DRASTIC TIMES CALL FOR
DRASTIC MEASURES: SELLING SEX

Throughout the Caribbean and Latin America, tourism destinations such as the Dominican Republic, Jamaica, and Brazil exemplify the geographic landscapes within which these realities are being acted out. International labor statistics estimate that "25 per cent of all Caribbean employees in all industries are working directly or indirectly for the tourism sector, which is double or more than in most other tourist destinations" (International Labor Organization 2000). Tourism is now the principal economic industry within the Dominican Republic (Cabezas 1999) and is hailed as "a mainstay of the economy," which has contributed to a pattern of remarkable growth and prosperity in the British Virgin Islands (Cohen 1995, 405). Hidden behind the statistics of gross domestic product and labor, however, is a phenomenon of exoticization that markets blackness as a sexual commodity. This recolonization of the black female body comes at a time when desperation is at a maximum and many women lack the power to resist the wholesale marketing of their sexual labor.

As a major component of the tourism industry, sex tourism has transformed one small town on the north coast of the Dominican Republic, Sosua, into a sexual landscape where German men and young, poor, black single mothers exchange fantasies (Brennan 2001).[2] Denise Brennan (2002) suggests that there are two dominant factors that propel young women to migrate from all over the Dominican Republic to engage in sex tourism in Sosua: poverty and single motherhood. Many of the fifty sex workers Brennan interviewed had never sold sex before migrating to Sosua, yet their belief in the possibility of meeting and possibly establishing a relationship with one of the many German men who frequent the city was enough to persuade them to try. This fantasy of escaping poverty via sex tourism (referred to as the "opportunity myth"), coupled with the globalization of capitalism in the Dominican Republic (Brennan 2001), has created a powerless group of Dominican women ripe for exploitation.

Throughout Jamaica, the reliance on tourism as a strategy of development has resulted in the infamous all-inclusive resort (Kempadoo 1999), a strategy that "incorporates poor countries into a consolidated global system under conditions established by the wealthier nations" that will enjoy them (Cabezas 2002). With World Bank statistics reporting nearly one-third of Jamaica's population living below the poverty level (Mullings 1999), coupled with access to millions of tourists per year, sex work gains legitimacy as an option for economic survival. Within this arena, the Jamaican female body becomes a form of "international currency" (Pettman 1997), appropriating both her sexual and physical labor. Faye V. Harrison (1997) suggests that this "misogynous symbolic assault against women" goes deeper than merely sex. In promotional materials from the early 1990s, aimed at soliciting foreign investment, images of the black female body suggest that there are many advantages to doing business in Jamaica. One example showcases protruding female buttocks in Jockey briefs (National Labor Committee 1992) with the caption "From jeans to jackets— from suits to shorts—smart apparel manufacturers are *making it* in Jamaica" (emphasis added by Harrison 1997). This type of marketing suggests there are many things on the auction block in Jamaica.

Selling sex as an aspect of tourism has become national business in Brazil as well, where state agencies present tourist destinations as spaces within which women are easily available (Gilliam 2001). The unfortunate truth is just that— privatization of public services in Brazil, as well as their growing dependence on the tourism industry, has pushed women to an economic periphery from which sex tourism seems a viable option for escaping unstable living conditions. Consequently, for many of the poor women in Brazil, their identity is tied to nationalist characterizations of them as sexual, erotic, exotic beings of difference constructed around blackness (Gilliam 2001). It is within this racialized space of inequality and exploitation that deep and troubling similarities emerge concerning sex tourism in the various destinations under present consideration, within which shades of blackness are equated to the "naturalized" hypersexuality of African-descended populations.

EROTIC COMMODIFICATION AND POSTCOLONIALISM: EXOTICIZING RACISM AND INEQUALITY

In an attempt to legitimize the sexual exploitation of female sex workers, they must be cast as the Other, more appropriately referred to as the "erotics of difference" (O'Neill 2001; see also, Mackie 2000). Tourism, as a strategy to solicit visitors and injections of capital, is almost always embedded in relations of inequality between host and guest. It is, by design, also about power (Enloe

1990).[3] Therefore, the relationship between sex and tourism must be contextualized as a social arena in which class, gender, race, and power intersect to reinforce the inequalities between rich and poor, and tourist and sex worker, ultimately resting upon the inequalities between the First and Third World (Truong 1990). Such inequalities strongly correlate with the imagined and legitimized binary opposition of whiteness and blackness, creating neocolonial instruments of racialized oppression for the twenty-first century.

The colonial connections among power, difference, and sexual exploitation, particularly of ethnic and racial Others, have been documented in the histories of various countries around the globe. Sex tourism as economic development also has a history as organized sex tours in a number of Asian countries in the 1970s (Brock and Thistlethwaite 1996) but existing as early as the 1950s (Mullings 1999). Asian women were marketed throughout Southeast and East Asia as "erotic commodities," both promiscuous and passive (Mullings 1999). These histories further intersect with a "worldwide reinvestment in patriarchal capitalism" (Gilliam 2001), supported and reinforced by multinational capital and white male consumers' desires for "exotic sexual experiences" (Mackie 2000, 44). This desire, more appropriately referred to as "post-colonial fantasy" (Sanchez-Taylor and O'Connell 2001), is fueled by First World male desires to consume the dark skinned "native" bodies of the developing world at cut-rate prices (Brennan 2002). Within the various "sexscapes" (Brennan 2001) of the Dominican Republic, Brazil, Jamaica, and Cuba, the fantasy is nurtured through racialized, sexualized images of bodily commodities, reminiscent of earlier relations between the colonizer and the colonized (Brennan 2001).

There is a well-known saying throughout the Caribbean and parts of Latin America that encapsulates the dynamics of gendered, racialized inequality so necessary for producing and sustaining power-mediated relationships between powerful men and powerless women. The saying in Brazil, "A white woman is for marriage, a *mulata* woman for fornication, a Black woman for work" (Gilliam 2001), carries the same message as the saying in Cuba, "white women for marrying, black women for work, and *mulatas* for making love" (Zúñiga 2001). This ideology, long a part of many national identities with mixed populations rooted in the enslavement of Africans, serves to reinforce an association between the *mulata* and sex (Gilliam 1998, 2001; Zúñiga 2001), which inadvertently justifies First World men's desires to experience the exotic Other. This interaction between race and sexual power allows sex tourists to affirm their masculine, racialized power in ways not possible back home (Enloe 1990; Sanchez-Taylor and O'Connell 2001).

Sex tourism, as an economic industry, remains ambiguously illegal. Therefore, the "trade in human bodies" must operate within, or in some cases outside of, the many bars, casinos, and dance clubs within the tourism sector

(Kempadoo 1999). Consequently, advertisements for sex tourism must be subtle, allowing for the continuation of the tacit agreement between government officials and globalized sex tourism. Travel brochures and hotel advertisements present island resorts as "fantasy islands" (Davidson and Sanchez-Taylor 1999), featuring brown-skinned, scantily dressed women. Colleen Ballerino Cohen notes the ways in which promotional videos for the British Virgin Islands link pristine allure with the allure of virginity, coupled with notions of the naturalness of exoticized sexual difference (1995). Here and elsewhere, racialized and ethnic differences are used to construct an Otherness, as well as notions of authentic blackness. Ethnographic accounts conducted among repeat clients reveal the catch-all category—*LBFM: little brown fucking machines*—invented by white men who frequent the sex industry of the Caribbean to describe the female sex workers (Davidson and Sanchez-Taylor 1999).

This type of racist, gendered ideology has become part and parcel of the sex industry within many Caribbean countries. In Cuba, prostitutes who service the tourism sector are known as *jineteras*, literally meaning "jockeys" because they are viewed as riding the tourist (see O'Connell Davidson 1996). Nadine Fernandez (1999) suggests that the racialized, and highly sexualized, image of the Afro-Cuban *jineteras* greatly contributes to their appeal as objects within Cuban sex tourism. Dominican women are also exoticized and racialized through tourism advertisements that construct them as "hypersexual workers" (Cabezas 1999, 112). Amalia Lucia Cabezas reports that one of the most common sights in the Dominican Republic is the middle-aged European man accompanied by a young Dominican female. These racialized images are blatant examples of symbolic violence (see Harrison 1997), which reinforce the dominant identity of white males, thereby reassuring male tourists of their inalienable right to be served and serviced by "others" (Davidson and Sanchez-Taylor 1999). Ultimately, the sex industry is about purchasing fantasy (O'Neill 2001,149). By casting sex workers as women who are naturally "hot for it," sex tourism creates racialized boundaries that legitimize the sexual exploitation of women, particularly women of color. This "commodification of otherness" (hooks 1992) must be addressed in light of the glaring human rights abuses associated with selling sex under the guise of generating tourism revenues (Harrison forthcoming).

REPRESENTATION AS LEGITIMACY:
SEX WORKER AS NATURAL "WHORE"

Within systems of structural violence and inequality such as the sex-tourism industry, there must be hegemonic forces in place to effectively legitimize the myriad ways in which the powerful exploit the weak. This is established in two distinct ways: through an ideology that represents sex workers as natural "whores" and by characterizing sex workers as immoral and deviant members of society. Such women are presented (and represented) as beings with insatiable sex drives for which sex comes naturally and brings the utmost pleasure. Women of color are often portrayed as being wildly sexual, comparable to animals, which welcome sex at any time (Brock and Thistlethwaite 1996; see also, Harrison 1997). In ethnographic data gathered among Caribbean sex tourists, sex was portrayed as being more "natural" in Third World countries, with white male informants insisting that these women love sex and "are doing it all the time anyway" (Davidson and Sanchez-Taylor 1999).[4] In Jamaica the female sex worker is stereotyped as a "whore" by both clients of the trade and Jamaican men. Not only is their involvement naturalized by such imagery, but it also serves to reveal the glaring double cultural standard of female sexuality (Kempadoo 1999). In many Caribbean societies it is acceptable, and sometimes socially expected, for men to flaunt their sexuality. For women, however, this is not the case, although increasingly Jamaican women are contesting that restriction and claiming their prerogative as sexual beings.

Another powerful way in which the exploitation of women is legitimized occurs through a discourse of deviance and immorality aimed at the character of women involved in the sex trade, further victimizing those caught in this vicious cycle while minimalizing the economic turmoil that prompts women to seek sex work as an alternative to available low-wage work (Ryan and Hall 2001). Furthermore, if these women can be believably represented as deviant and immoral "whores," who naturally enjoy their sexual encounters, it makes them "invisible as workers" and unworthy of human rights (Mellon 1999). The Dominican Republic offers food for thought concerning these issues. Recently, the sex industry has received considerable attention in the transnational media, forcing government officials to acknowledge the situation. In 1997, the Minister of Tourism suggested a red-light district to contain the activity; however, strong public opposition quickly shifted his perspective. The blame was summarily displaced onto the work of "pathological individuals" (cited in Cabezas 2002). Such distancing between the sex industry and the state, as well as the transnational conglomerates of the tourism industry, reinforces popular opinions of sex workers as deviant, pathological perpetrators of immoral activities.

These strategies, coupled with the illegality of the sex trade, prohibit sex workers from protection under their own national laws. Even more harmful from a human rights perspective are the ways in which such portrayals affect policy and action. When women sex workers are defined as promiscuous, their involvement is deemed "self-inflicted harm," and UN committees frame the discourse as one in which the workers must be protected from themselves in order to have their human rights protected (Brock and Thistlethwaite 1996). Ultimately, the larger question becomes "whose power, status, and privilege is being protected and why?" (Brock and Thistlethwaite 1996, 180).

An important point made by Julia O'Connell Davidson and Jacqueline Sanchez-Taylor (1999) serves to further clarify the ways in which the sex tourism industry is legitimated and reinforced:

> That the Western sex tourist's pocket can contain sufficient power to transform others into Others, mere players on a pornographic stage, is a testament to the enormity of the imbalance of economic, social, and political power between rich and poor nations. (53)

Presented in such blinding light, it becomes clear that women involved in sex tourism around the globe "lack access to rights that are enshrined in the conventions of the United Nations along with the basic tenets of labor rights covered by the conventions and recommendations of the International Labor Organization" (Mellon 1999, 309). Let us not, however, overlook the role of governmental corruption and police abuse within this intricate web of exploitation and structural violence.

CORRUPTION AND ABUSE: HUMAN RIGHTS VIOLATIONS

To better understand the ways in which power and difference intersect, we must broaden our perspectives to include all actors, as well as their actions and intent, within the wider social arena of institutionalized power (Wilson 1997). Among those countries pursuing sex tourism as an economic development strategy, street pimps are not the only ones getting rich. Police, government officials, and military officers have much to gain financially through fines, bribes, and kickbacks (Brock and Thistlethwaite 1996). Economic structures of power and dominance make it possible for these social actors to exploit the system without detection by others, serving to further blame the victim. In the ethnographic research that Cabezas conducted in the Dominican Republic, all of the sex workers interviewed depicted the abuses, both physical and sexual, suffered at the hands of police as the worst part of sex tourism (Cabezas 1999). High levels of corruption, due to the gray area that sex tourism occupies within the legal system of the Dominican Republic, make it impossible to expose the true crimes being committed by those occupying positions of power.

A more recent article by Cabezas (2002) suggests that the situation in the Dominican Republican is intensifying. Women both within and outside the trade reported victimization by a new form of state-inflicted violence that stigmatizes all women as potential sex workers. Women reported being beaten, verbally abused, and sometimes even raped by the police for the mere suspicion of their involvement. There were also multiple reports of arbitrary arrest and detention without probable cause. The blanket application of guilt and gender-based violence being enacted upon women of the Dominican Republic constitutes a serious human rights concern.

REALITIES OF GLOBALIZATION
AND TRANSNATIONAL PROCESSES

Within all societies engaging in sex tourism, the central government and transnational enterprises are aware that sex has a market value (Cabezas 1999). Global capitalism, as it engulfs the furthest reaches of the world, elevates economic success above human lives (see Nash 1994). This type of dehumanization is an important component of power in legitimizing women as sexual objects and the body as commodity (Brock and Thistlethwaite 1996). Globalization, therefore, is not concerned with human rights, social justice, or human welfare. It has, in effect, replaced one form of human exploitation with another (Cabezas 2002). Further characterized by Harrison as a "gendered phenomenon marked by masculinist logic" (1997), globalization entraps many of the world's women into service work (Gilliam 2001). Clearly, when the service work available cannot sustain these women and/or their dependents, their choices become few. Yet, emerging from this social inequity is a rising tide of human agency, as sex workers demand to be recognized for the "services" they render.

Adding insult to injury, transnational processes contribute to the persistent inequalities of globalization in the Caribbean and Latin America in seemingly invisible ways. Media outlets all over the world reinforce the racialized exoticization of these women for the benefit of their global male cohort. The promotion of sex tourism via the Internet, for example, expands male access to women as sexual commodities (Vanaspong 2002) while reinforcing the racialized and sexualized identity of Caribbean and Latin American women (Sanchez-Taylor and O'Connell 2001). Technological advances in computing have allowed for an online merger of prostitution and pornography, resulting in the development of specialized sex sites, such as the World Sex Guide. The WSG (as is it known to frequent users) is an online hodgepodge of information, personal testimonies, and suggestions concerning where to go and whom to see (Bishop and Robinson 2002). These sex guides, written by white Western men, reveal the projection of racially dominated fantasies presently fueling the sex tourism industry. Entries pertaining to the Caribbean,[5] in particular, demonstrate how sex tourists are buying "blackness" (Brennan 2001; Sanchez-Taylor and O'Connell 2001):

> I find that sipping a beer and watching a fine brown-sugar Dominican teenager take off her clothes and shake her ass like only Dominican chics can does wonders for clearing your mind and getting up your guts (not to mention your cock) for the bargaining process.

> You think of those incredible women, ranging in color from white chocolate to dark chocolate, available to you at the subtle nod of your head or touch of your hat.

Along with diaries are tips about how to negotiate the lowest prices for the best sex. The following entries suggest a conscious effort to reinforce the unequal relations between sex tourists and desperate sex workers:

> Tips: it all comes down to how many babies this chic has crying at home.

> You will have more power to negotiate in countries with lots of poverty.

In the end, after painstakingly enduring this misogynist environment of racist opportunists, one is left with the problematic of the white male imagination.

> About half the girls have a shot at being decent with you—even pleasant. I mean, who wants to fuck a bitch? Prostitution is a fantasyland, but without the fantasy what do you have?

Nearly halfway around the world another unseen culprit contributes to the bodily commodification of "dirt cheap colored girls," in the words of a German sex tourist describing the sex trade in the Dominican Republic (Brennan 2001). Within the German and European media blackness is exoticized, and women of the Caribbean are advertised as sexual commodities (Brennan 2002). The transnational movement of German males between the Dominican Republic and Germany has created an expatriate community in Sosua. Complete with German bakeries and access to German products, news, and magazines, Sosua is being recolonized by Europeans. Real estate signs now appear in German (Brennan 2001). In a recent daily newspaper from Cologne, *Express*, the following statement suggests that it is a conscious and deliberate effort:

> After Columbus and the Spanish colonizers, the Germans are the new masters on the Island.

This type of blatant exploitation is secured in the sex trade, as desperate Dominican women try to establish relationships with these German men. Also important is the German male notion that Dominican women are more sexual, more compliant, and have fewer commodity needs (Brennan 2001). The stories chronicled by Brennan (2001, 2002) illustrate a variety of outcomes regarding such relationships; however, most are regulated by the persistent inequalities between wealthy white men and poor black Dominican sex workers.

WOMEN'S RIGHTS AS HUMAN RIGHTS

Within the discourse on women's involvement in sex tourism, there are varying positions concerning the human rights status of sex workers. Much of the current human rights language ignores women's sexual agency, as well as the lived experiences of women who may have entered the sex trade without being coerced (Cabezas 2002). I settle on the proclamation that the industry is nothing more than "sexual slavery," utilizing the following definitional criteria:

> Female sexual slavery is present in all situations where women or girls cannot change the immediate conditions of their existence; where regardless of how they got into those conditions they cannot get out; and where they are subject to sexual violence and exploitation. (Barry 1984, 40)

There are also articles within both the Universal Declaration of Human Rights and the Convention on the Elimination of All Forms of Discrimination against Women that proclaim the "inalienable right of all human beings to work and to freely choose their job or profession" (Mellon 1999). In a clear step toward self-determination and empowerment, sex workers have begun to mobilize as political activists, demanding equality as "workers" who contribute their labor to the market (Cabezas 2002). One such group of Dominican sex workers, Movimiento de Mujeres Unidas (MODEMU), has gained significant political ground by employing a rights-based discourse in their strategy for recognition as women, as workers, and as citizens (Cabezas 2002).

Groups such as this are a step in the right direction toward raising global awareness of the current "feminization of poverty" (Harrison 1991) being played out in countless communities all over the globe. Another step, which constitutes one of the few positive aspects of globalization, is the utilization of global technological possibilities concerning collaborative networks, which are essential for building support and providing information. We are connected in ways never before possible through the Internet, print, and media, as well as through the circuits and networks of the UN since 1975 when the UN sponsored its first international conference on women. Many important questions arise from these new connections, such as the role of academic researchers reporting on these struggles for global human equality. Where do we stand, as anthropologists, in the human rights arena? This question is gaining volume as concerned intellectuals work to negotiate an answer.

ANTHROPOLOGY AND HUMAN RIGHTS

As scientists ultimately interested in human experience, anthropologists seem likely candidates for fiery support of universal human rights. We have, however, been much too quiet for much too long, allowing the constraints of academic rigidity to suppress our emotional human connection to those we witness in situations of desperation. The political economy of globalization has left billions in worse economic conditions than were experienced prior to capitalist penetration. Anthropologists have in the past made, and continue to make, important contributions concerning human rights, particularly in the area of documenting the impact of human rights violations (Harrison 2000). But have we used the tools of our trade in the most effective way to provoke positive change? Fredrik Barth (2000) suggests we have not, due to our limited vision of what is necessary to analyze the processes we seek to understand and change. Barth makes clear that we are, at the moment, ill-equipped to make change, until we build models capable of illustrating the complex interactions unfolding in front of us (2000).

Within the various "sexscapes" (Brennan 2001) discussed here, the complex interactions are overwhelming, as are the resulting human rights abuses. As Harrison (2000) reminds us, anthropologists have the ability to make positive contributions through our insights into the subtle logics of culture, power, and political economy, particularly in situations of racial domination. These forces interact in ways that produce the economic stagnation and individual desperation that lead women to sell their bodies in the global market. Yet it is not enough to simply document and lament such tragedies. We must get involved on new and different levels, beginning with public policy. This is not to suggest that ethnographic inquiry is inadequate. On the contrary, it is extremely effective at illuminating the lived experiences of real people so glaringly absent in economic models (Barth 2000; Harrison 2000). What I am suggesting, as many are, is the merging of various kinds of knowledge aimed at mutually agreeable solutions.

Within the anthropological discourse on the global economy, there is a dominant ideology that economic models, such as those utilized by international lending institutions, must be abandoned if there is ever to be real change. Barth, however, provokes us to stop and consider the global situation from another angle. In a recent essay regarding activism in anthropology, Barth suggests a type of "If you can't beat 'em, join 'em" logic. He suggests that if we are truly interested in affecting these situations, we must "devote time to coming up with models of culture and economy that allow us to analyze the interdependence of human lives, social relations, and macro-systems of economy and politics" (2000, 158). We cannot simply show resistance and write about it—we must come up with our own models to deliver a competing representation of what is really going on in the world, to convince those who work with economistic models that there are other ways to look at the world. Perhaps even harder to comprehend is Barth's position that policymakers (possibly well meaning) are trapped by the means of implementation at their disposal and the roles they are locked into. Well-argued anthropological analyses, Barth suggests, could actually free policymakers. Stated another way, perhaps our ethnographic contributions could illuminate and expand their range of options.

In considering that suggestion, I was reminded of a personal experience I had while in South Africa at the World Conference against Racism. It was my first trip out of the country, so navigating around Durban on foot was intimidating. While trying to figure out where to stand to cross the busy intersection, a middle-aged gentleman nearby (obviously sensing my anxiety) struck up a conversation. He was wearing a badge from the conference as well, so I knew he was headed in my direction. I followed his lead, and we began to walk toward the cricket stadium, and it was obvious he had been here before. As we walked, we talked about the city, the weather, and different aspects of Durban and South Africa. I asked what organization or university he was affiliated with, and he replied he was with the World Bank. Realizing this rare opportunity, I could not contain myself. To soften the blow, however, I jokingly replied something along the lines of "You know, the way you guys have treated people all over the world has made you very unpopular!" He replied respectfully, after a slight chuckle, "Well, Melissa, we know people feel this way about our involvement, but I have never met anyone willing to just come out and tell me that." We discussed various issues concerning the global economy, and he expressed sincere frustration about the lack of success of many World Bank programs. As we neared the stadium, he asked about my affiliation. "I am a cultural anthropologist from Tennessee." He immediately burst out laughing and said, "And you think we've done some damage! You guys aren't the most popular folks in the world either!" We both got a good laugh out of that, and in retrospect that conversation offers food for thought. Perhaps Barth's suggestion has merit, and we can meet with those in positions of power to negotiate a mutual ground. Some may be like the gentleman I met, who seemed genuinely concerned about the welfare of all people. Perhaps various perspectives can bring growth to all sides if we engage those institutions and establishments we formerly sought to destroy in a way that promotes understanding.

The first step toward such engagements is to begin where we are, using accessible local-level political circles to tackle issues of human injustice (Barth 2000; Messer 2002). It is also important to consistently step out from behind the lens of academia to recognize the multiple fronts of "a collective struggle for a better world" (Harrison 2000). Universities are essential in the production and dissemination of knowledge, but there is much to be learned from real people engaged in real struggle in our own backyards. Additionally, we all have the agency to act upon the world. Through the choices we make—our course content and instruction, community involvement, purchases, support of organizations, parenting, relationships—we inadvertently influence sex workers and all issues of human rights. When we are no longer willing to purchase items made under inhumane conditions comparable to slavery, we effect change. When we educate our students, families, children, and communities about the realities of globalization, capitalism, and racial domination, we dislodge Western concepts of normality associated with economics and racial inequality. When we creatively combat and delegitimize racism and sexism in our everyday lives, we transform ideologies. As we advocate for the global right to human agency, let us not forget to exercise our own. Undoubtedly, it will take both to disempower the structured inequalities of our globalized world.

NOTES

1. See Barbara Ehrenreich and Arlie Russell Hochschild (2002).
2. D. Brennan (2001) discusses the situation in terms of dual fantasies: the sexual fantasies of German men and the economic fantasies of Dominican sex workers.
3. Cynthia Enloe (1990) goes on to suggest that sexual desire is a central component of tourism ideology in general.
4. See Enloe (1990) for further discussion of the ways in which notions of the naturalness of sexual difference in the British Virgin Islands are used to promote tourism.
5. Diary entries on the World Sex Guide are organized by region of the world and then subcategorized by country.

REFERENCES

Barry, Kathleen. 1984. *Female sexual slavery*. New York: New York University Press.
Barth, Fredrik. 2000. Reflections on theory and practice in cultural anthropology: Excerpts from three articles. In *The unity of theory and practice in anthropology: Rebuilding a fractured synthesis*, ed. Carole E. Hill and Marietta L. Baba, 147–63. NAPA Bulletin 18. Arlington, Va.: National Association for the Practice of Anthropology.

Bishop, Ryan, and Lillian S. Robinson. 2002. Travellers' tails: Sex diaries of tourists returning from Thailand. In *Transnational prostitution: Changing patterns in a global context*, ed. Susanne Thorbek and Bandana Pattanaik, 13–23. London: Zed Books.

Brennan, Denise. 2001. Tourism in transnational places: Dominican sex workers and German sex tourists imagine one another. *Identities* 7 (4): 621–63.

———. 2002. Selling sex for visas: Sex tourism as a stepping-stone to international migration. In *Global woman: Nannies, maids, and sex workers in the new economy*, ed. Barbara Ehrenreich and Arlie Russell Hochschild, 154–68. New York: Metropolitan Books.

Brock, Rita Nakashima, and Susan Brooks Thistlethwaite. 1996. *Casting stones: Prostitution and liberation in Asia and the United States*. Minneapolis, Minn.: Fortress Press.

Cabezas, Amalia Lucia. 1999. Women's work is never done: Sex tourism in Sosua, the Dominican Republic. In *Sun, sex, and gold: Tourism and sex work in the Caribbean*, ed. Kamala Kempadoo, 93–123. New York: Rowman & Littlefield.

———. 2002. Tourism, sex work, and women's rights in the Dominican Republic. In *Globalization and human rights*, ed. Alison Brysk. Berkeley: University of California Press.

Cohen, Colleen Ballerino. 1995. Marketing paradise, making nation. *Annals of Tourism Research* 22 (2): 404–21.

Davidson, Julia O'Connell, and Jacqueline Sanchez-Taylor. 1999. Fantasy islands: Exploring the demand for sex tourism." In *Sun, sex, and gold: Tourism and sex work in the Caribbean*, ed. Kempadoo, 37–54. New York: Rowman & Littlefield.

Ehrenreich, Barbara, and Arlie Russell Hochschild, eds. 2002. Introduction. In *Global woman: Nannies, maids, and sex workers in the new economy*, 1–13. New York: Metropolitan Books.

Enloe, Cynthia. 1990. *Bananas, beaches, and bases: Making feminist sense of international politics*. Berkeley: University of California Press.

Faulkenberry, Lisa V., John M. Coggeshall, Kenneth Backman, and Shelia Backman. 2000. A culture of servitude: The impact of tourism and development on South Carolina's coast. *Human Organization* 59 (1): 86–95.

Fernandez, Nadine. 1999. Back to the future? Women, race, and tourism in Cuba. In *Sun, sex, and gold: Tourism and sex work in the Caribbean*, ed. Kempadoo, 81–89. New York: Rowman & Littlefield.

Gilliam, Angela M. 1998. The Brazilian mulata: Images in the global economy. *Race and Class* 40 (1): 57–69.

———. 2001. A black feminist perspective on the sexual commodification of women in the new global culture. In *Black feminist anthropology: Theory, politics, praxis, and poetics*, ed. Irma McClaurin, 150–86. New Brunswick, N.J.: Rutgers University Press.

Goodwine, Marquetta. L., ed. 1998. *The legacy of Ibo Landing: Gullah roots of African American culture*. Atlanta, Ga.: Clarity Press.

Harrison, Faye V. 1991. Women in Jamaica's urban informal economy: Insights from a Kingston slum." In *Third World women and the politics of feminism*, ed. Chandra Talpade Mohanty, Ann Russo, and Lourdes Torres, 173–96. Bloomington: Indiana University Press.

———. 1997. The gendered politics and violence of structural adjustment: A view from Jamaica. In *Situated lives: Gender and culture in everyday life*, ed. Louise Lamphere, Heléna Ragoné, and Patricia Zavella, 451–68. New York: Routledge.

———. 2000. Facing racism and the moral responsibility of human rights knowledge. In *Ethics and anthropology: Facing future issues in human biology, globalism, and cultural property*, special issue of *Annals of the New York Academy of Science* 925:45–69.

———. Forthcoming. Everyday neoliberalism in Cuba: A glimpse from Jamaica. In *From the outside within: Reworking anthropology as a labor of love*. Urbana: University of Illinois Press.

hooks, bell. 1992. *Black looks: Race and representation*. Boston: South End Press.

International Labor Organization. Caribbean Office and Multidisciplinary Advisory Team. 2000. *The importance of employment conditions, training, and good labour relations for tourism development in the Caribbean*, www.ilo.org/public/english/region/ampro/portofspain/speeches/ctoshort.htm (accessed April 11, 2001).

Kempadoo, Kamala. 1999. Continuities and change: Five centuries of prostitution in the Caribbean. In *Sun, sex, and gold: Tourism and sex work in the Caribbean*, ed. Kempadoo, 3–33. New York: Rowman & Littlefield.

Mackie, Vera. 2000. Sexual violence, silence, and human rights discourse: The emergence of the military prostitution issue. In *Human rights and gender politics*, ed. Anne-Marie Hilsdon, Martha Macintyre, Vera Mackie, and Maila Stivens, 37–59. Advances in Asia-Pacific Studies 4. London: Routledge.

Mayorga, Laura, and Pilar Velasquez. 1999. Bleak pasts, bleak futures. In *Sun, sex, and gold: Tourism and sex work in the Caribbean*, ed. Kempadoo, 157–82. New York: Rowman & Littlefield.

Mellon, Cynthia. 1999. A human rights perspective on the sex trade in the Caribbean and beyond. In *Sun, sex, and gold: Tourism and sex work in the Caribbean*, ed. Kempadoo, 309–22. New York: Rowman & Littlefield.

Messer, Ellen. 2002. Anthropologists in a world with and without human rights. In *Exotic no more: Anthropology on the front lines*, ed. Jeremy MacClancy, 319–37. Chicago: University of Chicago Press.

Mullings, Beverley. 1999. Globalization, tourism, and the international sex trade. In *Sun, sex, and gold: Tourism and sex work in the Caribbean*, ed. Kempadoo, 55–80. New York: Rowman & Littlefield.

Nash, J. 1994. Global integration and subsistence insecurity. *American Anthropologist* 96:7–30.

National Labor Committee. 1992. *Preliminary report: Paying to lose our jobs*. New York: National Labor Committee Education Fund in Support of Worker and Human Rights in Central America.

O'Connell Davidson, Julia. 1996. Sex tourism in Cuba. *Race and Class* 38 (1): 39–48.

O'Neill, Maggie. 2001. *Prostitution and feminism: Towards a politics of feeling*. Oxford: Blackwell.

Pettman, Jan Jindy. 1997. Body politics: International sex tourism. *Third World Quarterly* 18 (1): 93–108.

Ryan, Chris, and C. Michael Hall. 2001. *Sex tourism: Marginal people and liminalities*. London: Routledge.

Sanchez-Taylor, Jacqueline, and Julia O'Connell. 2001. Tourisme sexuel dans la Caraïbe. *New West Indian*, www.awigp.com/default.asp?numcat=sextour (accessed March 6, 2003).

Stivens, Maila. 2000. Introduction: Gender politics and the reimagining of human rights in the Asia-Pacific. In *Human rights and gender politics*, ed. Anne-Marie Hilsdon, Martha Macintyre, Vera Mackie, and Maila Stivens, 1–36. Advances in Asia-Pacific Studies 4. London: Routledge.

Truong, Than Dam. 1990. *Sex, money, and morality: The political economy of prostitution and tourism in South East Asia*. London: Zed. Books.

Vanaspong, Chitraporn. 2002. A portrait of the lady: The portrayal of Thailand and its prostitutes in the international media. In *Transnational prostitution: Changing patterns in a global context*, ed. Susanne Thorbek and Bandana Pattanaik, 139–55. London: Zed Books.

Wilson, Richard A., ed. 1997. Human rights, culture, and context: An introduction. In *Human rights, culture, and context: Anthropological perspectives*, 1–27. London: Pluto Press.

Zúñiga, Jesús. 2001. Cuba: The Thailand of the Caribbean. *New West Indian*, www.awigp .com/default.asp?numcat=sextour2 (accessed March 6, 2003).

· 7 ·

Intersections of Gender, Race, and HIV/AIDS in Africa

Esther I. Njiro

*T*he HIV/AIDS pandemic represents a crisis for development in Africa, as it threatens to rapidly reverse the social and economic achievements of the past half century (World Bank 2002). During the 1980s, the most serious pandemic disease of modern times was first identified. The syndrome was called AIDS (acquired immuno deficiency syndrome) and is caused by the human immunodeficiency virus (HIV), which was first identified in 1983. This infection has now spread across the globe and is growing fastest in the developing world. Out of an estimated 40 million people in the world living with HIV, 28.1 million live in Africa (UNAIDS 2001). A region that has only 10 percent of the planet's population has 72 percent of the people infected with HIV and an estimated 4,500 new infections occurring daily. In actual numbers, there are 29.4 million people living with HIV/AIDS and approximately 3.5 million new infections in 2002. This chapter describes a historical evolution of racism, gender, and poverty in South Africa and gives examples from other African countries to show the links among gender, HIV, and race in the context of development in Africa.

Links among race, gender, and HIV/AIDS are found in the macroeconomic institutions and institutions of development that are in place in most African countries. Colonial racism forcefully moved Africans from their ancestral lands to live in rugged, congested, and degraded environments. African men were reduced to underpaid and undervalued laborers. Forced male migrations disrupted family ties and opened up risky sexual relationships for men in towns, commercial farms, mines, and industries. Unstable family and social relationships in racist capitalist African countries altered the social-cultural gender division of labor, leaving most of the uneconomically viable productive work to women. Women's dependency on husbands' remittances puts them at high risk in sexual relationships. Unable to negotiate safe sex or leave a risky union, women were (and still are) forced to stay with nonmonogamous partners for survival.

One of the most important strides made in understanding the nature, scope, and impact of HIV/AIDS on individuals and communities is the role that gender plays in fueling the pandemic, influencing its impact. Gender in this context is defined as a social-cultural construct that differentiates women from men and prescribes the two groups' way of interacting with each other. Each culture has widely shared expectations about appropriate male and female behavior, characteristics, and roles that ascribe to women and men differential access to power, including productive resources and decision-making authority (UNAIDS 1999). A consistent finding is that social construction of gender and sexuality interferes with women's and men's knowledge about sexual risks of HIV/AIDS and sexually transmitted diseases. A gendered perspective facilitates the effective address of societal vulnerability to this pandemic.

GENDER, HUMAN RIGHTS, AND HIV/AIDS

Human rights have been central to the response of the international community to the HIV/AIDS epidemic, but emphasis has been on the individual rights of privacy, confidentiality, and nondiscrimination rather than on social and collective rights. There are constraints in using a human rights framework to locate AIDS prevention, treatment, and care. Because human rights were based on male norms, addressing women's human rights was only accomplished as recently as 1993 at the Vienna World Conference on Human Rights. Until recently, the human rights framework did not adequately take gender into account, and debates about injustice and inequality have historically excluded a gender analysis (Tallis 2000).

In African and other developing countries, the pandemic mirrors conditions of global inequality. HIV flourishes where there are poverty, conflict, and inequality and where states are weak and have few resources to meet the basic needs of their citizens. In these situations, women and girls bear the brunt of the pandemic because they are more vulnerable in a range of ways—they lack power in sexual relations, and they cannot control their own bodies, especially in situations of poverty where culture and gender norms force them into precarious lifestyles.

Evolution of Racism, Gender, and Poverty in Africa

The evolution of a gendered and racist South Africa can be traced to the nineteenth century, when European explorers discovered other human beings who did not resemble them in appearance and in their cultural practices. Needing to create a way to comprehend and explain the difference, they employed the notion of race to legitimize their biases and acts of injustices and exploitation based on differentiation (Duncan 1993).

Both gender subordination and racism are forms of discrimination that use similar criteria against their targets—that is, the differentiated, outward physiological features of human anatomy. As forms of ideology, they operate to justify privileged positions of a dominant group over another. Racists assume that persons with a different skin pigmentation and different cultural identity from theirs are inferior and stupid and deserve to be oppressed. In South Africa, apartheid racism dispossessed Africans of their ancestral land by forceful and systematic removals from the rich and fertile lands to the rugged native reserves where overcrowding and environmental degradation were the order of the day. S. Sibanda (2003) states this clearly when he says,

> A land situation where less than 2% of the whites had a monopoly control of 87% of agricultural land in 1936 and by 1990 14% of whites still have a monopoly control of 82% of the country's agricultural land is at the heart of the land questions in South Africa. Today, about 2.4 million rural households representing about 13 million African people live in the 13% of the land allocated to the African people in terms of the Native Land Act of 1913. Africans continue to eke a living under conditions of insecure and precarious customary and communal tenure systems. In addition there are about 6 million Africans living on white commercial farmland some of the most underpaid and exploited labourers with no hope of tenure. (11)

Blacks, as Africans were called, had and still have congested living arrangements with massive out-migrations of the men from the former native reserves. Out-migration by men started a process that destroyed family ties and human development for many African communities. By systematically subjecting Africans to inhumane housing (usually makeshift shacks), lower standards of education and health facilities, and a life deprived of all recreation and creative opportunities, the current scenario of abject poverty and passive vulnerability to HIV/AIDS was created for them.

The violence of racism against the psychological well-being of Africans on the continent has not been adequately documented, but anecdotes and public speeches tell of alienation, a sense of worthlessness, and perpetual despair that have played a major part in making them vulnerable to diseases and other maladies (Boonzaier 1988). Table 7.1 depicts an overview of the links between patriarchy and apartheid.

Racial capitalism under apartheid unleashed processes of underdevelopment and impoverishment, which affected both men and women, but women's

Table 7.1. Apartheid, Racism, and Gender

	Apartheid	Patriarchy
Root of the problem	Unequal power relations	Unequal power relations
Manifestation	Based on race	Based on sex
Social attitudes	Patronizing attitude of whites: "Our blacks are happy/grateful"	Patronizing attitudes of men: "Our women like staying at home"
Complexes	Inferiority complex: "I am very happy working for my baas"	"I like it when my husband exercises control over me"
Focus on the physical	White myths/stereotypes around the physicality of blacks	Women seen as sexual objects
Stereotypes	"Blacks are loud/lazy"	"Women gossip/have nothing better to do"
Legal	Blatant legal discrimination based on race	Blatant legal discrimination based on sex
Land	87 percent black population forced onto 13 percent of land	Women in many South African communities are not allowed to own land or property
Education	Vastly inferior education system for blacks; few opportunities in mathematics, science, and technology	Equal numbers of boys and girls at primary and secondary school, but huge drop in girls at tertiary level; only tiny percentage in science and technology careers
Participation in the economy	Confined to lowest paid jobs; high unemployment	Black women confined to even lower-paying jobs; even higher rates of unemployment
Participation in politics	Until 1994, blacks barred from politics	Still very unequal representation of women, especially in provincial and local governments
Violence	Very violent system; gross human rights abuses	Rape, domestic violence, sexual harassment of women by men
Fighting the system	Blacks in the forefront but supported by some progressive elements from other racial groups who recognize that transformation is in their interest	Women in the forefront but supported by progressive men who realize that transformation is in their interest

Source: Adapted from Commission of Gender Equality (1998, annex 1) and Agenda (1997).

experiences of poverty and dispossession differed by color of their skins. The system of controlled labor migration under apartheid (which denied Africans residence in urban areas while requiring them to work there) created gendered patterns of poverty and affected gender relations within households. Since the system specifically discouraged rural women from entering towns, particularly with the introduction of pass laws for African women in 1959 and since most labor demand was for African men, women's options were (and remain) largely confined to rudimentary agriculture, informal earnings, or reliance on remittances and transfers (Wilson and Ramphele 1989). To the extent that women accessed urban employment, it was mostly in the form of insecure and low-paid domestic work.

Women's lack of residence rights in urban areas made them vulnerable to arrests and removal when visiting husbands. This made them vulnerable to the whims of partners and employers on whom their presence in urban areas depended. Separation from male partners made it difficult for women to access their income for household purposes. It also deprived women of male labor for agriculture or other labor around the homestead and rendered them vulnerable to attack and theft while living alone in rural homesteads. Women's access to land and other resources in rural areas was also weakened due to male absence and was dependent on the discretion of relatives or male chiefs (Wilson and Ramphele 1989). While the restrictions on movement and residence have formally ended today and efforts are being made to redress imbalances in access to resources and social provision, much of racist discriminatory legacy still affects the daily realities of poor Africans.

Women are particularly hard hit by racism. Although under apartheid all women to differing extents were subjected to formal discrimination, various pieces of legislation differentiated them by racial groups. African women, like their male counterparts, had no political representation, while white women had the vote by 1921. White women used their vote to elect to power the apartheid governments, notwithstanding their gender and racial injustices (Baden, Hassim, and Meintjies 1998). In addition, the white female voters condoned power relations whereby interactions between white and black women were madam–maid relationships depicting economic differences rather than cooperation between women.

Today legacies of the past have compounded the multiple legacies of gender, race, and class discrimination. African women have been consigned to rural areas where amenities such as running water, water-borne sanitation, electricity, shopping facilities, and other conveniences are very limited. Thus, women are at the lowest rungs of the socioeconomic ladder. The root cause of this is patriarchy, the common denominator of all of South Africa's eleven ethnic groups. Albie Sachs, a constitutional court judge, gives some insights into patriarchal unity:

> It is a sad fact that one of the few profoundly non-racial institutions in South Africa is patriarchy. Among the multiple chauvinisms that abound in our country, the male version rears itself with special equal vigour in communities. Indeed it is so firmly noted that it is frequently given a cultural halo and identified with the customs and personalities of different communities. Thus to challenge patriarchy, to dispute the idea that men should be dominant figures in the family and society, is to be seen not as fighting against the male privilege but as attempting to destroy African traditions, or subvert Afrikaaner ideals, or undermine civilised and decent British values. Men are exhorted to express their manhood as powerfully as possible, which some do by joining the police or the army or vigilante groups and seeing how many youths they can shoot, whip or tear gas, club or knife, or how many houses they can bulldoze, or how many people they can torture into helplessness. Patriarchy brutalises men and neutralises women across the colour line. (Quoted in Commission on Gender Equality 1998, 14)

Gender and HIV/AIDS: Critical Concerns and Insights

Gender inequalities are a major driving force behind the HIV/AIDS pandemic. Gender roles and relations powerfully influence the course and impact of HIV/ AIDS. Different societal assignments to males and females affect their ability to protect themselves from HIV/AIDS and cope with its impact. Models of response to this pandemic have relied on individual behavior-change interventions to control the transmission of HIV without addressing the gender-based inequalities that overlap with cultural economic and political inequalities that affect women and men of all ages.

Although HIV/AIDS is a disease affecting both women and men, there are trends that show that the increase in the number of women who are becoming infected at very young age is growing rapidly. Women constitute 41 percent of the 30.6 million adults living with HIV (UNAIDS 2000). A variety of factors increase the vulnerability of women and girls to HIV/AIDS, and these include social norms that deny women sexual health knowledge and practices that prevent them from controlling their bodies or deciding the terms on which they have sex. We shall outline these by examples.

Lack of information, misinformation, and untruths about the disease is one factor for acceleration of the pandemic. In many African societies, gender determines what and how women are expected to know about sexual matters. Some local languages have no positive terms for discussing sexuality, which in many cases is shrouded in myths of secrecy and pornography. Sexuality encompasses how a person feels about her body, her relationships, and sexual activities. It is a social construction of a biological drive, determined by a range of factors, including society's implicit and explicit rules as well as internal drives and underlying motives. The expressions of sexuality are determined by interactions, practices, partners, pleasure (or pain or pressure), procreation, and power.

Many cultures consider female ignorance of sexual matters a sign of purity and, conversely, knowledge of sexual matters and reproductive physiology a sign of easy virtue (Ankomah 1992; Caldwell, Caldwell, and Quiggin 1989; Carovano 1991). "Good" women are meant to be ignorant about sex and passive in sexual interactions. Even if they are informed, they struggle to be proactive in negotiating safer sex.

Fundamental to both gender and sexuality is the issue of power. A complex interplay of social, cultural, and economic factors determines the distribution of power. Imbalance in power between women and men restricts women's sexual autonomy and expands men's sexual freedom. Both these factors increase women's and men's risk and vulnerability to HIV/AIDS (Baylies and Bujra 1995).

A statement by a Senegalese woman reflects the general misconceptions regarding this disease. The words she spoke could have been spoken by any person unaware of the true realities regarding HIV/AIDS:

> I don't need condoms because I'm not a prostitute. I have a husband and children. It is rare that during my travels I fall to the advances of a man. When I do, it is with someone I trust. I only choose to have sexual relations with men who are clean and visibly healthy, polite, and capable of respecting me. These men know me, trust me and know that they don't have to use condoms with me.[1]

Myths and stereotypes about AIDS are such that some women fear to use the condom because they fear that the condom will fall off inside the vagina and get lost or travel to the throat. Some even say that their reproductive organs will come out when the condom is removed. Although information on sexuality is lacking for both women and men, women have to be prepared for reproduction while men have no chance of reliable information sources.

The social and cultural construction of gender and sexuality, with its inherent myths and values around morality and fertility, projects differential social values and norms for women and men and ascribes different sets of knowledge and experiences for women and men. In many societies, multiple sexual partnerships are accepted and condoned for men. Women have to take care to protect their reputation as "proper and reproductive women." Female monogamy and male infidelity and promiscuity are accepted as social norms, putting married women at risk (Jobson 2001).

Women, for example, are not expected to be sexually assertive. If a woman suggested safe sex to her spouse, she might get in trouble, for it is an indication of infidelity. Women are not safe even from their protectors (fathers, grandfathers, brothers, and uncles, to name a few), as shown by the statistics on the perpetrators of sexual abuse, mainly male relatives and family friends (Baylies and Bujra 2000).

Women are physiologically more vulnerable to HIV and sexually transmitted disease infections because of the following:

- They tend to marry older men who have had more sexual partners and are therefore likely to be infected.
- As receptive partners, women have a larger mucosal surface exposed during sexual intercourse. If the intercourse takes place at an age when the mucosal surface is still tender or when it is damaged due to rituals such as female genital infibulation, early marriage, the infection rate is higher.
- Semen has far higher concentration of HIV virus than do vaginal fluids.
- Women often require blood transfusion during childbirth and abortions, thus increasing their chances of infections.

Although women are productively engaged in both formal and informal sectors of production in most African economies, there are gender-related differentials in women's and men's access to and control over productive resources such as land, technology, property, credit, employment, training, and education. The social construction of women's sexuality also requires that women spend most of their lives pregnant or rearing children and caring for the ailing elderly persons for society to continue. Men, on the other hand, are not inclined to passive procreation; rather, they acquire power and status from engaging in outside activities, a construct that condones promiscuity in men. The consequences of this have been an enormous gap between what women want sexual relationships to be and the realities of their lives. In many cases, they have sex not necessarily as an expression of love and pleasure but for a need to become pregnant, a duty to make men happy, or a profession for making a living in situations where there are no choices and to secure survival and social position. Denial of choices is an aspect of human rights violations. As stated by the United Nations Development Program (1995), "human poverty" is more than "income poverty." It is a denial of choices and opportunities for living a tolerable life.

The fact that until recently men were never targeted in interventions to prevent HIV/AIDS has meant that women continue to be in danger. The social construct of masculinity is such that sexual conquest is the main goal for men, irrespective of how adversely it affects women. Women have limited resources to resist this pattern. When men's power is challenged, their resistance might militate against change. Men must be sensitized and mobilized to a greater extent for an effective response to HIV/AIDS and sexually transmitted diseases. Understanding constructions of masculinity in the relevant settings will enhance any positive impact of interventions.

Linkages among HIV/AIDS, Gender, and Poverty

Although there is no agreed-on poverty line to establish absolute poverty levels in Africa, household surveys reveal the continuing concentration of poverty among Africans (as opposed to other racial groups), who carry over 95 percent of the poverty burden (Baden, Hassim, and Meintjies 1998, 38). Lack of economic options open to poor women is clearly a factor in promoting sexual survival strategies, which carry high risks of HIV/AIDS infection, particularly in urban areas. "Substantial numbers of urban women exchange *sex for* money, security and favours. The definition of what constitutes sex work is fairly complex in this setting; ranging from escort agencies to town-wives for migrant men" (Frohlich 1997: 6).

HIV prevalence figures show a higher rate of infection for females than for males and a particularly high risk of contracting HIV among young African women.[2] The rate of infection among women has also risen rapidly since 1990. Women tend to become infected at an earlier age, fifteen to twenty-five years, while infection rates peak in their late twenties to mid thirties. Heterosexual transmission of HIV is dominant in Africa; but perinatal transmission is also a route of transmission from infected mothers to children, and breast-feeding may be associated with higher perinatal infection rates (Frohlich 1997).

Higher-than-average levels of HIV infection have been observed among partners of migrant workers, some of the poorest groups living mainly in refugee camps. Border provinces in African countries and along long-distant transport routes have particularly high HIV prevalence rates, a fact that contradicts poverty's being a directly causal factor of HIV infection.

Poor people are less likely than better-off groups to seek treatment, and they tend to travel further and wait longer for the treatment. While richer groups rely heavily on private doctors, the poor use subsidized hospitals and health centers in a much higher proportion (Reconstruction and Development Programme 1995, 22–23).[3] Cost and time in travel and waiting to be seen are given as major reasons for not seeking care.

Why Are Women More Vulnerable to HIV Than Men?

One of the many manifestations of this disease is the male power and control in nonconsensual sex. Many women are increasingly denied the freedom to control their sexual behavior and are forced to have intercourse against their will both within and outside their consensual unions (UNAIDS 1999).

Many women live in a situation of forced domestic sexual compliance. If they speak out or if they offer resistance to unsafe sex, they may be perceived as being adulterous. It is considered unthinkable that a husband would bring disease into his home, so a woman who is found to be HIV positive may be accused of being the one who brought disgrace to the family. An example of this scenario comes from a medical student in South Africa who sought advice on how to cope when her husband returned from working in another city. Her first concern was to avoid becoming pregnant. She produced a condom and asked him to use it. He threw it away, declaring, "I am not a child."

Other circumstances of violence include rape, sexual trafficking, and slavery. Violence is a transmitter of HIV. Women may be assaulted by their partners for being disobedient or for talking back, refusing sex, or not having the food ready on time. Women who have been sexually abused are more likely to engage in unprotected sex, have multiple partners, and trade sex for money or drugs. Further significant findings are that men having extramarital affairs who report sexually transmitted disease symptoms are more likely to be reported on wife abuse.

In many African cultures, motherhood, like virginity, is considered a feminine ideal. Economic realities and social pressures reinforce the value of motherhood. Children are viewed as sources of labor for the family and as sources of security for their parents in old age. In polygynous families, they maintain the balance among co-wives and bring in status via schooling and employment as resource networks for men. In this context, behavior options to prevent HIV infection through use of condoms present difficulties for women and men who have to maintain fertility. The following statement from a woman in Kenya shows the problems of a woman who dares be sexually assertive:

> I told my husband that it was better to use condoms; the doctor said so. The doctor had also given me some to take home. My husband became angry and asked me who gave me permission to bring those condoms home. (SAFAIDS/KIT and World Health Organization 1995)

Men's Vulnerability to HIV/AIDS

Women and men are trapped by cultural as well as social conventions that require women to be subservient. They both need to be freed from the constraints of their social conditioning to achieve fairer relationships. Men's greater power in gender relations places them at risk of HIV for a range of reasons. Gender analysis is usually employed to describe women's vulnerability to HIV; however, this discussion highlights some of the ways gender and cultural norms contribute to men's vulnerability.

Women and men often subscribe to beliefs that a variety of sexual partners and sexual variation are essential to men's nature since "real men" take risks, supporting norms concerning sexuality. Prevailing norms of masculinity expect men to be more knowledgeable and experienced sexually. Such norms prevent young men from seeking information or admitting their lack of knowledge about sex or protection. Many young men experiment with sex in unsafe ways at a young age to prove their manhood. In many rural societies, older men grant license to youth to "sow their wild oats," while they themselves assume authoritative and wise leadership. In the context of the AIDS pandemic, this has led to young men coming home to die (Jobson 2001).

There are numerous myths among young people in Africa. One particularly common one is that if a man does not have sex to release his semen, it will go to his head and make him mad. That is why long-distance truck drivers stop every 400 kilometers (248 miles) to release their "heat" through sex. Some notions of masculinity emphasize sexual domination over women as a defining characteristic of being "a real man." Men are expected to use alcohol and drugs more than women are, and, insofar as these impair judgment, they lead to high-risk behavior and unprotected sex. Men who have sex with men may fear homophobia and keep their sexual behavior secret, often increasing their own risks to themselves and to their partners, whether male or female.

HIV/AIDS AND DEVELOPMENT

The ultimate aim of development is social upliftment. This is the goal of the World Bank when investing in development projects in Africa. However, vulnerable communities can sometimes be more marginalized in the development process. The relationship between HIV/AIDS and development is a complex one. On the one hand, HIV/AIDS is destroying the development gains of the last few decades, and on the other, development itself is promoting HIV transmission through its impact on vulnerable groups such as people living with HIV/AIDS and poor women. This negative cycle is further exacerbated by widespread poverty throughout the continent. For this cycle to be broken and replaced by a positive response to HIV/AIDS, it is necessary to understand these complex interactions.

The Impact of HIV/AIDS on Human Development

Across the globe, issues of health and disease are viewed as falling within the domain of the health care sector and, to varying degrees, the religious sector. The approach to the HIV/AIDS epidemic was no different, and, until recently, this latest threat to human health was considered a severe health crisis that needed to be handled solely by the health authorities. However, during the 1990s, the devastating impact of this pandemic on social, economic, and environmental development became apparent and resulted in the pandemic being increasingly recognized as a developmental crisis (see table 7.2). Indeed, the impacts of HIV/AIDS are so serious that in 2000 the United Nations took the unprecedented step of labeling the pandemic a threat to global security (Annan 2000).

The impacts of HIV/AIDS on some key human development indicators highlight why this disease is the greatest threat to public health that Africa has ever faced. Almost all measures of mortality are becoming worse. In those countries where HIV infection is well established, it has become the leading cause of adult death and a major cause of infant and child mortality (Lagu et al. 1997). UNAIDS (2001) estimates that in those countries where more than 15 percent of adults are infected, at least 35 percent of boys now aged fifteen will die of AIDS. In countries with as high a prevalence as that of South Africa, this figure may reach 50 percent. Life expectancies in many countries are now falling and by 2005 are expected to drop by as much as twenty years and approach levels not seen in Africa since the early 1950s.

HIV/AIDS typically attacks and kills young adults who often have families and are economically productive. It is not surprising, therefore, that the pandemic is having a profound effect on almost every aspect of social and economic life. Although it is difficult to measure the exact impact of HIV at a national level, there is a growing body of evidence on its negative impacts on households and institutions.

Household providers infected with HIV become dependents as their health steadily deteriorates and scarce resources are used for their care and eventual burial. UNAIDS (2000) reports that in families where the breadwinners developed AIDS, such as in urban areas in Côte d'Ivoire, the outlay on school education was halved, food consumption went down 41 percent per capita, and expenditures on health care more than quadrupled.

The rising mortality of young adults is creating a growing number of AIDS orphans (defined as children who, before the age of fifteen, lost either their mothers or both parents to AIDS). Of the fourteen million living AIDS orphans globally, over 95 percent are in sub-Saharan Africa. Before AIDS, about 2 percent of all children in developing countries were orphans, but by 1997 the proportion had escalated to 7 percent in many African countries and in some cases 11 percent. Due to the stigma attached to AIDS, UNICEF reports that AIDS orphans are at greater risk of malnutrition, illness, abuse, and sexual exploitation than children orphaned by other causes. A UNAIDS (2000) report quotes studies in Uganda that have shown that following the death of one or both parents, the chance of orphans going to school is halved

Table 7.2. Impacts of HIV/AIDS on Social, Economic, and Biophysical Environments

Social	Economic	Biophysical
Dissolution of households	Decrease in monthly income per capita, monthly consumption per capita and savings for households	Change in demand for natural resources as the population changes
Poor morale and stress	Loss of economically active people	Inability to utilize natural resources efficiently and effectively as labor resources are lost
Destruction of community social cohesion	Loss of institutional memory of an organization	Pollution of groundwater resources through improper burial processes
Stigmatization and isolation of people living with HIV/AIDS	Inhibition of private sector growth	Air, land, and groundwater pollution from disposal of health care waste
Abandonment and abuse of women infected with HIV	Loss of productivity	Increased vulnerability of people living with HIV/AIDS to changes in environment, particularly environmental health problems leading to stricter pollution controls
Increase in numbers of street children and in amount of abuse and sex work among orphans	Increased costs of training and replacement	Overall impediment to sustainable development progress
Overburdening of public social support systems	Loss of investment in South Africa due to unstable workforces	
Decrease in the Human Development Index	Decrease in gross domestic product of the country	
Decrease in school attendance; children heading households no longer attend school		

Source: World Bank (2002, 9). Data sources from Centre for AIDS Development, Research, and Evaluation (2000); LoveLife (2001); and Ashton and Ramasar (2001).

and those who do go to school spend less time there than they did formerly. Other work from Uganda has suggested that orphans face an increased risk of stunting and malnourishment.

Using South Africa as an example at the national level, UNAIDS (2000) predicts that as HIV prevalence rates rise in South Africa, both total and growth in national income will fall significantly. According to a study by ING Barings

Bank (quoted in UNAIDS 2000), the overall economic growth rate over the next decade is likely to be 0.3 to 0.4 percentage points lower every year than it would have been without AIDS. A further study suggests that by 2010, the real gross domestic product will be 17 percent lower than it would have been in the absence of AIDS. These figures suggest an alarming future for Africa, especially considering that South Africa has one of the strongest economies in the region. For Tanzania, the World Bank predicts that gross domestic product growth will be 15 percent to 25 percent lower for the 1985–2010 period as a result of AIDS (UNAIDS 1998).

There is not space here to discuss all the impacts of HIV/AIDS, but there is substantial literature that documents these impacts on virtually all aspects of society, including education, the health sector, agriculture, business, and numerous others. The tragedy of the AIDS epidemic is that it hits the poor the hardest and is rapidly erasing decades of slow but steady gains in standards of living. The much-vaunted notion of an African renaissance is at risk of being undermined by the HIV/AIDS pandemic.

The Impact of Development on HIV/AIDS

When integrating HIV/AIDS into analyses of economic environments, it is important to recognize the underlying factors that drive HIV transmission. A simplistic approach to HIV/AIDS can be detrimental, and the present section provides a background to the dynamics of HIV/AIDS. It is widely believed that the spread of HIV in Africa is almost entirely through sexual intercourse and from infected mother to child.

The transmission of HIV occurs in a social, cultural, and economic milieu that strongly influences individual behavior. In other words, risky sexual practices do not automatically change once communities are provided with appropriate information. This vital fact was not appreciated in the early days of the pandemic; instead, once the mode of transmission had been established, it was believed that education and awareness raising would be sufficient for people to modify their sexual behavior and hence eliminate or reduce their risk of becoming infected. While this approach worked relatively well in the wealthy, industrialized world, it has failed in most developing countries.

The concept of vulnerability is useful in understanding why HIV/AIDS spreads differentially within different populations (Whiteside 1998). For example, inferior economic and social status limits the ability of many women to refuse unwanted or unprotected sexual intercourse regardless of how much they know about AIDS or their desire to adopt safe practices. Societal vulnerability focuses on the contextual factors that strongly influence and constrain an individual's personal choices.

It is important, therefore, that programs aimed at mitigating the impact of development projects on HIV/AIDS are not limited to only education and condom provision but rather that such programs should consider other potential interventions. A scheme of the chain of causation that precedes an individual's becoming infected with HIV includes issues of poverty, political instability, and addressing the role of women; that is, the determinants of HIV infection will have to be addressed before the pandemic can be brought under control. Development project managers and those responsible for addressing HIV/AIDS issues need to have this bigger picture in mind when approaching the issue of HIV/AIDS.

While there is a substantial body of literature on the impact of HIV/AIDS on development, little has been written on the reverse relationship—that is, the impact of development on the transmission of HIV and management of AIDS. However, this situation may be changing, as there is a growing interest in addressing these impacts among the bigger development agencies, including GTZ (Deutsche Gesellschaft für Technische Zusammenarbeit, or German Agency for Technical Cooperation), United Nations Development Programme, and the World Bank. It is likely that this resurgent interest has been prompted by the realization that, in the absence of a clear strategy, a development project may actually promote the transmission of HIV and hence undermine key developmental objectives.

CONCLUSION

Women's and men's knowledge, attitudes, and related sexual behavior are highly influenced by gender norms, and socioeconomic and political factors. Macroeconomic institutions of racist capitalism determine the poverty levels for the most affected communities in Africa. Understanding individual and community risks of HIV from a gender and racial perspective reveals the many gaps of knowledge that need to be filled if the struggle against the pandemic is to succeed. Comprehensive prevention and care programs that take into account a wide rage of social, cultural, and political factors are more likely to stem the pandemic. Given the facts of gender contradictions and the condoning of multiple partners for men and that of fidelity for women, the current line of response to HIV/AIDS cannot lead to any breakthrough. Emphasis on individual behavior change that does not address the institutional imbalances that render African communities poverty stricken are futile. Racist inequalities that leave Africans and women without property rights and ownership of productive resources have to be challenged. Discrimination in the form of poor education, lack of viable employment, lack of recreation facilities, and lack of access to health services has to stop if vulnerability to HIV/AIDS is to be stemmed.

Preventive programs should also be aware of the way HIV affects, and is affected by, development. Africans should be enabled to take control of their own lives, a process that requires markedly high levels of political commitment and deliberate steps to address the gender dimension of the pandemic. The ability of men and women in Africa to engage in consensual safe sex is a human rights challenge.

NOTES

1. As quoted in UNAIDS, *Facing the Challenges of HIV/AIDS/STDs: A Gender-Based Approach* (Geneva, Switz.: UNAIDS, 1998), www.unaids.org/NetTools/Misc/DocInfo.aspx?LANG=en&href=http%3a%2f%2fgva-doc-owl%2fWEBcontent%2fDocuments%2fpub%2fTopics%2fGender%2fFacingChallenges_en%26%2346%3bpdf (accessed February 23, 2005).

2. Studies in KwaZulu-Natal in 1990–1992 found that HIV infection rates were 3.2 times higher among women than among men. A 1994 survey in Hlabisa, in rural KwaZulu-Natal, found HIV prevalence of 13.4 percent among women compared to 5.8 percent among men (Frohlich 1997, 5–6).

3. Some sources claim that poor people also use private facilities due to the lack of available public facilities, although this, if true, is probably diminishing with the expansion of free health care (Debbie Budlender, personal communication).

REFERENCES

Agenda. 1997. AIDS: Global concern for women [journal theme], no. 44: 6–23.

Ankomah, A. 1992. Premarital sexual relationships in Ghana in the era of AIDS. *Health Policy Planning* 7:135–43.

Annan K. 2000. Address to United Nations Security Council, January 10, 2000, New York.

Ashton, P., and V. Ramasar. 2001. Water and HIV/AIDS. Some strategic considerations in Southern Africa. In *Hydropolitics in the developing world: A South African perspective,* ed. A. Turton and R Henswood. Pretoria, South Africa: African Water Issues Unit and International Water Management Institute.

Baden, S., S. Hassim, and S. Meintjies 1998. *Country gender profile: South Africa.* Brighton, Sussex, U.K.: Institute of Development Studies.

Baylies, C., and J. Bujra. 1995. Discources of power and empowerment in the fight against HIV/AIDS in Africa. In *AIDS: Safety, sexuality and risk,* ed. P. Aggleton, P. Davies, and G. Hart. London: Tylor and Francis.

———. 2000. *AIDS, sexuality and gender in Africa: The struggle continues.* London: Routledge.

Boonzaier, E. 1988. Race and the race paradigm. In *The use and abuse of political concepts*, ed. E. Boonzaier and J. Sharp. Claremont, South Africa: David Phillips.

Caldwell, J.C., P. Caldwell, and P. Quiggin. 1989. The social context of AIDS in sub-Saharan Africa. *Population and Development Review* 15:185–234.

Carovano, K. 1991. More than mothers and whores: Redefining AIDS prevention needs of women. *International Journal of Health Services* 21:131–42.

Centre for AIDS Development, Research, and Evaluation. 2000. *The economic impact of HIV/AIDS on South Africa and its implications for governance: A bibliographic review.* Pretoria, South Africa: Joint Centre for Political and Economic Studies.

Centre for AIDS Development, Research, and Evaluation. 2000. *The economic impact of HIV/AIDS on South Africa and its implications for governance: A literature review.* Prepared on behalf of USAID through the Joint Centre for Political and Economic Studies, Pretoria, South Africa

Commission on Gender Equality. 1998. *Annual report from March 1997 to March 1998.* Bramfontein, Johannesburg, South Africa: Commission on Gender Equality.

Duncan, N. 1993. Discourses in racism. PhD diss. University of Northern Cape, Beleville, South Africa.

Frohlich, J. 1997. *National STD/HIV/AIDS review: Comprehensive report.* Vols. 1–4. Pretoria, South Africa: Medical Research Council.

Jobson, M. 2001. The intersections of gender, HIV/AIDS, and human rights. Paper presented at the Centre for Gender Studies, University of Pretoria, South Africa.

Lagu, M., K. De Cock, N. Kaleeba, S. Mboup, and D. Tarantola. 1997. HIV/AIDS in Africa: The second decade and beyond. *AIDS* 11 (suppl. B): S1–S3.

LoveLife. 2001. *Impending catastrophe revisited: An update on HIV/AIDS epidemic in South Africa.* Parklands, South Africa: Henry J. Kaiser Foundation.

Reconstruction and Development Programme. 1995. *Key indicators of poverty in South Africa.* Pretoria, South Africa: Ministry in the Office of the President.

SAFAIDS/KIT and World Health Organization. 1995. *Facing the challenges of HIV, AIDS, STD: A gender-based response.* Southern Africa AIDS Information Dissemination Service, Zimbabwe; Royal Tropical Institute, Netherlands (KIT); World Health Organization, Geneva, Switzerland.

Sibanda, S. 2003. An overview of the land question in South Africa: The political and policy issues related to the strategy for implementing land reform. Paper presented at the South Africa Land Reform Conference, Johannesburg, South Africa.

Tallis, V. 2000. Gendering the response to HIV/AIDS: Challenging gender inequality. *Agenda* 44:6–21.

UNAIDS. 1998. *HIV/AIDS and the workplace forging innovative business responses.* Geneva, Switz.: UNAIDS.

———. 1999. *Gender and HIV/AIDS: Taking stock of research and programmes.* Geneva, Switz.: UNAIDS.

———. 2000. *AIDS epidemic update, December 2000.* Geneva, Switz.: UNAIDS.

———. 2001. *AIDS epidemic update, December 2001.* Geneva, Switz.: UNAIDS.

United Nations Development Programme. 1995 *HIV and the challenges facing men.* By Kathryn Carovano. Issue Paper 15. New York: United Nations Development Programme, HIV and Development Programme.

Whiteside, A., ed. 1998. *Implications of AIDS for demography and policy in southern Africa.* Scottsville, South Africa: University of Natal Press.

Wilson, F., and M. Ramphele. 1989. *Uprooting poverty: The South African challenge.* Report for the Second Carnegie Inquiry into Poverty and Development in Southern Africa. Cape Town and Johannesburg, South Africa: David Phillips.

World Bank. 2002. *The integration of HIV/AIDS issues into the environmental assessment process for World Bank funded projects.* Report 1. Washington, D.C.: World Bank.

The Role of Sexual Violence against Zanzibari Women in the Human Rights Conflict with Tanzania over Sovereignty

Fatma Jiddawi Napoli and Mohamed Ahmed Saleh

$\mathcal{I}$t may seem unusual to begin the introduction of an important and sensitive subject such as "sexual violence" with a geographical presentation of the country Zanzibar. The truth is, there is no way of separating the two in this study, as they are closely intertwined. Sexual violence has been used throughout history, in varying degrees, by different colonizing powers in this northwestern Indian Ocean archipelago, as a political weapon to subjugate the population and assert their hegemonic control over the islands. This was true during the period of non-African colonial occupation and remains true today, with the colonization of the islands by fellow Africans under the guise of the Union government of Tanzania.

For the majority of Zanzibaris, the union is a tool in the hands of the mainland Tanzania politicians to colonize the islands and reduce them to a mere region of Tanganyika. For elaboration on this issue, it is important to understand that today the Union government is identified and seen as the same as the mainland government. Therefore, what is referred to as Union government is in fact the mainland government, which is the government of Tanganyika. Hence, it is the government of Tanganyika that is dominating Zanzibar, which is why Zanzibaris have been in constant conflicts with their mainland counterparts over the question of sovereignty.

BACKGROUND TO THE PROBLEM

As an island country situated in the Indian Ocean at the crossroad between Africa and Asia, Zanzibar has an average area of 2,460 square kilometers (1,525 square miles)[1] and almost one million inhabitants. Geographically and culturally,

159

Zanzibar belongs to the Swahili world.[2] It is one of the areas where this coastal mercantile culture and civilization took shape and flourished (Pearson 1998; Saleh 1996; Mazrui and Shariff 1994; Middleton 1992). Zanzibar developed into an important melting pot where migrants from the four corners of the globe were integrated into the society and became part of the social, cultural, and political construction underlying Zanzibari identity and nationalism. In 1832, the sultan of Oman, Seyyid Said bin Sultan, established the capital of his empire in Zanzibar. In 1890 the British imposed their protectorate over the islands, and in the process the sultan of Zanzibar lost his political power and became a figurehead. Seventy-three years later, Zanzibar acquired its independence after a prolonged struggle against the British colonialism. It was on December 10, 1963 that Zanzibar became an independent and sovereign state. On December 16, 1963, the prime minister of the newly independent country, Muhammed Shamte, raised the red, green, and golden flag of Zanzibar in front of the United Nations building in New York to mark the entrance of Zanzibar into the world body. This symbolic gesture, which brought back one of the most ancient and historical states of Africa into the concert of nations, becoming once again "a state in the society of states," is fundamentally important to understand the ongoing resistance in Zanzibar. It is a clear indication that old sovereignties die hard.

The current problems are the aftereffects of the independence struggle and largely stem from the geostrategic position of the islands. As a cosmopolitan society, Zanzibaris developed throughout history a strong notion of tolerance, which allowed different religious as well as communal groups to live together in mutual respect and harmony (Al Barwani 1997; Bakari 2001; Saleh 2002). Nevertheless, the notion of tolerance—which is an important Swahili cultural value, one inculcated into the society from birth to death—was not able to shield the Zanzibaris from the divisive policies of British colonialism. As a result, the era of fighting against British rule was the most divisive, and it brought to the forefront a racist and heinous discourse in the political debate. When the independent movement against colonial rule in Zanzibar started in the late 1950s, the ancestral origin of the cosmopolitan society of Zanzibar was utilized by populists and some fascist-oriented elements in the society—notably, racist politicians within the Afro Shirazi Party and colonial authorities—to create misunderstanding between Zanzibaris of different ancestral origins in the country. In the context of its policy of divide and rule, the British authorities accentuated the ethnic diversity of the population and sowed the seeds of discord among Zanzibaris, which made them vulnerable to the conniving schemes of external forces.[3] For instance, this situation favored the machination of the future first president of the union, Julius Nyerere, who had a lot of influence on the Afro Shirazi Party. It was through this party that he managed to assert his political control over Zanzibar. Ultimately, a bloody revolution conducted by his surrogates, the Afro Shirazi Party (then a major parliamentary opposition), took place on January 12, 1964, one month after independence, overthrowing the first postcolonial coalition government of the Zanzibar Nationalist Party and the Zanzibar and Pemba People's Party. However, Zanzibar's independence was not to last long, as one hundred days after the Revolution, the country was forced, under Cold War circumstances,[4] into a union with Tanganyika. On April 22, 1964, Abeid Amani Karume, president of the People's Republic of Zanzibar, and Nyerere, president of the Republic of Tanganyika, signed an agreement that led to the formation of the United Republic of Tanganyika and Zanzibar on April 26, 1964, to be known later as the United Republic of Tanzania. Neither of the populations of the said two countries was consulted directly by means of a referendum or indirectly through their representatives. The terms of agreement have never been faithfully fulfilled. No ratification by the Council of Ministers and the Revolutionary Council of Zanzibar was obtained. The Constituent Assembly, scheduled to be summoned within a year of the signing of the agreement between the two presidents, has not yet met. It is now forty-one years. To date, the law ratifying the articles of the union of 1964 does not exist on the statute books of Zanzibar; they were never published in the official gazette.

Although for many years a one-party system, Zanzibar and Tanganyika were ruled by two different political parties: Afro Shirazi Party, sole ruling party in Zanzibar, and Tanganyika African National Union, sole ruling party in Tanganyika. It was only in 1977 that the two ruling parties merged to form a new single political party for the whole United Republic of Tanzania under the name of Chama Cha Mapinduzi, literally "party of the revolution." In 1992, a multiparty system was introduced, but the Chama Cha Mapinduzi remains, to date, the ruling party. Many Zanzibaris oppose the present union setup, from which Tanganyika is seen to benefit at the expense of Zanzibar. Many Zanzibaris believe that Tanganyika, under the guise of the union, not only turns a blind eye to abuses of the Zanzibar government but may also be the driving force behind them. It is interesting to note here that Tanzania has not, up to this day, ratified the international convention on torture and other cruel, inhuman, or degrading treatment or punishment. In the present setup, the implementation of international human rights standards into the constitution is dualistic. Although Zanzibar has a separate constitution, the islands do not have the capacity to ratify the international covenants, as this power falls in the domain of the union. The obligations and rights enshrined in the constitution of the Union government of Tanzania supersede the constitution of Zanzibar. Therefore, the Union government is first and foremost responsible for all the violations of human rights in the country. However, it has little interest in the rights of the Zanzibari nationals, and the abuses serve to silence them from talking about and asserting their political and human rights, with one of the fundamental issues being Zanzibaris' rights for culture and self-determination. Numerous reports from international human rights organizations, such as Amnesty International, Human Rights Watch, and Unrepresented Nations and Peoples' Organisation, have recently reported on human rights abuses in Zanzibar—for example, laws that limit the freedom of expression and the press; and the torture and ill-treatment of people by the police, including floggings and beatings as well as harsh prison conditions and arbitrary arrests and detention.

The situation became even more desperate in the past four decades, as the Union government's coercive forces used all the means at its disposal, including sexual violence, to demoralize the Zanzibari masses from struggling for their inalienable human and democratic rights. It is a weapon that has been used consistently to prevent Zanzibaris from playing an active role in the political process that would eventually allow them to attain self-determination and their country to regain its status as a sovereign state on the world map. This is why, as we have indicated earlier, the strategic geographical position of Zanzibar and its political and social evolution are closely linked. From the annals of history, it cannot be denied that Zanzibar is one among the most ancient city-states in the world. Today, however, Zanzibar is on the brink of being completely swallowed by the "big brother" and reduced to being just another region, if not district, of Tanganyika. During the last four decades, Zanzibar has been gradually but surely driven into the backyard of Tanganyika; hence, it is condemned to disappear as a specific sovereign entity of the Swahili world. This is why, for many Zanzibaris, it is almost a moral duty in each and every one of their publications to start by describing their country, notably by emphasizing its specificity as an independent entity, separate from Tanganyika. This is not only an act of resistance by Zanzibaris, but it is also a form of therapy against the trauma that has been inflicted on the majority of the population of these islands. This has been Zanzibar's history in the past forty years, full of tyrannical brutalities and insidiousness as a result of a bloody revolution that ended the country's multiparty democracy until its resumption in 1992. It is estimated that about five thousand Zanzibaris, most of whom could trace their ancestral origins along the Indian Ocean basin and the Persian-Arab gulf, were slaughtered during this bloody event.

Since the creation of the union, the question of self-determination of the islands of Zanzibar has become crucial. On the one hand, the Tanganyika politicians under the guise of the union would like to obliterate Zanzibar from the world map since it reminds them of an existence of an old sovereign nation; on the other hand, Zanzibaris oppose the move with a strong resistance. This aspect is important to know in order to understand current political, social, and cultural issues at stake. It provides a practical means of refreshing and reminding the individual readers as well as the international community that the United Republic of Tanzania was formed by two different sovereign states—that is, two peoples with two different histories, cultures, and identities. Each of these peoples has its own social, political, cultural, and economic aspirations and has a legitimate right to exist and be respected. The following statement, by Hassan, a Zanzibari fisherman, clearly reflects the sentiments of the majority of the islands' population: "Everybody is tired of the way it is. Tanganyika is the big fish eating the little one. All the fish should be the same" (quoted in Robinson 2000). The Zanzibaris, although a minority group within the union, are proud of their national heritage and are not keen to accept their disappearance as a people with its own history, culture, and identity. Zanzibari women have always been in the forefront of the national struggle.[5] This was true during the independence struggle in the 1950s and 1960s against the British colonial rule and remains true today against social and cultural domination, hence ethnocide and the direct political control of the islands by Tanganyika. In both cases, Zanzibari women have been giving momentum to the movement whose ultimate goal is to create the necessary conditions for the eventual political emancipation of Zanzibar.

UNION AS A FORCED MARRIAGE

The debate on the union between Zanzibar and Tanganyika has often revolved around the gender question. Tanganyika, being the main partner of the union, always takes a macho position, considering itself as a man and Zanzibar as a woman who does not have a say in the matters pertaining to the couple. As a man, Tanganyika has a right to repudiate his wife (Zanzibar) and not the other way around. Zanzibaris have for some time now been considering divorce, but in vain (Robinson 2000). In the islands, the union, which was forced onto Zanzibaris, is to date compared allegorically to a forced marriage. To the majority of Zanzibaris, a marriage could only have taken place if there were consent between the two parties. The said consent could have been obtained only through a referendum. Zanzibaris were never consulted in this matter, so for the majority of them, the union remains a political rape and hence a nightmare. Right from the outset, the Tanganyika government under the guise of the union confiscated power and, by proxy, banned all political parties except the ruling Afro Shirazi Party, which was just an extension of the Tanganyika ruling party. To consolidate its hold and maintain its hegemony in all sectors of Zanzibari life, the Tanganyikans managed to convince their local puppets of the need to be protected if they have to remain in power against the Zanzibaris' popular will. In this manner, they created a relationship of dependency with their Zanzibari protégés. The latter could not imagine holding onto power without the protection of the former. Slowly but surely by using the same tactics as their former colonial masters of divide and rule, as well as by changing one article after another of the constitution in its favor, Tanganyika managed to consolidate its hold on Zanzibar. Furthermore, in its endeavor to maintain its colonization over Zanzibar and maintain the power of an unpopular government in the islands, the repressive apparatus of the union, does not hesitate to use sexual humiliation as one of its major tools in ensuring the physical and mental torture of Zanzibaris.

SEX AS AN INSTRUMENT OF POLITICAL SUBJUGATION

Violence against women has been and continues to be used by the undemocratic regimes in Zanzibar and Tanzania as a weapon of political intimidation. This tool has effectively silenced many Zanzibari women and caused them to be marginalized from active participation in the democratic process of their country. Such divisive and exploitative means of political intimidation emerged in Zanzibar during the bloody revolution of 1964, when hundreds of Zanzibari women and children were raped. The rape was racially motivated against Zanzibari women of Arab, Indian, and other foreign or mixed ancestry. It was done mostly by lumpen elements, mostly originating from Tanganyika, who formed the revolting forces against families of the former establishment. Some men were sodomized. Due to a great sense of shame and fear of reprisals, families did not dare to expose these disgraceful incidents to the public and had to live with their trauma, vowing never again to participate in the political process. In the course of our field research on the Zanzibari diaspora in Scandinavia, we came across a Danish woman whose Zanzibari husband had to go into exile after the revolution of 1964. She could still recall how traumatized her husband was at the beginning of their marital life, and she could not understand why her husband was having terrible nightmares every night. It took some time before the husband could verbalize and explain to his wife his tragedy of seeing his sister being raped in his very presence during the revolution. This is only one example among many others. There is quite a lot of testimony on this subject; if collected it would provide enough material to write a whole book.

In the case of Zanzibar, no one has been brought to trial for these crimes against humanity. Even if there were a trial, like that in the Bosnian case, experience has shown that, for religious and cultural reasons, Muslim women who have been raped find it difficult to testify. Violence against women has also been effectively used to silence some men who, due to what happened to their families, wives, sisters, and relatives in 1964, decided not to be politically involved. This political passivity has been further accentuated by the union. It significantly contributed to the dormancy of the political process within the islands for many years and the continual subjugation and colonization of Zanzibaris by Tanganyika. This trend of violence against women has proven to be an extremely effective weapon for the rulers of Tanzania and has continually been used through the years to this day.

FORCED MARRIAGES: INSTITUTIONALIZED RAPES

The same racist criteria were employed to justify forced marriage in the aftermath of the 1964 revolution. This organized rape by the state apparatus was geared to appease the sexual fantasies and obsessions of the ruling clique, notably, members of the Zanzibar Revolutionary Council (Baraza la Mapinduzi) and their cronies, under the guise of promoting racial harmony in the society. In its January 1971 issue, *Drum* magazine reported one of the incidents of forced marriage:

> One fateful Sunday morning, four beautiful teenagers . . . Badria Mussa, 20, Fawzia Mussa, 17, Wajiha Yusuf, 14, and NV Mohammed Hussein, 16, were abducted and carried off to be married to elderly revolutionaries. These unfledged youngsters were relaxing at home in Zanzibar Town when armed soldiers stormed in and asked the girls to accompany them on a "special" mission. . . . But the girls resisted and a battle of words ensued with the agitated girls' relatives joining in. . . . The reluctant girls were escorted to a place where there was a crowd of anxious people including government officials, and most important, a Muslim priest, locally known as a Kadi. The Kadi was already in ceremonial robes. He sat majestically and then turned to the girls: "The ceremony we are celebrating today is of great moment. It is under order from the government, and by the will of the Almighty that our performance today should open a new era in the history of our country."

The *Drum* narration further continued:

> When the girls realized that they were about to be married, pandemonium broke out. They became hysterical and bathed in streams of tears, and together with their parents and relatives screamed in chorus: "No, no, no, no, How can it happen?" But the matrimonial blessing was made. The girls became the official wives of four tough and forceful men about 30 years their senior. After the weddings the brides were carried away in a stately fashion, with all ceremony, pomp and pageantry. But they were carried away in marked haste. As they continued to weep bitterly, they spent the first night

of their honeymoon at Ziwani Prison where they were held for the night, together with three of their fathers. The 11 men who had accompanied the girls were in turn detained at Malindi Police Station. Early next morning they were taken to the People's Court and sentenced to one year's imprisonment and 24 strokes for contravening the island's marriage code. It was alleged that they refused to consent to the marriage of the four girls on racial grounds. (Smyth and Seftel 1998)

According to the aforementioned publication, the president of Zanzibar, Abeid Amani Karume, justified his forced marriage code by saying,

> In the colonial times the Arabs took African concubines without bothering to marry them. Now that we are in power the shoe is on the other foot. We have the rifles. (217)

During this period, hundreds of families fled the country with their young daughters, leaving everything they owned behind. Those who remained were at the mercy of the ruling regime. Some families arranged marriages between cousins to save their children from these heinous crimes.

RAPE AND SEXUAL ABUSE

Sexual crimes were common throughout the period of the rule of President Karume, the father of the present president of Zanzibar.[6] Not only the father and the members of his Revolutionary Council were involved in the crimes but also his children. Before the October 2000 elections, a group of Zanzibaris for human rights distributed an e-mail message on www.zanzinet.org and other websites about the incident of rape that led to the death of the victim and involved the present president of Zanzibar and his brother who is presently ambassador of Tanzania in Germany. This happened after the victim, a young girl, refused to concede to the sexual temptations of the princes, who would not take a no for an answer. This particular incident has remained in the memories of many Zanzibaris: the victim tried her best to resist, but in vain. At the height of his eight years of dictatorial and oppressive rule, the first president of postrevolutionary government of Zanzibar, Karume was gunned down in his ruling party headquarters by a group of young Zan-zibari army officers. They were led by Captain Mohamed Hamud, whose father was killed a few years earlier by the same president. Karume's assassination remains to date enigmatic, for nobody knows the real motive behind the killing. Some people advance the thesis of revenge while others, an attempt to get rid of a dictatorship and pave the way for democratic process in Zanzibar. A substantial number of innocent Zanzibaris, particularly those with connections to the former Umma Party,[7] were arrested and imprisoned for many years. Torture was the major means of obtaining information from the suspects, including beatings and sexual assault. There were also some cases of sodomy in the process of humiliating and mentally torturing the suspects. A recently published novel (Shafi 2003), one based on the author's prison experiences during this particular period, provides insight into understanding the barbaric prison system in Zanzibar and Tanzania and the inhuman treatment reserved for the suspects of treason.

In 2001, rape was used again by the police, the military, and the intelligence service to intimidate the opposition. This was witnessed during the January 27, 2001, massacre of Zanzibaris, and the launch of a witch-hunt campaign of opposition activists, when hundreds of women were raped, some in the sanctity of their own homes. Victims of rape were women who supported individually (or with their family) the opposition party, notably, Civic United Front. Initially, the police murdered opposition members and later raped their sisters, daughters, and wives. Some men were also sodomized. The findings in the report from the African Division of Human Rights Watch, especially those documenting what happened on the sister island, Pemba, are revealing:

> In the aftermath of the demonstrations, as the police made their rounds from house to house searching for demonstrators and opposition supporters, there were a number of cases of rape and other instances of sexual abuse perpetrated largely by militia as well as police. After the round-ups, sexual abuse also occurred in the prison holding cells. In Wete, Pemba, militia members sexually assaulted both men and women in the course of house-to-house searches. One woman told Human Rights Watch that she was living with her three young children when five men came to her house after nightfall on January 27, 2001, one in an army uniform and the rest in green militia uniforms, but all wearing black stocking masks over their faces. After breaking down her door and searching, they took her gold jewelery and several items of clothing. Then, while the militia searched, the soldier pointed his rifle at her chest and pushed her down onto her bed with his rifle, where she was raped in turn by two militia while the others watched and her children cried in the hallway. They threatened her that they would return the next day, and the next.[8] (Human Rights Watch 2002, 40).

In another testimony, Human Rights Watch (2002) reported a case of a female school student who was raped in the sanctity of her home by militia members while police watched. In Chake Chake, one of the three districts of Pemba, according to Human Rights Watch findings, four armed and masked police wearing Field Force Unit (military police) uniforms forcibly entered a woman's house in the morning of January 27, 2001, and demanded to know where her husband was. As she could not answer accordingly,

> One of them began to beat me on the head and neck until I was dizzy and fell down. Then he picked me up twice and dropped me on the ground. He said, "If you want us to leave you alone, give us money. . . ." Then the policeman pulled up my dress, and then he inserted his fingers inside me and told me to urinate. My relative told them that I could not have sex, and gave them US$50 dollars, but they wanted more, so I got them US$120 dollars, and then they left. We hid inside for two days and heard a local policeman leading mainlanders to the houses of [Civic United Front] members and telling them to rob and harass Arabs.[9] (40)

Human Rights Watch indicates in its report that there is evidence of other rapes in Chake Chake, including those of a mother and a daughter. The report further emphasizes that, according to a police officer from Zanzibar Town who spoke to Human Rights Watch researchers under condition of anonymity, police also sexually abused and assaulted detainees in holding cells:

> The situation was very bad; there was a lot of confusion. Police were going into cells and treading on people and beating them. They [the female prison guards] were doing things to them that are unacceptable, such as searching women, grabbing their buttocks, genitals, breasts. The cells in Madema are designed to hold thirty people, but there were more than 200 in there.[10] (quoted in Human Rights Watch 2002, 41)

According to the Human Rights Watch findings, in a Pemba prison (Wete), "police inserted twigs and sticks into the anuses of male prisoners as they searched them" (41). According to one witness whose testimony is published in the Human Rights Watch report,

> We were stripped in front of all the askaris [police]. We were fully searched, our entire bodies. They also search in your private places. Women were searched in another area. Sometimes an askari would use a stick to do the [anal] searching, then show that stick to others. I know the guards who did this by name. (41)

The repression campaign and humiliation of Zanzibaris continued with a reported number of house searches, looting, and destruction of people's properties. While carrying out house-to-house searches, police and other forces threatened residents, looted and destroyed property, beat and arrested people found out of doors, and raped a number of women, particularly targeting known opposition supporters, the wealthy, and people of Arab origin. Human Rights Watch reports that in Chake Chake, forty-three people claimed to have experienced losses in excess of US$28,000 dollars due to police damage to property and looting (Human Rights Watch 2002, 41).[11] As hundreds of men fled their homes to avoid arrest, many women who were left home alone faced violence at the hands of security forces and their ruling party (Chama Cha Mapinduzi) accomplices (41). One would have to read the Human Rights Watch report (2002) thoroughly to get a hint of the extent of violence and human rights abuses against women in particular and Zanzibari people in general in January 2001.

History has shown to date that in many areas of the world where oppressive regimes face popular challenge, most of the time they resort to sexual violence to crack down the resistance. In apartheid South Africa, Bosnia, Chile under Pinochet, and Indonesia, sexual abuses and rape have been used as a political weapon to neutralize the opposition, to alienate the opposition from its popular basis, to settle political scores or enact revenge, and to humiliate and exhibit the perverted arrogance of power. In Zanzibar, it seems that the state was used for the same purpose, as both the Union government and the Zanzibar puppet government—one imposed on Zanzibaris by the mainland Tanzania[12]—have lost popularity while the opposition has apparently gained credibility. On two occasions, 1995 and 2000, the Union government disregarded the will of the majority of Zanzibaris and imposed a president on them. To effect his imposition in 1995, as well as in October 2000, the president unleashed a reign of terror in the islands that was witnessed even by international press. A well-known mainland Tanzanian journalist, Jenerali Ulimwengu, who dared to organize a debate on the local television station about these violations of human rights, was deprived of his Tanzanian nationality and became stateless. Another journalist from Zanzibar, Ally Nabwa (executive editor of a local newspaper *Dira*), had to face the same fate and was forced to surrender his passport for expressing ideas that are different from those of the ruling clique. During the last presidential elections (October 2000), the army took all the ballot boxes and kept them for a few days before they announced a landslide victory for the ruling party. It is on the basis of this prevailing situation that Zanzibaris consider the mainland's imposed president of Zanzibar as an unlawful president, as he was not elected by Zanzibaris. Ever since, they have been requesting the world not to force them to accept what is unlawful. They have been pleading to the international community to exert pressure on the Union government so as to make it stop its infringement on the islands' internal matters and respect the democratic process launched with the introduction of multiparty system in the country.

CONCLUSION

During the last four decades, Zanzibar has witnessed the worst human rights violations, which continue unabated (Article 19 2000). Since the union with

Tanganyika and the ultimate consolidation of Tanganyika's hold on Zanzibar state structures, the people of Zanzibar have been subjected to all forms of humiliation, oppression, and suppression of their democratic rights. They have patiently endured the suffering that goes with those evils. As we have already seen throughout this chapter, sexual violence has always been one of the major aspects of violations of human rights perpetrated in the islands by the union forces. Robert Hayden's paradigm (2000), which points to the conditions under which mass rape is avoided in ethnonational conflicts, could be applied only with a great deal of caution in the present situation in Zanzibar. It seems his paradigm would be valid only in situations where there is mutual understanding and recognition of fundamental values. However, in the situation where those who hold power have an inferiority complex, the situation becomes very problematic. Sexual violence becomes a means of looking down on the others and of affirming one's superiority. In the context of Zanzibar, which is a traditional society with taboos and strong beliefs (customs and traditions), sexual violence, notably rape, is the ultimate humiliation to women and their families, resulting in the deprivation of women of their womanhood, their marginalization, the destruction of mental and sociocultural harmony (a raped woman is traumatized and will face difficulties in marriage), the dispossession of self as a free, independent human being, and the loss of a nation.

Human Rights Watch's findings show that Tanzanian security and state officials were responsible for serious violations of domestic and international law. Security forces were responsible for extrajudicial executions and an excessive use of force resulting in killings and assaults of unarmed civilians, including those assisting the wounded. Despite all the constant oppressions, Zanzibaris are still persisting in their struggle for the restoration of a democratic and peaceful Zanzibar. Their sense of historical past and destiny revives in their collective memories the remembrance of resistance against all forms of cultural as well as political subjugation. Today, they have difficulties accepting the loss of their identity. Whether inside Zanzibar or outside the isles, they remain attached to their maternal land where their umbilical cord is buried and to the culture that nurtured them. They have a strong cultural self-consciousness, which demonstrates itself inside Zanzibar as a form of resistance against cultural and political hegemony of mainland Tanzania and, outside the isles, as a means of maintaining Zanzibari identity. This is why the international community has a duty to intervene in the conflict over the question of self-determination in Zanzibar. This will help to both reduce constant political violence, where in many occasions women are victimized, and consolidate emerging values of democracy and human rights. Concerted efforts should be made to pressure both the union and Zanzibar governments to reform their restrictive legislation. A truth and reconciliation commission should be formed to clarify the past human rights abuses, killings, and disappearances and create conditions for a sustainable peace and reconciliation process based on the principles of pardon (forgiveness). Perhaps the biggest challenge to addressing the question of human rights in Zanzibar is the need for the international community to recognize it as having issues and problems that are often unique and different from those on the mainland. Hence, there is the need to act upon human rights knowledge as a moral and political responsibility (Harrison 2000). Any approaches to human rights reform and protection of rights need to be seen in light of that perspective, particularly recognizing Zanzibaris' economic, cultural, and political rights to freedom and self-determination.

NOTES

1. The main island (Unguja) has an average area of 1,464 square kilometers (908 square miles) and its sister island, Pemba, 868 square kilometers (538 square miles).

2. Extends along 3,000 kilometers (1,860 miles) on the eastern coast of Africa, from Brava (Somalia) to Sofala (Mozambique), as well as the adjacent islands, notably, Lamu, Mombasa, Pemba and Unguja (Zanzibar), Mafia, Kilwa, and the Comoros.

3. The British authorities encouraged communal identifications. During the British colonial time, there were about twenty-three officially registered associations (see Babu 1989).

4. The U.S. State Department played an important role in the creation of Tanzania (see Wilson 1989).

5. The names of Bi Mvita and Bi Kessi Salim were famous among the Zanzibaris for their militant stand on social, political, and human rights.

6. The first president of Zanzibar (1964 to 1972); his son Amani, present president of Zanzibar, imposed on Zanzibaris by the Union government.

7. A Marxist militant group that split from the Zanzibar Nationalist Party (ZNP) in 1963.

8. "In the aftermath of the demonstrations . . .": Organized to protest the 2000 elections, which were considered by all national and international observer groups as a shambles (see Commonwealth Observer Group 2001).

9. The term *mainlanders* is used to distinguish Zanzibaris from Tanganyikans, who are also called Tanzania mainlanders.

10. Madema is a notorious police station on the other side of Zanzibar Town, where quite often the police take the opposition party members and activists for interrogations.

11. This is a huge sum of money in a country such as Tanzania, where an ordinary citizen's wage is far less than US$100 dollars per month.

12. Zanzibar retains a certain autonomy under the union. The union president, Benjamin Mkapa, does not have to interfere with Zanzibar elections. However, in total violation of the union arrangements, he has been directly involved in choosing and

imposing a president on Zanzibaris. In the 1995 elections, as well as the October 2000 elections, he was fully and openly involved in the whole Zanzibar electoral saga.

REFERENCES

Al Barwani, Ali Muhsin. 1997. *Conflicts and harmony in Zanzibar.* Self-published memoirs, Dubai, United Arab Emirates.

Article 19. 2000. *Zanzibar: Democracy on shaky foundations.* London: Article 19.

Babu, Abdulrahman. 1989. Background to Zanzibar revolution. Introduction to *US foreign policy and revolution: The creation of Tanzania*, by Amrit Wilson. London: Pluto Press.

Bakari, Mohammed Ali. 2001. *The democratisation process in Zanzibar: A retarded transition.* Hamburg, Germany: Institute of African Affairs.

Commonwealth Observer Group. 2001. *The elections in Zanzibar, United Republic of Tanzania: 29 October 2000.* London: Commonwealth Secretariat.

Harrison, Faye V. 2000. *Facing racism and moral responsibility of human rights knowledge.* New York: New York Academy of Sciences.

Hayden, Robert M. 2000. Rape and rape avoidance in ethno-national conflicts: Sexual violence in liminalized states. *American Anthropologist* 102 (1): 27–41.

Human Rights Watch. 2002. *"The bullets were raining": The January 2001 attack on peaceful demonstrators in Zanzibar,* www.hrw.org/reports/2002/tanzania (accessed February 16, 2005).

Mazrui, Alamin, and Ibrahim Noor Shariff. 1994. *The Swahili: Idiom and identity of an African people.* Trenton, N.J.: Africa World Press.

Middleton, John. 1992. *The world of the Swahili: An African mercantile civilization.* New Haven, Ct.: Yale University Press.

Pearson, Michael. 1998. *Port cities and intruders. The Swahili coast, India, and Portugal in the early modern era.* Baltimore: Johns Hopkins University Press.

Robinson, Simon. 2000. A whiff of revolt on Spice Islands: Thirty-six years after its union with Tanzania, Zanzibar considers divorce. *Time Europe* 156, no. 18 (October 30).

Saleh, Mohamed Ahmed. 1996. Zanzibar et le monde Swahili. *Afrique contemporaine*, no. 177 (janvier–mars): 17–29.

———. 2002. Tolerance: Principal foundation of the cosmopolitan society of Zanzibar. *Journal of Cultures of the World,* www.unescocat.org/cultmon/dossiers/zanzibaresos .html (accessed March 30, 2005).

Shafi, Adam. 2003. *Haini.* Nairobi, Kenya: Longhorn Books.

Smyth, Annie, and Adam Seftel. 1998. *Tanzania: The story of Julius Nyerere from the pages of* Drum. Kampala, Uganda: Fountain.

Wilson, Amrit. 1989. *US Foreign policy and revolution: The creation of Tanzania.* London: Pluto Press.

IV

NEW DIASPORAS:
REFUGEES AND IMMIGRANTS

· 9 ·

The Second Coming: African Women as a Racialized Transmigrant Group in a Canadian Context

Philomina E. Okeke

*T*his chapter briefly explores the impact of global restructuring, contemporary immigration patterns, and the racist practices and policies they nurture on African immigrant women's life chances in Canada. Based on a recently completed study, the chapter examines the experiences of African female immigrants in Canada and their fight against racism, especially the modes of resistance deployed in a struggle that extends beyond the borders of their new homeland. The spotlight on a group of new Africans in diaspora exposes the specificities of the black experience and raises some important questions around the homogenization of differences afforded by the use of the term *immigrants*. While the analysis highlights the challenges these women face in their struggle to establish a second niche abroad, it also celebrates their active resistance to various forms of racialization that undermine their efforts.

Analysis of global racism must pay attention to the commonalities shared as well as the specificities of particular social contexts that define the experiences of individuals and groups. For immigrant communities around the world, the World Conference against Racism (WCAR) provided yet another forum to reexamine their place in the mainstream societies they find themselves in—in comparison to similar communities—and in relation to the benchmarks that delegates arrived at as a global community. For new African diasporas in particular, WCAR brought into the limelight the various forms of racism and racialization embedded in globalization, which significantly define their prospects in these relatively new homelands. Since the early mid-1960s, the United Nations has played a crucial role in promoting international efforts at combating racism.[1] The political conflicts and economic crisis of the past two decades have further expanded the UN's role as the major world body charged with policing and regulating the conduct of nation-states. Indeed, since the early 1990s, the UN has increasingly promoted international awareness of new and varied experiences of racism, pressing for measures of intervention that the world community should be held responsible for implementing. The WCAR forum also yielded itself to the showcasing of minority social groups such as Africans in diaspora, which often find themselves in the "black pool" with stereotyped labels that mask their own unique characteristics. For new Africans in diaspora, WCAR afforded yet another base for developing or strengthening networks and solidarity with other groups involved in similar social movements. It also readily created a forum for the critical analyses of their experiences as immigrant black communities who share some common characteristics with others but face their own unique challenges, given their historical origins and relation to the mainstream society.

For the most part, the existing literature on blacks in North America concentrates largely on the history of slavery, the experiences of descendants of this history, and the progress they have made in the contemporary society. This literature significantly belies the voice of newer immigrants from the African continent who can neither relate to this history nor share many of its basic characteristics.[2] African immigrants are no longer a negligible minority among North American blacks. With respect to Canada, immigrants constitute the majority among blacks at both the national level and in some of the provinces.[3] The economic downturn and political unrest across the African continent have encouraged a continuously rising trend of immigrants to North America. But not much is documented so far about the conditions that compel these immigrants to flee their homeland, their experiences in new settlements abroad, and the prospects for progress over time. Although emerging debates in African studies have raised some crucial questions about African–North American immigration, the discourse has, for the most part, focused on male-defined experiences such as the brain drain from the mid-1980s, the impact of African immigrants on the democratization movements across the continent, and the social status of new settlers in the United States.[4] Scholars of African studies are wrestling with the collapse of academic and research infrastructures across the continent, the gap left by waves of highly trained personnel leaving the continent, and the erosion of long-established linkages with institutions abroad that must adjust to sharp decline in public funding.[5] As the analysis here reveals, existing data on the immigration of Africans to the West, particularly North America, point to the rising number of middle-class families leaving the continent in search of better economic pastures. However, many groups of African immigrants across North America are increasingly mobilizing themselves to influence the political, economic, and social trends in their home countries.

The existing literature on new Africans in diaspora not only is sparse but has also misrepresented the gender profile of the relevant immigration trends and experiences. However, the poverty of literature on African women immigrants is also not unconnected to the global and Canadian trends in the prevailing social discourse.[6] Although women constitute the majority of the world's migrants, the factors that decide their emigration to other parts of the world and the challenges they face in their new environments remain ancillary to analyses of male experiences.[7] The treatment of gender in the analysis of international migration has been influenced by the differing emphases placed on immigrants from specific regions. As noted earlier, the analysis of international migration has not critically interrogated the trends in African immigration to North America and the peculiarities that follow and help define the African immigrant in the New World.[8] The emerging discourse on new settlers in particular has so far received minimal attention in Canada. More importantly, the gender component remains grossly unrecognized.

Although research on female immigrants from the developing world is gradually emerging into a small but growing body of literature in Canada, African women in Canada have gained little or no profile in any existing discourse on international migration. Thus, the recently completed study of black female immigrants in Edmonton, Alberta, constitutes one of the few attempts at highlighting the diversity of black experiences in Canada.[9] This study contributes to building literature that speaks to gender implications of global restructuring in a racialized world. The lives of African women in this study portray in various ways their struggle with global racism. Their experiences speak to their social location as transmigrants rather than as immigrants who have cut links to their homelands in order to establish new homes elsewhere. They are placed in a situation where they have to establish homes away from home with very strong links to Africa for themselves and their families—especially the children.

THEORETICAL PERSPECTIVES

Although feminist writings have contributed greatly to the development of what presently exists as the database on African women, it is safe to say that feminist authors have not quite stayed on course with regard to the significant developments happening in African women's lives. For the most part, debates on the conditions of African women's lives have followed the WID-WAD-GAD triad: Esther Boserup's groundbreaking book *Women's Role in Economic Development* (1970) laid the groundwork for women in development (WID), a gender perspective to the analysis of development theory and practice.[10] The critiques of WID gave rise by the late 1970s to women and development (WAD), a set of Marxist-based approaches that exposed the gender division of labor in the national and international economies that exploits women's labor in both the private and public spheres with little or no rewards for their efforts.[11] Gender and development (GAD) in the early 1980s focused on the relations of gender, recognizing the larger social milieu in which women's productive and reproductive roles are constructed. The contributions of African female scholars to the postmodern and postcolonial discourses since the mid-1980s appear to have shifted the course of this debate by raising crucial questions about its contents and loci. These scholars point to African women's marginal presence in the forums where their concerns are addressed. The consistent homogenization of "Third World" women in Western feminist literature, they argue, has not allowed a rethinking of African women's role and place in the contemporary society.[12]

However, despite the impact that African scholars have made in the relevant forums, the debate on the political economy of knowledge production—who speaks for whom—does not appear to have waded into prevailing debates on the gender implications of South–North immigration. To some extent, the same can be said of the larger, Western feminist forum. Very little groundwork has been done in terms of catching up with the rapidly growing literature on globalization and transmigration trends. Indeed, it is only at the close of the last decade that critical feminist perspectives focusing on women's global–local interactions and agency in the everyday world began to emerge.[13] Following the tentative stances of proponents, this chapter embraces the formulations of transnational trends and characteristics of social groups for analyzing the multiplicity of identities, connections, and experiences of African Canadian women.[14] As N. Glick Schiller, L. Basch, and C. Blanc-Szanton observe, "By maintaining many different racial, national, and ethnic identities, transmigrants are able to express their resistance to the global political and economic situations that engulf them, even as they accommodate themselves to living conditions marked by vulnerability and insecurity."[15] In similar terms, transnational feminism is slowly replacing the idea of global feminism, with the recognition that locations are linked to each other in ways that demand we pay attention to the flows of capital, labor, culture and knowledge.[16] The globalization process has necessitated a search for identity in an international context where individuals and social groups are forced to develop multiple and fluid identities. For instance, Nakanyike Musisi notes that in the Canadian context the search for identity is not a matter of "choice" for African diasporic communities. She insists, "Part of the process of survival in a multicultural state entails negotiating socio-cultural space for the multiple identities."[17] This chapter takes a similar stance, asserting that the experiences of African female immigrants are better understood in the context of the emerging discourses on immigration and transnational feminism than from the insights provided by the existing development literature.

GENDER AND INTERNATIONAL IMMIGRATION: VOLUNTARY AND INVOLUNTARY IMMIGRANTS

The notion that men and women are equally involved in making decisions about when and where to migrate has not been seriously questioned in studies of international migration. The gender implications of voluntary and involuntary migration greatly affect the prospects of female immigrants, especially in the early stages of settlement. Given their subordinate status in most societies, women immigrants who accompany family members abroad do not often share equally in making decisions about when and where to emigrate.[18] Women may also be less prepared to leave behind the networks of social support they have always counted on for the emotional and social challenges of a new environment. Male and female immigrants must deal with the immediate demands of survival in a new environment. But often, male immigrants are better equipped when it comes to settling down as newcomers. Canadian immigration selects candidates from three major groups: an independent class, of professionals and financial investors; the family class, applications by a parent on behalf of an entire nuclear family and its immediate dependants; and the class of refugees and political asylum seekers, considered on the basis of UN international criteria for qualification. The majority of African female immigrants come into Canada as part of the family class—on the strength of their husbands' status. These women's chances of building a new life in Canada, especially at the early stages of settlement, are largely tied to the quality of their relationship with their husbands.

In general, male and female immigrants to Canada must deal with widespread racism, social isolation in various forms (appearance, language, associations, etc.), and economic insecurity even as they struggle to stabilize changes in the relations of gender within and outside the domestic sphere. Further, they must go on to establish the relevant social, economic, and political niches to anchor themselves as new members in a larger social arrangement. The settlement process requires that African immigrants must re-create their culture, formulate new patterns of social interaction, and seek out aggressive strategies to establish economic autonomy.[19] Often, many African immigrants, especially those from West Africa, arrive on Western shores with little if any experience of racism and how it defines their social worth in the new culture in which they find themselves. Not only are they forced to confront the many faces of racism on a daily basis, but they also find themselves struggling to properly situate their children for the struggle ahead. Whether they work outside the home or not, these women are usually the caregivers and home keepers. Hence, they are likely to shoulder these challenges more than their male counterparts are. Female immigrants are also more prepared than their husbands to take on any job in order to keep the family afloat. In any case, the typical menial jobs that are easily available are stereotypically classified as being women's work. Female immigrants are therefore more likely to find employment (often in menial jobs) than their male counterparts are. In some cases, such new developments call for a renegotiation of gender roles, as well as household and familial responsibilities. However, the configuration of gender relations would certainly differ given the commonalities, as well as the significant features, that define each social context.[20]

Although the study drew its sample from African and Caribbean female groups, the analysis here focuses exclusively on the experiences of African women, the subjects of a subsequent study.[21]

BEING BLACK AND AFRICAN
IN CANADA: STATISTICAL REPRESENTATIONS[22]

Canada is a nation of immigrants. However, the racial gulf between whites and nonwhites, which continues to mediate the life chances of social groups, can be traced to two major historical factors: the international configuration of power forged by imperialism, slavery, and colonization; and Canada's colonial ties to Britain.[23] These factors have helped to nurture discriminatory policies that favored Canadians of Anglo-Saxon background. This means that those outside the group must find "ways to weave their history, identity and aspirations into the fabric of the Anglo Saxon mainstream."[24]

There are three major demographic categories: mainstream whites, natives, and visible minorities.[25] According to the 1996 national census, visible minorities constitute 11 percent of Canada's population (3.2 million), recording a 6 percent increase since 1986.[26] The terms *visible minority* (in simple terms, a nonwhite Canadian) and an *immigrant* (a Canadian by immigration) are clearly defined in Canadian official statistics. However, in social terms, they blur. For instance, blacks constitute one of the groups in Canada who are usually treated as immigrants simply because they are visible, regardless of whether they are born in Canada or not. Black Canadians trace their history to the arrival of enslaved settlers, mainly from the United States in the 1600s. Subsequent immigration waves included loyalists to the British throne who were offered settlement after the 1776 revolution, black veterans of the 1812 war, and the streams of fugitives from slavery before the consolidation of international efforts toward abolition. By the turn of the twentieth century, black immigration to Canada began to attract a more diversified group of settlers from the Caribbean and Africa.[27] Although each group of black immigrants confronted racism in its subtle and overt forms, their experiences reflected the diversity of their histories and social backgrounds. Moreover, changes in Canada's fundamentally racist immigration policies mediated the trend and nature of black immigration, increasingly reflecting in the twentieth century the actions of individuals and groups in search of better economic opportunities abroad.[28] Sunera Thobani points out in her critical review of Canada's immigration act that the current arrangement justifies overt forms of discrimination "through the unequal allocation of resources for immigrant recruitment and processing which favored 'developed' countries with large white populations, and . . . through allowing immigration officers discretionary powers which allowed their subjective prejudices to influence their allocation of points and the processing of immigrants."[29] African immigrants typify this trend. The experiences of those interviewed for the study, the challenges they faced in obtaining Canadian immigration papers, and their struggle to settle down in their new communities underscore Thobani's point. The analysis of female immigrants' lives in Canada certainly lend credence to her assertion that the act "accomplished more than simply allowing the racist and sexist biases of immigration officers to be exercised. It organized the racialization of the nation and of immigrants, as well as the gendering of immigration."[30]

Although they differ in many ways, the experiences of immigrant Canadian blacks are often subsumed within those of native black settlers in both Canada and the United States. Given the stereotypes of native experience often transported from the United States and marketed in Canada, immigrants from the Caribbean (70 percent) and Africa (15 percent), who constitute the majority of Canada's black population of a half million, assert distinctive identities. With respect to the total national population, black women (52 percent) outnumber black men (48 percent), the gender imbalance increasing as the population ages.[31] The influx of Caribbean female immigrants since the onset of the Canadian program for foreign live-in domestics in 1955 significantly boosted the increase in the black female population.[32]

The few existing studies on Canadian blacks dispel many prevailing stereotypes, which greatly tarnish their image as a social group. For instance, blacks represent one of the most educated groups in Canada. Within the group, however, men fare better than women, especially at the tertiary education levels.[33] Further, contrary to the accepted stereotypes of black employment patterns, Canadian blacks record fairly high employment levels despite the multiple forms of inequalities they encounter in the labor market. Evidently, black Canadians, regardless of their historical roots, struggle with employment instabilities and underemployment in a labor market segregated along racial, gender, and ethnic lines. Black women in particular often find themselves at the bottom rungs of paid work when compared to other female immigrants. Decades of feminist activism have resulted in significant legal dictates in women's favor, but white women in the mainstream appear to have reaped most of the accruing benefits. The employment records of immigrant blacks in Canada point to their resilience in countering the levels of social barriers erected against them.

BLACK WOMEN IN ALBERTA

Most recent data place Alberta's black population at 24,915. Albertan blacks are mostly immigrants.[33] The majority reside in the two most popular metropolises: Edmonton, the provincial capital, and Calgary, its commercial base. Similar to the national and provincial patterns, Caribbeans (6,620) and Africans (4,280) constitute the majority within the black population in Edmonton.[34] The study focused primarily on black Edmontonian women's economic autonomy as a crucial base for attacking other facets of social equality. The sample was made up of approximately two hundred women within the age range of eighteen to fifty-five years, with Caribbean (45 percent) and African (38 percent) representing the major groups. Questionnaires and focus group discussions within the community were the main sources of data collection for the study.

The study identified the following factors as the major barriers to black women's economic autonomy in Alberta. Foremost among these barriers is black women's inadequate access to facilities for orientation to life in a new environment as well the lack of social support, especially for families with young children of preschool age. African women, most of whom came under the family class, were forced to either stay at home with children or manage child care and paid work under difficult conditions (e.g., night shifts, irregular hours, and lack of leisure time). Moreover, women in the sample make the point that their educational attainments, previous work experience, and employment history (especially outside Canada) are not often recognized by employers. Usually, those without "Canadian training" face the difficult challenge of updating their qualifications. But this is not the end of the struggle. The racist connotations around "Canadian experience" mean that even those who trained in Canada (53 percent of the sample) have a hard time finding decent employment. Often, black women are forced to accept available opportunities and gradually seek out better alternatives. Most of the women interviewed are either underemployed or poorly remunerated in seemingly high positions as compared to their Canadian counterparts. About 34 percent of the participants in the study earned monthly incomes under $1,500 and a little over 70 percent have incomes below $30,000. Often, female preserves such as teaching, nursing, social work, and child care, with consistent labor shortages, provide a step-in ladder for these women.

In many ways and at various levels these women encounter barriers in their struggle to establish economic autonomy in Canada. But what is even more interesting is their resilience in confronting these barriers. African women's resourcefulness in fighting this battle and the lengths to which they have taken it, in particular, have spurred many female scholars in the field to challenge the negligence of gender in the analyses of racism and global restructuring.

AFRICAN WOMEN IN CANADA: THE ALBERTA EXPERIENCE

Beyond the commonalities shared with their Caribbean sisters, African women, who constitute 38 percent of the sample, reveal in their experiences yet a different struggle against racism and other forms of social inequality that has resulted in the gradual establishment of networks of female activism that extend beyond Canadian borders.

For the most part, these women have made considerable economic strides despite the initial barriers they faced as family-class immigrants accompanying husbands who came into Canada either as students or, more increasingly, as professionals granted permanent residence. Except in the case of those who came to Canada as refugees, the decision to emigrate, the women explain, was largely arrived at by the male "head of household." Although only a few of the women came to Canada on their own, a good number within the sample are highly trained professionals in their fields. In their struggle to establish economic autonomy as individuals and family units, not only do these women display incredible resistance to forces that attempt to racialize their lives into existing stereotypes of black experience, but they also deploy effective strategies for pursuing their goals in the short and long terms.

Foremost, many of the focus-group participants emphasize a strong resolve to stay away from any form of social assistance ("welfare"), as it denigrates in their view the social standing and economic status they held in their home countries. Even refugees who initially depended on social support for their immediate basic needs were often anxious to break away from what they view as a potential vicious circle. Although the exigencies of immediate survival led to some shifts in gender roles, women are expected to carry the major burden of domestic responsibilities, as men struggle to establish their status as the primary breadwinners. But as mentioned earlier, women are more likely than men to seek out available (often menial) jobs to ensure the family's economic survival in the early stages of arrival. Hence, many of the African women in the study have worked or are still employed as day care attendants, home care givers, and cleaners; those with younger children settle for nights shifts, leaving the children with their husbands. However, a good number of the women have moved on to better jobs (many with Canadian training), even though the majority within this group still consider themselves underemployed and/or poorly remunerated. Except for a few women who have established (formally or informally) their own small home-based businesses (e.g., selling African food items and running day homes), the majority of the women pursue opportunities in paid work. Regardless of their economic status, African women in the study, including those who came in as refugees, struggle to assert their preference despite the challenges they face in the settlement process. They exhibit a strong resolve to survive on their own efforts, rather than surrender to the social net, in order to shape their life chances in Canada as individuals and family units.

Further, the women consider their flexibility to career change an effective strategy for accessing the limited labor market opportunities available to them. For instance, those who earn annual incomes of about $40,000 and above have had to change careers virtually in midlife, moving, for instance, into professions in social work, where labor shortages often guarantee them at least entry-level or part-time positions. A few women in the study work or volunteer with nongovernmental agencies. Previously, Asian and Latin American women were favorably represented in social agencies that catered to immigrants. These establishments are gradually attracting African women. In Edmonton, such centers include the Edmonton Immigrant Settlement Association, Changing Together: Center for Immigrant Women, Catholic Social Services, and the Mennonite Center. African women's rising profile as employees, volunteers, and clients is gradually providing a base for the coordination of support services in their local communities.

Moreover, African women in the study also place a high premium on their children's education. Despite the limitations that paid work has placed on leisure time, these women (and male spouses, especially professionals who can afford to take time off work) go to great lengths to monitor their children's progress at school (e.g., assistance with homework, meetings with teachers, private learning resources at home). Education is considered the most important asset for social mobility, especially for immigrant children, and African women are taking important steps to ensure that their children excel in school. Those interviewed stress the fact that they want their children to start life as adults in Canada on a much higher socioeconomic platform than to that of their parents. In addition, these children have more recent social ties to Africa and, unlike native black children, have inherited an African cultural heritage. The immigrants includes a large network of successful extended-family members within independent African countries where blacks excel as individuals in their own rights. This heritage is very much alive not only in terms of the outstanding professional role models (including many parents) children can look up to but also through community social interaction that promotes specific African cultures, languages, and traditions.

Most important, African women in the study, along with other female members of the community, are gradually building formal and informal social networks of support within the community. At the informal level, word of mouth as well as social gatherings at the family and organizational levels (e.g., country, ethnic, and religious associations) serve as important forums for welcoming new immigrants and disseminating crucial information about housing, job opportunities and affordable (private and public) child care arrangements. At the formal level, women's associations of specific countries have also established outreach programs with support networks revolving around the concerns of new or stay-at-home mothers and new immigrants. Forums are also organized to raise awareness about women's active roles in the community's welfare and to mobilize women to participate.

It is interesting to note that African women's social activism, as revealed in this study and subsequent follow-ups, is transmigratory in nature. The efforts of African women to establish themselves in Edmonton represent, to some extent, part of a growing national and international effort. The National Association of Eritrean Women in Canada (with branches across the provinces, including Alberta) blazes the trend along this line. The association has not only developed well-established networks of support programs for women's concerns in specific communities across Canada but has also mobilized female members into extending support to women back home. For instance, the association provides funding for day care programs and income-generating activities in Eriteria. It has also played a crucial role in expanding women's political participation and representation in government. While the social acceptance of women's presence in the public sphere has yet to catch up with the progress women have made so far, association members have gained considerable support from their men in Canada, who strongly back their effort at civic education, ensuring that immigrant Eritrean women exercise their voting rights for elections back home. As noted, African women's rising profile in social agencies has had a salutary effect on these efforts in Alberta.[35]

African women immigrants have also had to shed those vestiges of social divisions from Africa that might constitute additional barriers to their progress in Canada. As the experiences of the participants in the study convey, African women have to rally around one another as individuals and groups in order to establish crucial support bases, regardless of the ethnic, national, class, and religious divisions. Back in Africa, these divisions have created social inequalities that keep groups of women apart. They continue to pose a serious barrier that militates against women's social mobilization at the grassroots and national levels. But it seems that the common barriers that African women face in Canada have become a basis for uniting them in a struggle for their survival as a racialized group.

Moreover, it appears that despite the burden of domestic responsibilities that African female immigrants carry, there has been a significant shift in the overall structure of gender relations to accommodate women's social activism in Canada. The prevailing gender ideology in Africa has posed a strong barrier against women's participation in formal politics and representation in government. Historically, women entered the elite colonial and postcolonial circles of most African countries as wives to civil servants and the male ruling class.[36] Although African women are gradually emerging from this subordinate status, their access to the spheres of power and influence is still significantly tied to their relationships with men in the military and political classes.[37] Often, the state-reinforced gender ideology is based on women's social roles rather than on their status as full-fledged citizens and equal partners with men in nation building.[38] It seems that the exigencies of life in Canada for African men and women alike have weakened to some extent the gender ideology in which they were raised.

On the whole, African women in Alberta and in Canada are exploiting their multiple identities in confronting local barriers and the global forces that mediate their living conditions. At various levels and in different social contexts, they identify themselves as women, black women, black Canadian women, Christian or Muslim women, African Canadian women, and women from specific African countries (Nigeria, Togo, Eritrea, etc.) and of different ethnic groups within them. The fluidity of their identities, though a key feature in their racialization in Canada and globally, is being effectively harnessed to confront the barriers they face within and outside the domestic sphere as wives, mothers, paid workers, and social activists for their local communities and the African continent. These multiple identities have become a crucial weapon in the development of a strong support base as Canadians and transmigrants who are hardly immune to the challenges of global restructuring.

NOTES

1. In November 1963, the UN General Assembly adopted the declaration on the elimination of all forms of racial discrimination. In December 1965 the General Assembly adopted the UN International Convention on the Elimination of All Forms of Racial Discrimination. Subsequently, 1971 was declared the international year for ac-

tion to combat racism and racial discrimination. The UN brought the first and second decades (1973–1982, 1983–1992) of the global struggle against racism to a close with international conferences held in Geneva. WCAR marks the third decade of UN involvement in the struggle.

2. This vacuum is clearly demonstrated in the parallel forums and discourses maintained by African and black studies, especially in the United States. Until the past decade, which ushered in social movements and intellectual forums toward the reparation to blacks for slavery, the former focused largely on social issues within Africa while the latter concentrated on the experiences of native blacks. The Pan-African movement that united blacks across continents did not make any appreciable headway until its recent resurgence in the 1990s, with a united forum around issues of reparation for slavery. For instance, see A. Ajayi and M. Vogt, eds., *Proceedings on the First Pan-African Conference on Reparations* (Addis Ababa, Ethiopia: Research and Documentation Committee of the Organization for African Unity Group of Eminent Persons for Reparation, 1993). Such efforts have spurred a new era for discourses in African studies that link Africa's future with that of its descendants in diaspora.

3. In Canada, for instance, the province of Nova Scotia has a huge native black settlement dating as far back as the 1600s, while Alberta has a largely immigrant black population. See J. Torczyner, *Diversity, Mobility and Change: The Dynamics of Black Communities in Canada* (Montreal, Quebec: McGill Consortium for Ethnicity and Strategic Social Planning, 1997). As the background data used for the recently concluded study of black women in Edmonton show, immigrants constitute the majority of Canada's black population.

4. For analyses of the brain drain resulting from this migratory trend and its impact on African studies in Africa and the United States, see T. Mkandawire, "Problems and Prospects of Social Sciences in Africa," *International Sciences Journal* 135 (1993): 130–40; Jane Guyer, *African Studies in the United States: A Perspective* (Atlanta, Ga.: African Studies Association Press, 1996).

5. T. Mkandawire, "The Social Sciences in Africa: Breaking Local Barriers and Negotiating International Presence; The Bashorun M. K. O. Abiola Distinguished Lecture Presented at the 1996 African Studies Association Annual Meeting," *African Studies Review* 40, no. 2 (1997): 15–36. Guyer, *African Studies.*

6. Afua Cooper, "Constructing Black Women's Historical Knowledge," *Atlantis* 25, no. 1 (2000): 39–50.

7. D. L. Spitzer, "Women, Migration and Immigration Policy in Canada," paper presented during International Week 2001, University of Alberta, Edmonton.

8. For instance, over the past few years the proceedings of the annual meetings of the American African Studies Association have reflected an increasing attention to international migration and new Africans in diaspora. The Canadian counterpart has not demonstrated a comparable level of concern.

9. The study titled "Black Women and Economic Autonomy in Alberta: Barriers to Accessing Equal Opportunities" was carried out by the Black Women Working Group: Dr. Philomina E. Okeke (principal researcher), assistant professor, Women's Studies Program, University of Alberta; Dr. Christina D. Nsaliwa, executive director, Edmonton Immigrant Services Association; Mary Ebinu, head of department, Grande Prairie

Composite High School; Jenny R. Kelly, doctoral candidate, Department of Educational Policy Studies, University of Alberta; Dr. Adenike Yesufu, project coordinator, Young Women's Christian Association; and Dr. Malinda Smith, assistant professor, political science, Center for Legal Studies, Athabasca University. The research began in early 1999 and was completed in December 2000. The study was funded by the Status of Women, Canada.

10. A. Banderage, "Women in Development: Liberalism, Marxism and Marxist Feminism," *Development and Change* 15 (1984): 495–515. S. Stichter and J. Parpart, eds., *Women, Employment and the Family in the International Division of Labor* (London: MacMillan, 1990).

11. M. Mies, *Patriarchy and Accumulation on a World Scale: Women and the International Division of Labor* (London: Zed, 1986). E. Rathgeber, "WID, WAD, GAD: Trends in Research and Practice," *Journal of Developing Areas* 24 (July 1990): 489–502.

12. Oyeronke Oyewumi, *The Invention of Women: Making an African Sense of Western Gender Discourses* (Minneapolis: University of Minnesota, 1997). Ifi Amadiume, *Male Daughters and Female Husbands: Gender and Class in an African Society* (London: Zed Books, 1987).

13. D. Smith, *The Everyday World as Problematic* (Boston: Northeastern University, 1987).

14. A. Appadurai, "Global Ethnoscapes: Notes and Queries for a Transnational Anthropology," In *Recapturing Anthropology*, ed. R. Fox (Santa Fe, N.M.: School of American Research Press, 1991), 191–210. N. Glick Schiller, L. Basch, and C. Blanc-Szanton, "Transnationalism: A New Analytic Framework for Understanding Migration," in *Towards a Transnational Perspective on Migration: Race, Class, Ethnicity, and Nationalism Reconsidered*, ed. N. Glick Schiller, L. Basch and C. Blanc-Szanton (New York: New York Academy of Sciences, 1992), 1–24. L. Malkki, "National Geographic: The Rooting of Peoples and Territorialization of National Identity among Scholars and Refugees," in *Culture, Power, and Place: Explorations in Critical Anthropology*, ed. A. Gupta and J. Ferguson (Durham, N.C.: Duke University Press, 1997), 52–74.

15. Glick Schiller, Basch, and Blanc-Szanton, "Transnationalism."

16. S. Razack, "Your Place or Mine? Transnational Feminist Collaboration," in *Antiracist Feminism*, ed. A. Calliste and G. Safa Dei (Halifax, N.S., Canada: Fernwood, 2000), 39–53.

17. Nakanyike B. Musisi, "Catalyst, Nature, and Vitality of African-Canadian Feminism: A Panorama of an Émigré Feminist," in *Emigré Feminism: Transnational Perspectives*, ed. Alena Heitlinger (Toronto: University of Toronto Press, 1999), 131–48, 138.

18. Spitzer, "Women, Migration and Immigration Policy."

19. Dr. Denis Spitzer and I are completing a three-year province-wide research project (2002–2005) titled "In Search of Identity, Longing for Homeland: African Women in Alberta." The project is funded by Social Science and Humanities Research Council of Ottawa, Ontario.

20. Okeke and Spitzer, "In Search of Identity."

21. Spitzer, "Women, Migration and Immigration Policy."

22. The statistical information used in this section is taken from the study.

23. Malinda Smith, "Quilting Canada's Race Policy," *Africa Link* 6, no. 4 (1998): 12, 29–30.

24. "Black Women and Economic Autonomy," 5.

25. The term *visible minorities* gave official recognition to nonwhites, a social group defined by visible characteristics (especially skin color) whose well-being calls for some degree of state intervention. This term has become a homogeneous label for a diversity of persons and groups devoid of their struggles against racism. See Linda Carty and Dionne Brand, "'Visible Minority' Women: A Creation of the Canadian State," in *Returning the Gaze: Essays on Racism, Feminism, and Politics*, ed. Bannerji Himani (Toronto: Sister Vision Press, 1993), 207–22.

26. "Black Women and Economic Autonomy," 4.

27. J. Kelly, *Under the Gaze: Learning to be Black in White Society* (Halifax, N.S., Canada: Fernwood, 1998). B. Pachai, *Beneath the Clouds: The Survival of Nova Scotia's Blacks*, vol. 2, *1800–1989* (Halifax, N.S., Canada: Black Educator's Association, 1990).

28. "Black Women and Economic Autonomy," 5.

29. S. Thobani, "Closing the Nation's Doors to Immigrant Women: The Restructuring of Canadian Immigration Policy," *Atlantis* 24, no. 2 (2000): 16–26, 17.

30. Thobani, "Closing the Nations's Doors," 18.

31. Background data from "Black Women and Economic Autonomy," 7.

32. See A. Calliste, "Canada's Immigration Policy and Domestics from the Caribbean: The Second Domestic Scheme," in *Race, Class, Gender: Bonds and Barriers*, ed. Jesse Vorst et. al (Toronto: Garamond, 1991), 136–68; Silvera Makeda, "Speaking of Women's Lives and Imperialist Economics: Two Introductions from Silenced," in *Returning the Gaze: Essays on Racism, Feminism, and Politics*, ed. Himani (Toronto: Sister Vision Press, 1993), 242–69.

33. See J. Torczyner, *Diversity, Mobility, and Change*, background data in the "Black Women and Economic Autonomy," 7.

34. Background data from the "Black Women and Economic Autonomy," 7.

35. Data collected during an interview with one of the officials at the provincial level. Given the association's political involvement in negotiations within the local communities in Canada and those back home, the official prefers to remain anonymous.

36. R. Fatton, "Gender, Class, and the State in Africa," in *Women and the State in Africa*, ed. J. Parpart and K. Staudt (London: Lynne Rienner, 1989), 47–66.

37. Amina Mama, "Feminism or Femocracy? State Feminism and Democratization in Nigeria," in *Africa Development* 20, no. 1 (1995): 37–58. S. Tamale, "When Hens Begin to Crow: Gender and Formal Politics in Contemporary Uganda" (doctoral dissertation, University of Minnesota, 1997). Aili Tripp, "Women's Movements and Challenges to Neopatrimonial Rule: Preliminary Observations from Africa," *Development and Change* 32 (2001): 33–54.

38. P. E. Okeke and Susan Franceschet, "Democratisation and State Feminism: Gender Politics in Africa and Latin America," *Development and Change* 33, no. 3 (2002): 439–46.

10

Weaving Identities: Refugees, Immigrants, and Local People in a European World of Differences

Jan Delacourt

$\mathcal{D}$iscrimination works in myriad ways and assumes many forms: this chapter explores some of the different ways of conceiving and perceiving differences, the ways they interlock, and the consequent effects on access to rights and services. I began in 1998 with an ethnographic study of the lives of women in Ivrea, a town in Northern Italy, observing what differences were salient for them. Life story interviews with local and immigrant women provided depth and subtlety, particularly through the process of reviewing the outcomes of the interviews with small groups of the women themselves. Together, we looked at what seemed obvious, what was ambivalent, and what seemed contradictory, working from the root imagery of holistic everyday experiences to tease out the basis of a critical epistemology.

In 1999, the town council invited a small group of refugees from Kosovo to settle in the area. The refugees were supported by an organized group of local volunteers and others, who assisted various parts of the settling process. Similar groups of refugees went to other places in Northern Italy, but "our" system of integration and support was deemed more successful by the local people. The term *integration* was once used to mean "to complete what is imperfect by the addition of the necessary parts" (*Shorter Oxford English Dictionary* 1968). Pragmatically, I use mutual adaptation and a dialogic process to frame what counts as being successful integration, based on observations and interviews with supporters and refugees. Drawing on both studies, I highlight some of the processes of working with differences that reflect the positive nature of confrontations among people, belief systems, and ways of behaving that support growth and integration.

Three modes of perceiving difference weave their way through the material. The first is a common use of difference that divides, usually so that one part rules over the other or others. Binary divisions have been a basic tenet of modernism. The International Convention on the Elimination of All Forms of Racial Discrimination (1965) lists race, color, descent, and national or ethnic origin as the grounds used to divide and oppress. Add to these gender, sexual orientation, physical ability, social class, and even so-called culture, which can operate in anthropological discourse to enforce separations, and all these divisions can carry a sense of hierarchy (Abu-Lughod 1991, 137).

A pragmatic approach to these multiple divisions in the world at large is to build into practice (in politics, law, economics, social policies) a series of checks and balances. For example, in the European Union, different principles underlie the directly elected European Parliament, where the number of seats per country depends on the size of the electorate; and the Council of Ministers, where each country sends its government's minister, regardless of the size of the country. The presidency of the council rotates so that each country has six months in which to set the agenda. The United Nations, consisting of representatives of national governments, has parallel ways of working with nongovernmental organizations (NGOs)and with cross-national groups such as indigenous peoples and migrants.

A third approach moves away from the previous ones and inquires how each of us, individually or in a group, lives our own difference. Carla Lonzi, an Italian feminist, writes,

> Difference is an existential principle which concerns the modes of being human, the peculiarity of one's own experiences, goals, possibilities, and one's sense of existence in a given situation and in situations one creates for oneself. . . . Equality is what is offered as legal rights to colonized people. And what is imposed on them as culture. (quoted in Kemp and Bono 1991, 41)

THE DIFFERENCES THAT DIVIDE

I start from the assumption that racism preceded "races": the "master race" was created to make logical and natural its domination over the rest. In this way, slavery and indentured labor systems were created and sustained in colonies for the enrichment of the colonizers. Growing up in Rhodesia, Southern Africa, in the 1950s, I learned that race was marked by skin color and hair type but named as some kind of ethnic origin: Africans were distinguished from Europeans. My Australian parents found "our" label problematic, being proud of their long history of separation from Europe! Race determined all aspects of life: place of abode, access to health care and education, and employment and levels of pay in a system that was as unjust as apartheid.

Only we called it "separate development." This masking of systems of privilege—making them so bland as to be invisible to the perpetrators, rendering inaudible and indeed out of order voices of protest from the oppressed—is an important feature of racism. This "norm against noticing" highlights the problem that "racism is widely discredited as a heinous offense perpetrated 'somewhere else but not in our country' or 'in our home'" (Harrison 2000). The NGO Forum Declaration, the document agreed upon by the nongovernmental organizations present at the United Nations World Conference against Racism (2001), stresses this point in its opening sentence: "The declaration and program of action is based on the understanding that . . . the voices of the victims of racism, racial discrimination xenophobia and related intolerance must be heard."

I asked the women in the first study just one question: What kinds of difference have had an impact on you and your lives? The immigrant women had greater experience to draw on for cultural and social differences, though all mentioned changes of culture: school, work, even moving from village to town or town center to periphery. The experience of being forced to reflect about oneself in new circumstances is universal; so are the experiences of meeting blocks to one's hopes and ambitions. Noella loved languages and longed to travel: she chose to do the three-year course to become a waitress, only to find that females would never be given the work she wanted on cruise ships. Grazia gave up her teaching career to help her husband in his business. Dina insisted that class was the deciding factor that kept her poor; after the end of the war, the only work available was agricultural labor, hard and poorly paid. Dina told me that when her daughter of twenty-one wanted to marry a man ten years older, "I cried all the tears I had. I told her: get yourself a life, there will always be someone to marry!" Her older daughter had been fortunate: uninterested in teaching or accountancy, the two areas most open to women, she was selected for the first course in physiotherapy in the area in the 1970s.

In Italy, after unification in 1861, the ruling Piedmontese found that the Southerners were rebellious. Then some Italian emigrants to other parts of Europe and America began earning a criminal label for all Italians. Great pains were taken to distinguish between Northern and Southern Italians. The latter were portrayed as being dark, short, and with characters prejudged as those who were criminal, unintelligent, brutish, lazy, and so on (Gribaudi 1996, 75). *African* is a term of abuse for Sicilians and Calabrians. One of the women in my first study is a Ghanaian. She said, "Although I am well-accepted here personally, I know I can never really be an Italian. That was one reason I decided to keep my Ghanaian nationality and passport."

Dominant systems do not read or listen to their critics. By the 1950s, black intellectuals "understood fascism not as an aberration from the march of progress, an unexpected right-wing turn, but a logical development of Western Civilization itself" (Kelly 2000). Aimé Césaire, originally published in 1955, wrote, "It would be worthwhile . . . to reveal to the very distinguished, very humanistic, very Christian bourgeois of the twentieth century that . . . what he cannot forgive Hitler is not the crime . . . against man, it is the crime against the *white* man, the humiliation of the *white* man, and the fact that he applied to Europe colonialist practices which until then had been reserved exclusively for the Arabs of Algeria, the 'coolies' of India and the 'niggers' of Africa" (2000, 36).

Fascist rule in Italy forbade internal migration; it also rewarded mothers of large families for their "true work." These values continued to have effects even on the lives of women born after fascism. Those who were children during World War II remembered the fear of all soldiers, how their young aunts would be hidden away for protection, and how the period of the civil war involved personal feuding and killing as well as political battles. Their accounts were echoed in the horrors of the Kosovo refugees. Those born later suffered from lack of educational and career opportunities for women; those who moved to pursue their aims were viewed with suspicion. Susanna's mother was told, "Your little daughter has discovered America here, hasn't she?"

Xenophobia is a term widely used in Europe for these divisive differences that are not necessarily physically marked but that are just as powerful in deciding political, economic, and social status. Ernest Gellner defines the problem thus:

> Cultural difference and social boundaries have existed at most times and in most places: quite often, there was tension and hostility at those boundaries. This is xenophobia, hostility to the Other. . . . By linking dislike of the Other to citizenship rights, nationalism turns xenophobia from what may, in favorable circumstances, be a mere human foible, into a destructive, dangerous force. (1995, 7)

In Italy, a person has rights also as a resident in a *comune* (local council) and province. These include access to education, health services, and employment placements. When the Kosovo refugees arrived, one of the mayors caused a stir because he gave "his" refugees residency rights, while other mayors were more cautious because humanitarian aid was not a category yet in their printed documentation. This sense of caution is deeply embedded in Italian bureaucracy: a common excuse for inaction is "Non è nella mia competenza," roughly equivalent to the English "It's not part of my job."

Nationalism in Europe has a long, destructive history of war and displacement of people. Hannah Arendt raises the particular problem for those who found themselves part of no nation:

Civil wars . . . spread over the twenty years of uneasy peace were not only bloodier and more cruel than all their predecessors; they were followed by migrations of groups who, unlike their happier predecessors in the religious wars, were welcomed nowhere and could be assimilated nowhere. Once they had left their homeland they remained homeless, once they had left their state they became stateless; once they had been deprived of their human rights they were rightless, the scum of the earth. (1973, 267)

Internal displacement because of war still had an effect on Grazia, a local woman, born in the area but whose grandparents had been moved from the Veneto during the First World War to make space for the Italian defense against the invading Austrians. "I'm not really Piedmontese, I was brought up with the values of the Veneto," she said. Opinions on the time it took for an immigrant family to feel part of the new place ranged from three to four generations.

Scott Pegg raises another issue about nation creation:

If one takes 1960 as a convenient shorthand date for an ending of the vast majority of the decolonization processes, then it can be argued that the three decades which followed that year were characterized by the greatest level of territorial stability ever seen in the history of international relations. . . . Once acquired, sovereign statehood has become almost impossible to lose. (2000, 90)

The corollary, of course, is that for minority groups within nations, it is almost impossible to create a new state. This was clearly visible in the struggles of Kosovo, which had a de facto status as a republic under the 1974 Yugoslav constitution but was stripped of its autonomous powers by proposals first made by Slobodan Milosevic, president of Serbia, in 1988. Kosovo had approximately two million ethnic Albanians, loosely Muslim in their religious faith, and a Serbian minority of two hundred thousand; it also had important mineral and natural resources. In the late 1980s and early 1990s, six hundred thousand mostly young Kosovo Albanians emigrated to Western Europe and began the support of the shadow republic of Kosovo with a voluntary 3 percent tax.

Wars between and within nations were and are often struggles around the presumed equivalence of people, nation, state, and territory. According to Andreas Wimmer,

The nation became an imagined community of solidarity with clear territorial boundaries which held political, social and economic rights as collective goods. . . . The ethnicization of bureaucracy and bureaucratic practices had the combined effect of state, culture and territory seeming to belong to members of the nation. . . . The state in this sense is owned by the people who have been united into a nation. (1997, 29)

The legacy remains in discrimination against immigrants, as Wimmer explains. Given the evidence of very different abilities to absorb other cultures in various immigration contexts, "discursive constructions of 'otherness' and the related perception of differentness and menace are linked rather with political vested interest than with objective cultural differences" (25). The NGO Forum Declaration recognizes this in points 15 and 16. Popular versions of nationalism assign European nations, and indeed Italian regions, to a hierarchy of acceptability and prestige. This well-known, although shifting, hierarchy is based roughly on geopolitical and economic grounds: Northern Italy being better than Southern Italy, its wealth often based on long-established industries and/or colonial exploitation and a vaguer cultural basis related to levels of education and a history of production in the arts and music.

For the perpetrators of oppression, all these systems serve to maintain their power and privilege. The oppressed are silenced, even taught that this is the "natural way things are." The struggle for gender equality took a long time to become a mass movement: Mary Woolstonecraft published her *Vindication of the Rights of Women* in 1789, but the suffragette movement for votes for women in Australia and the United Kingdom did not gain sway until more than a century later. Women in Italy were given the vote only after the defeat of fascism and the establishment of the republic in 1945. Much of second-wave feminism's struggle against patriarchy and sexism was in the form of a claim to equality with men, particularly in the United States, Britain, and France. The issue of gender and its social construction runs throughout the following sections, within power struggles at the national and the European level, between locals and immigrants, within families and indeed within individuals.

CHECKS AND BALANCES: EUROPEAN IDENTITIES

Rosi Braidotti highlights how the project of a European Union identity raises "potentially explosive issues of entitlement and diversity" because of "the history of European nationalism and of intolerance towards the very cultural differences that compose the European region" (2001, 4). The very beginnings of the European Union lay in the foundation of the European Steel and Coal Commission, which unified the production of iron and steel so that "the solidarity in production will make it plain that any war between France and Germany becomes not merely unthinkable but materially impossible" (Holmes 2000, 26). It is perhaps ironic that an institution that began with the desire to stop wars between its members has taken such a long time to debate issues of culture and education and the thorny issue of the identity of a European. Cris Shore points out that "as if by default, an 'official' definition of European is being constructed. It can be seen emerging at the borders and boundaries of the new Europe, particularly in the spheres of immigration control and external customs barriers" (1993, 786). A glaring example of how belonging to one "club" can make one forgetful of other older memberships occurred when France had presidency of the Council of Ministers. Its strong emphasis on the prevention of unauthorized entry of immigrants caused serious concern to many NGOs and to the United Nations High Commission for Refugees as it "did not attempt to reconcile the proposed measures . . . with States' existing international legal obligations towards refugees and asylum seekers" (UNHCR 2000). Another ambiguity was apparent when in February 2000, the European Union swiftly deplored the rise to power of Jorg Haider and his far-right Freedom Party in Austria, elected on an anti-immigration platform. However, at the same time, the European Union negotiated with seventy-one poor countries to accept "draconian new immigration rules in exchange for renewing an aid and trade package" (Denny 2000).

The power to decide identity and subsequent entitlement rests also within bodies set up to assist processes of asylum seeking. In 1998 a group of Romanian Roma refugees arrived in Turin, fleeing persecution in Romania. They lived without support until, with some local activists and politicians, they began the process of applying for leave in order to apply for asylum status. After they were granted the leave to apply, the Red Cross provided them with tents. When their application to apply for asylum was turned down on the grounds that these individuals had not been persecuted, the tents were taken away.

Migrants of any kind—whether they are economic migrants, exiles, emigrés, refugees, or asylum seekers—understand soon enough that nothing can be taken for granted in their new location. Italians understood the process very well as emigrants establishing many clubs, associations, and even consulates in centers of settlement (between 1876 and 1976, nearly twenty-six million Italians left Italy, a number equal to half the current population). Facts of this nature are often used to preface any writings about immigration into Italy: the process of receiving migrants has clearly sparked a need to understand more of who and what this nation now is. However, as the tide of emigration ebbed, immigrant numbers included returning Italians but also those called *extracomuitari*, or those from outside the European Economic Community, the name for the European Union in the 1980s. Technically, extracomunitari includes Swiss, Americans, and Australians, but it is generally used as a marker of color and/or criminality, certainly for those low on the hierarchy of nations. The term has recently been enshrined in immigration law, and all foreigners, including Europeans who are non–European Union, and requesting or renewing permits to stay in Italy, are now fingerprinted.

Internal migration after Mussolini became a significant source of labor for industrialization, mostly from the South, impoverished by systems of absentee landlords to the North. Internal immigrants to Turin in the 1950s and 1960s faced great hostility from the Turinese and a lack of adequate housing. However, they had work and a regular income: they started off living in garages and overcrowded hostels, but many ended up in houses or apartments they bought or built. The struggle for basic services helped to galvanize collective action. The workers in these factories formed part of the "long hot summer" of social revolution in 1968. Previous poor access to schooling was compensated for by a trade union agreement with the industrialists for 150 hours of education for all workers, first to complete the requirements for compulsory schooling and then for work-related or general education purposes.

It also galvanized action from many existing religiously based charities and from spontaneous groups formed within "civil society." This lack of creative responses to new needs by local, regional, and national government in Italy was balanced by an upsurge of human response, which was rooted in internal migration processes but which continued and was strengthened to meet the needs of immigrants from outside Europe. The case of the refugee group received in Ivrea reveals the importance of a long history of civil action. The town had supported victims of the wars in ex-Yugoslavia in the early 1990s, and loosely linked groups continued to press for local government action and involvement in the international community. The second-stage reception in Ivrea was innovative and well ahead of national government plans.

Another often-mentioned fact about immigrants in Italy is that they tend to be heading for the more industrialized countries, the unspoken assumption being that they will move on. The assumption of the Build the Peace project in Ivrea was that refugees required a place to settle in order to decide the next steps in their project: return, settle, move on. The project arranged housing that would allow extended families to remain together; Italian lessons; and support for dealing with the complicated bureaucracy of local, provincial, and national governmental departments. Only one person was a refugee recognized under the Geneva Convention; the rest were receiving "humanitarian aid," a term that allowed response but without the clear rights and duties for refugees recognized internationally by the convention. The project's aim was "to do as you would be done by," very different from earlier reception centers. These were housed in old schools or emergency parish housing where the shape of the buildings determined living arrangements; men were often separated from women and children.

Access to work and education was crucial for the Kosovo refugees as it was for the internal immigrants in Turin. Then, the strength of the trade union movement after fascism helped to give rise to a women's movement that challenged traditional notions of a woman's role, the general unpaid provider of services. Industrialization brought many more women into the workforce and gave them access to the 150 hours of education. Specific courses for women were created using feminist principles of valuing individual experiences, questioning the roles ascribed to them and denied them, and investigating the oppressive forces that bore down on their lives. The left-wing ferment drew on their organizational skills and commitment to change. For many women, however, the change happened only outside the home: inside, their left-wing companions reverted to right-wing behavior.

Braidotti insists that difference must be dislodged from its disastrous history and made to sever its links with power and domination (2001, 27). It is also important to understand relationships constructed between birthplace and genealogical roots, nationality and citizenship. A letter to the *Guardian Weekly* newspaper in April 2003 signed by five previous heads of European nations urges that culture and education be given an important place within the constitutional treaty currently being drafted. It says, "Europe has new work to do. It must make possible a sense of belonging to Europe while maintaining the ties that link one to the land of one's birth" (Kok et al. 2003). The ambiguity about loyalties seems to lie between national and supranational claims within the European Union—but ignores the millions currently resident in Europe but not in the countries of their birth, which could very well be outside the union. Here again, the norm is assumed that people and territory are one, where the creation of "us" requires a blurring of "our" differentness. But Clara's grandparents came from four different parts of Europe and three religious traditions. How does she select or move among these very different heritages?

DIFFERENCE AS AN EXISTENTIAL PRINCIPLE

Resistance

Frances Angela, a photographer and working-class English woman, has used her work to create another perspective on sites of resistance. Her work is

> a place of resistance, not defined by poverty, deprivation and toil but a history that is acknowledged, that has a determining effect on personal and political identity. This place is neither the old margin nor the co-option of the center but a third space where new subjectivities, new politics and new identities are articulated. My new location has the resources of the center but remains outside to disrupt and resist, continually threatening the center with the contradictions of the margins. (1990, 73)

Those on the margins, those in their hard-fought "third space," remind us of Antonio Gramsci's subaltern, who as Lucia Chiavola Birnbaum recalls, maintains beliefs and a conception of the world and life that are very different from the hegemony of the educated classes (1993, 19). Birnbaum's history of the Italian feminist movement uses the process of creation of self through opposition to others as a way of charting developments. Anna, who tried to establish a self within marriage, finally initiated legal separation from her husband "to have peace to make my own life."

The metaphor of the Other has connotations of dissociation, yet it also holds positive implications when used in the sense of "difference." Using the metaphor of the Other, Italian feminists exhibited solidarity with all women while reserving the personal right to be different and the individual right of conscience (Birnbaum 1986, 184). Having understood what it is like to be treated as the Other, they went to meet the most despised and marginalized women; and from the prostitutes and other outcasts, they learned how living on the margins of a society gives a particular—and sharp—view of its laws, customs, and contradictions. They also saw that there was a danger of "Other-izing" the right-wing, more-traditional, often-religious women and that liberation was not something for individuals but for the whole. So there was a deliberate strategy to find inclusive ways of working with all women to further the rights of self-determination. (Their methods were successful: in this Catholic country, where women were given the vote only in 1945, divorce rights were granted in 1974 and abortion rights in 1978.) Their aim was to provide choices about ways of living. Their principles were inclusion, finding common ground, and respect for the rights of all people to self-determination.

It was fascinating to hear two very different accounts of these times in my first study. Grazia had married, partly to escape a tyrannical father, had given up her teaching to raise a family, and had thought that the 1968 revolution was about flower power in California. Only much later, when she had worked unpaid for a long time in her husband's business, she recalled, "I woke up and said to myself, 'Grazia you are back in a cage, you must have money of your own.'" Anna was very involved in the Italian version of political and industrial unrest of the late 1960s. When I asked her how this had affected her life, she said, rather sternly, "Well, I went to work, I looked after my husband and children, and then in the evenings I went to meetings to work out what needed to be done and then we did it." This included the local versions of national struggles for rights to abortion and divorce, plus local initiatives to assimilate internal immigrants and provide a high school sex-education curriculum. A major difference between Anna and Grazia was class: Anna's family had to make significant sacrifices for her education, and "migrating" into the middle classes, she lost none of her youthful insight into power balances in this society.

Migrants, simply by virtue of having a set of different experiences, raise questions about the host society. Jennifer, the Ghanaian woman, decided to look for work at a time when family finances were in difficulty. The prescribed role of immigrant women is cleaning: she soon had a good and steady income, but she said, "One day I had eleven carpets to clean all alone! I burst into tears, I decided I had to find a real job." She began working in a cooperative that assembles from tiny parts the small parts that go into photocopiers, windscreen wipers, telephones . . . whatever piecework can be bid for and whatever contract can be won. Although the pay was not much better, Jennifer was much happier, part of a community. Asked about racist incidents, she told the following story. A colleague signed that he had completed more work than he actually had. Jennifer said to him, "If you do that, it puts us all in difficulty; we are a co-op and we are all like bosses. There are no bosses to cheat." He replied, "This is the Italian way of doing things," adding that if she was unhappy she could "go back to slavery in Africa." She replied that she was in a good-enough situation in Ghana and only came to Italy because she married an Italian and that where she came from had no relevance to what was right and what was wrong for the co-op. She clearly delivered this message with passion, sitting tall and straight even as she told the story, showing no antagonism to the colleague beyond the defense of the work. He backed down and apologized.

Now, several of the refugees who settled in the area are working in the same cooperative. Jennifer, in her senior position, testifies that they are good workers, quick and accurate. They work hard to earn money for their immediate families and for the rebuilding in and of Kosovo: the habit of sending remittances extends even to families who have no intention of going back themselves. Remittances raise several issues: the need for extra money makes refugees part of a pool of labor willing to take poorly paid work, hence their involvement in the so-called Washington consensus on capitalist restructuring (Grillo 1998, 5). Globalization is made visible as women from several continents who are currently living in Italy bid for and obtain piecework such as assembling parts made in different places to go into office machines sold in the United States. The bidding process keeps down prices and pay, and there is no labor organization to insist on basic workers' rights within or across the cooperatives. This phenomenon also fits the assertion that "immigrants take the work Italians no longer want to do," an ambiguous argument in debates about Italian racism and immigration. It also demonstrates how globalizing forces create new ways of maintaining unequal power relations even within industrialized countries (see NGO Forum Delcaration [World Conference against Racism 2001], points 24 and 26—in particular, point 39, on women; and point 54, on migrants).

Integration

A significant finding of the first study was that for most of the women, there was a story of a figure I called "the midwife to a new consciousness." This person, usually another woman, variously gave time to listen to frustrated ambitions or simply spotted talents and commitments and helped to steer these into achievable goals. The experience was revelatory and sometimes revolutionary: "I found out there was more than one way to get to do what I wanted to do and that I could actually do it!" Clara said, "When I wondered how on earth I would support myself, my friend laughed and reminded me how useful it was to know so many languages. I had never thought of it as a way to live." Having another person accept one's needs, desires, and capabilities made it more possible for one to accept them as being valid and to take action.

Not all the refugee support-group members played the role of midwife; they were mostly older than the refugees and more left-wing politically than most of the native villagers. However, they found ways to spread the contacts, finding local people who, for example, knew the teachers and could ask after the children in school. Events were also staged so that all the refugees and supporters could meet and share food (the refugees, of course, did not all know each other). A broader network of supporters, including some of the refugees, grew from these and other interested persons, curious and also keen to support an integration process that included self-reflection in the light of different patterns of behavior.

Maja Korac (2001) identified similar networking in a different study: looking at settlement processes of refugees from the Balkans in Rome in the early 1990s, she found a "self-reception system" that facilitated their functional integration. There was so little organized provision for refugees that individuals and eventually cross-ethnic networks, including Italians, took the initiative to help one another to find work, housing, and education and to build personal paths to integration. This contrasts with highly organized systems in other places that provided much more in material terms but denied social agency to the refugees. It is crucial that stakeholders have some access to defining the domains of support, even when this creates disorganization and conflict (Hardy 1994, 278). Networks of support were also found to be highly significant in the integration of refugee men from the Horn of Africa. Where state funding was delegated to church groups, the number and breadth of personal contacts were significant not only in ensuring psychological well-being for the young men but in ensuring that they found the jobs and schooling they required (McSpadden 1998).

State funding for charitable works in Italy comes from a tiny percent of annual personal taxation. Called the *otto per mille*, it allows individuals to choose among recognized groups, including religious groups and the government, who then allocate funding to voluntary groups. But becoming and being recognized as a voluntary group has a long history in Ivrea: refugee support started with a local doctor persuading a group of friends, informally and then with some backing from local government, to provide material support for a Bosnian town during the war and free education in Italy for some young people from Bosnia. Following the election to power of a left-wing coalition in Ivrea in 1994, proposals were made and implemented for "solidarity" with groups in Palestine and Colombia. The communist councilor for political and social affairs saw the Kosovo project as a natural step in creating solidarity on the home territory; he worked to create an important support group among the local village mayors who helped to find housing and acted as guarantors for rent in the early stages. The councilor was also proud that the group's system of providing family homes, support, and the means for a normal life was actually much cheaper than running an institution. It also demonstrated how government structures and volunteers from civil society together can create imaginative responses to human needs.

Volunteers supporting the refugees had a support group themselves to understand the issues behind the puzzles they as volunteers faced. Many issues were to do with seeing and trying to accept that there was more than one way of doing things. Child care was an issue: young mothers among the refugees did not expect to stay home and look after their children; they soon found grandmother substitutes so that they could go out and work. Language learning was another: one supporter was disappointed that the group's care in providing transport and child care did not make all the women enthusiastic learners of Italian. And how did all the medical support and contraceptive advice fail for a young mother who arrived with one baby and soon became pregnant again? I heard several versions of the story before it was clear that when she went for a Pap smear, she thought she was being fitted with a contraceptive coil!

One of the immigrant women in the first study identified a significant issue when she said, "I didn't really choose to be in this place; I chose *not* to be where I was." The refugees had all been on long and complicated journeys, some over several years, self-financed. Ivrea was just one more stopping point for some, who accepted the offer of money to return to Kosovo in late 1999. The project of return was not necessarily valued by all the supporters; some were more anxious that the refugees recognize and enjoy the special wealth of support and opportunity on offer in Ivrea, and stay. Indifference seemed like a refusal, almost an affront, but for those Kosovars, Italy was a place of exile; their project was to return, rebuild, and reclaim their lives. However, more than half did stay, adapting to the bureaucratic nightmare that exists normally, let alone for those who belong to a nonexistent category such as humanitarian need.

Marina Bianchi stresses the importance of not asking direct questions of refugees. My original interviews with the refugees and a translator started by asking whether they had specifically chosen to come to Italy. (Only one family had.) Several asked me not to ask what it was like to be a refugee: they had been part of another project that looked at the psychological stress and responses to it. Often they told me anyway, but it was on their initiative. I learned Bianchi's gentle way of accompanying refugees as a viable alternative to formal interviews, and how to move from provider role to enabler role (Bianchi 2001). I became friends with a woman my age, widowed during the war. On one visit, I saw her peering at a TV guide, complaining about poor light and small print. I laughed and handed her my new reading glasses. She was delighted; how could she get some? Being an immigrant, I wasn't sure myself. I went and checked with the optician: yes, sight tests were free, and yes, standard reading glasses were available at low cost. I took her the information, and on my next visit she had her glasses.

LIVING DIFFERENCE TO CREATE COMMUNITY

How are asymmetrical relations of power shifted? From these two small studies, I conclude that a crucial early step involves a sense of personal agency, which may only develop with the support of a "midwife to a new consciousness," who listens and provides alternative choices and strategies and, above all, hope. The "coming to voice," first for self, then for and with others, builds resistance and helps to form alliances, networks, and contacts that may be temporary and shifting but that all demonstrate mutual recognition and support. These alliances encroach across rigid identities, such as "victim," "perpetrator," and "accomplice"; those apparently on different sides begin to ask questions of one another's experiences. The dialogue provides opportunities for providers, or those in comfortable situations, to understand what knowledge these "needy" ones have, often that of the dark side of their own nation. When I asked the supporters what they had learned from their experience, one elderly man who had been a partisan during World War II gripped the arms of his chair and almost exploded with rage before he changed his approach and said, "More patience to deal with this untrustworthy bureaucracy."

Some of the questions that seem important for those of European identity to ask themselves in their exploration of "whiteness" include the following: How has my whiteness limited my life? What areas of knowledge have been accidentally or deliberately closed off to maintain me in this state of sweet ignorance? And how does this simple ignorance lead to the abuse of human rights for other persons? An early step is to listen for and to the voices of those caught in the intersections of many forms of discrimination. Examples of victims refusing their status are coming into evidence: Geneviève Makaping, an anthropologist born in the Cameroon, has written a book called *Traiettori di sguardi: E se gli altri foste voi?* (*Trajectories of Gazes: And What if the Others were*

You?), which is selling well. In the recent amnesty for the employers of un-documented immigrant workers (first proposed for the immigrant women who take care of the elderly or children, then extended to all immigrant work-ers), the political rhetoric required that this not be an amnesty for immigrants but for employers to come out of the black market for labor. It was officially the employer who made the request for regularization and paid three months' worth of back taxes. However, it was soon evident that much of the money was coming from the immigrants' pockets. This grapevine knowledge perhaps strengthened the resolve of both the immigrants and the group of lawyers who have supported them over the years—in one case, when an employer refused to sign the application for regularization for an immigrant worker, he was taken to court and forced to do so.

Although they have existed for many years, these forms of civil society and professional support for those denied their rights now seem to be gather-ing strength and momentum from international events such as the United Na-tions conferences for women, for indigenous peoples, and against racism. Newer groupings, such as the local, national, and international social forums, bring together survivors of many forms of oppression who refuse the victim label and defy current power structures because to buy into such hegemonic thinking is to fall into a trap identified by bell hooks:

> Reading much of the popular contemporary literature on race and racism written by men in this society, I discovered repeated insistence that racism will never end. The bleak future prophesied by these writers stands in sharp con-trast to the more hopeful vision offered in progressive feminist writing on the issues of race and racism. This writing is fundamentally optimistic even as it is courageously and fiercely critical precisely because it emerges from con-crete struggles on the part of diverse groups of women to work together for a common cause forging a politics of solidarity. The positive revolutionary vi-sion in this work is the outcome of a willingness to examine race and racism from a standpoint that considers the interrelatedness of race, class and gender. In counter hegemonic race talk I testify to this writing, bear witness to the reality that many cultures can be remade,... that we can resist race and racism and in the act of resistance recover ourselves and be renewed. (1995, 6–7)

REFERENCES

Abu-Lughod, Lila. 1991. Writing against culture. In *Recapturing anthropology*, ed. R. Fox. Santa Fe, N.M.: School of American Research Press.
Angela, Frances. 1990. Confinement. In *Identity: Community, culture, difference*, ed. J. Rutherford. London: Lawrence and Wishart.

Arendt, Hannah. 1973. *The origins of totalitarianism*. New York: Harcourt Brace Jovanovich.

Bianchi, Marina. 2001. The responsibility of social scientists in the countries of reception: Interviews as potential risk factors—gentle and indirect ways to knowledge. Eurofor Conference, Maratea, Basilicata, Italy, 2001.

Birnbaum, Lucia Chiavola. 1986. *Liberazione delle donne: Feminism in Italy*. Middletown, Conn.: Wesleyan University Press.

———. 1993. *Black Madonnas: Feminism, religion, and politics in Italy*. Boston: Northeastern University Press.

Braidotti, Rosi. 2001. *Gender, identity, and multiculturalism in Europe*. San Domenico di Fiesole, Italy: European University Institute, Florence Robert Schuman Centre for Advanced Studies.

Césaire, Aimé. 2000. *Discourse on colonialism*. New York: Monthly Review Press.

Denny, Charlotte. 2000. EU tightens aid screw. *Guardian*, February 5, www.guardian.co .uk/eurocommission/Story/0,,193418,00.html (accessed March 30, 2005).

Gellner, Ernest. 1995 Nationalism and xenophobia. In *New xenophobia in Europe*, ed. B. Baumgartl and A. Favell. London: Kluwer Law International.

Gribaudi, Gabriella. 1996. Images of the South. In *Italian cultural studies*, ed. D. Forgacs and R. Lumley. Oxford: Oxford University Press.

Grillo, Ralph. 1998. *Immigration, racism, and multiculturalism in Italy*. Brighton, UK: Sussex University Centre for Migration Research.

Hardy, Cynthia. 1994. Underorganized interorganizational domains: The case of refugee systems. *Journal of Applied Behavioral Science* 30 (3): 278–96.

Harrison, Faye V. 2000. Facing racism and the moral responsibility of human rights knowledge. *Annals of the New York Academy of Sciences* 925 (December): 45–69.

Holmes, Douglas. 2000. *Integral Europe: Fast-capitalism, multiculturalism, neofascism*. Princeton, N.J.: Princeton University Press.

hooks, bell. 1995. *Killing rage: Ending racism*. London: Penguin.

Kelly, Robin. 2000. A poetics of anti-colonialism. In *Discourse on colonialism*. New York: Monthly Review Press.

Kemp, Sandra, and Paola Bono. 1991. *Italian feminist thought: A reader*. Oxford: Basil Blackwell.

Kok, Wim, Garret FitzGerald, Jacques Delors, Ingvar Carlsson, and Richard von Weiszacker. 2003. Rebuilding European identity. *Guardian Weekly*, April 17–23, 2003, 15.

Korac, Maja. 2001. Cross-ethnic networks: Self-reception system, and functional integration of refugees from the former Yugoslavia in Rome. *Journal of International Migration and Integration* 2 (1):1–26.

McSpadden, Lucia Ann. 1998. "I must have my rights!" The presence of state power in the resettlement of Ethiopian and Eritrean refugees. In *Power, ethics and human rights: Anthropological studies of refugee research and action*, ed. R. Krulfeld and Jeffery Macdonald. Lanham, Md.: Rowman & Littlefield.

Pegg, Scott. 2000. The 'Taiwan of the Balkans'? The de facto state option for Kosova. *Southeast European Politics* 1 (2): 90–100.

Shore, Cris. 1993. Inventing the "People's Europe": Critical perspectives on European Community cultural policy. *Man* 28 (4): 799–800.

Shorter Oxford English Dictionary. 1968. London: Oxford University Press.

United Nations High Commission for Refugees. 2000. Comments on the French presidency proposals for a council directive and council framework decision on preventing the facilitation of unauthorised entry and residence. Geneva, Switzerland, www.unhcr.ch/cgi=bin/texis/ (accessed March 2, 2005).

World Conference against Racism. NGO forum declaration. Durban, South Africa, September 2001, www.racism.org.za/declaration.htm (accessed March 2, 2005).

Wimmer, Andreas. 1997. Explaining xenophobia and racism: A critical view of current research approaches. *Ethnic and Racial Studies* 20 (1): 17–41.

11

My Country in Translation

Gina Ulysse

last sunday
i sat through a series of slides
one after another one after another
of haitian women children and men
in a hospital in limbé
slides one after another
one after the other
some of them i couldn't look at
without turning away
or covering my eyes
open gashes, tumors, abscesses
i heard a lot of medical terms
that i would forget an hour
after i sat through the slides
one after another one after another

meanwhile
my mind travelled
to lansing to miami
back to the slides
and back again
to lansing and miami
to when i first began
to translate for the refugees

the first time i translated
i'd laugh
when i couldn't understand when I couldn't explain
when I couldn't find english words for this man's words
i couldn't find the words

because even in kreyol or in french
they weren't part of my vocabulary
these words never were part of my vocabulary
because his life has never been mine
because the haiti i grew up in
the haiti i know didn't consist of these words
the haiti i knew didn't consist of these words

i continued to laugh
nervously
because i have never been to this haiti
but i was going back there
i was going back there with them
i was going back there with their words
as i translated
i even mimicked
pauses
hesitations
uneasy smiles
the quickness to say words
that once translated
would determine lives.
words determined young lives
i did that with all of them
in lansing and in miami

once while translating
my laughter got on the verge of
hysterics

when translating
i always asked them
if they understood me
then i would apologize
for not being able to translate properly
quickly enough
for not being familiar with some words
for not having understood everything.
politely they'd say:

kreyol ou bon gina
pa gen problem se lang ou.
ou pale kreyol tankou ayisien. ou ayisien

every time i think about lansing
about miami
i wonder if they know
that i remember those words
that i couldn't translate

those words that i didn't know
i wonder if they know
that these words give me
a little of the country that i didn't know
i wonder if they know
that these words give me
a little of the country that i used to know
a little of the country that i never knew

V

NEGOTIATING DIVERSITY
AND THE WAR ON TERRORISM

12

Diversity Training Doesn't Get to the Heart of the Matter

Camille Hazeur and Diana Hayman

$\mathscr{I}$t should come as no surprise to even the casual observer that the United States continues to struggle with significant human rights issues within its borders. Our universal proclamation of responsibility to promote human rights around the globe fades against our own record on human rights at home, particularly with regard to issues of race and gender. As two people who have been involved in "dealing with differences" in the education arena for over twenty years, we were eager to respond to Faye Harrison's call for presenters in an NGO Forum at the World Conference against Racism in Durban, South Africa. In her invitation to us, she writes that the goal of the conference is "to produce a 21st century blueprint and set of guidelines for more effective strategies to combat and redress racism and the related intolerances that intersect it"—a goal to which we have been committed for the whole of our professional and personal lives.[1]

Our lives intersected when the two of us met in 1979 when we were a grantee and a program officer (the former being Camille Hazeur and the latter Diana Hayman) for the U.S. Department of Education's Fund for the Improvement of Postsecondary Education.[2] The project was funded to design and implement a program at a small historically white private college to help white faculty in newly integrated classrooms discover and change attitudes and behaviors related to race that might negatively affect classroom teaching and relationships with students and colleagues. A Change Model was an early diversity training program built on Mark Chesler's assumptions (1971) about white teachers in newly desegregated schools. These assumptions ranged from common-sense knowledge that the average white teacher had little opportunity, because of historic segregation, to meet and know blacks and other people of color and that few, if any, teacher-education programs at the time prepared teachers to deal with racial/ethnic differences in the classroom, and so on. A Change Model is a long-term program comprising small group meetings of about four hours per week for six to eight weeks. It is an educational program based on the assumption that people need new and old information about one another and about how race and gender and other invidious distinctions have evolved throughout U.S. history. It provides participants with the time it takes to establish enough trust among them to examine and grapple with these issues in the workplace. Since 1979 the program has been replicated, but most administrators at institutions, organizations, and businesses that have shown an interest in the work have been hesitant to sign on. They all claim the time involved is too long and that potential participants will not want to do it.[3]

In 1987, the Hudson Institute, a conservative U.S. think tank, published a report called *Work Force 2000* (Johnston and Packer 1987). In it, researchers predicted radical shifts in the demographic makeup of the U.S. labor force. Of the estimated twenty-five million new people entering the workforce between the years 1985 and 2000, only 15 percent, they predicted, would be white males; 85 percent of new entrants would be members of a minority (see Diamante, Reid, and Giglio 1995, 1). According to Norma Riccucci (1997, 1), a professor of public administration who has written extensively on public personnel management, companies were "implicitly or explicitly warned" by these reports that failing to embrace diversity could jeopardize their viability, profitability, and competitiveness. A 1991 study by the Economic Policy Institute indicated that the Hudson findings were misleading (Mishel and Teixeira 1991), but the former's findings had little or no impact on the apparent inevitability that diversity would became *the* buzzword of the 1990s. Many organizations, both public and private, responded by developing "cultural awareness" or "diversity training" programs, all in an effort to "manage diversity" by making the workplace a comfortable environment for minorities and women—an acknowledgment early on that racial and gender diversity was or would be a problem.

We have both watched with collective interest the national proliferation of diversity training programs in government, public and private organizations, and the corporate sector. We have both taken part in several diversity training programs in the federal government and the private sector and found them sadly superficial. So we decided to take a look at available data on diversity training to gauge its effectiveness. A preliminary glance at the literature revealed that many blacks and other minorities believe that diversity training has been window dressing and has not addressed the continuing racism that characterizes many of their work settings (Kerka 1998). A more extensive review of articles and reports on diversity training turned up such phrases as "white male bashing or a pointless waste of time," "punishment for the insensitive,"

"PC's [political correctness's] final frontier," "sensitivity overload," and "confusion, disorder, and hostility" (Nemetz 1996, 434).

We were not surprised by these summations. In most reports we discovered that while human resource managers and training experts believed this was the first time many employees had ever discussed the issue of diversity, the programs were, overwhelmingly, no more than one day in length and, in many cases, lasting only a half day (Wentling and Palma-Rivas 1997a, 38). We agreed with the training experts that in theory, before conclusions are drawn about the programs' "effectiveness or efficacy," the programs themselves need to be analyzed to determine if they are "seriously flawed and distorted in the first place" (Riccucci 1997, 1); however, we found nothing in the literature that attempted such an undertaking, even though training is the most widely used strategy to manage diversity (Wentling and Palma-Rivas 1997a, 70).

We have both attended training sessions in which facilitators led the group through a barrage of activities designed to confront racial and gender stereotypes and bring forth negative feelings—all designed to encourage change and all in the course of a few hours. We have been present in other "training programs" in which facilitators have levied nothing short of threats to employees if they did not comply with established company policy and state and federal laws, mostly associated with what facilitators interpreted as affirmative action policy or equal employment opportunity law. But we have never attended sessions in which the focus was on the facts of our national past; its history of inequality based on race; and its intersections with gender, ethnicity, and class that characterize our workplaces.[4] In this chapter, we attempt to make the case that unless corporate leaders and private sector administrators are willing to hire facilitators who can teach the history of social inequality in the United States and allow employees the time it takes to make sense of it in their world of work, diversity training is a waste of time and fiscal resources.

DIVERSITY TRAINING: AN ANEMIC RESPONSE TO CHANGE

Diversity training is just one strategy under the larger umbrella of diversity initiatives. Designed to attract, recruit, and retain minorities and women, diversity initiatives are typically defined either as compliance with federally mandated affirmative action programs wherein companies devise special hiring practices and incentives to attract women and minorities or as diversity training for new and existing staff, defined broadly as "raising personal awareness about individual differences in the workplace and how those differences inhibit or enhance the way people work together and get work done" (Wentling and Palma-Rivas 1997b, 37). In the narrowest sense, according to the experts, it is education about equal employment opportunity law, defining diversity in terms of race, gender (including sexual harassment), ethnicity, age, national origin, religion, and disability. In the broadest sense, diversity training includes that about sexual orientation, values, personality characteristics, education, language, physical appearance, marital status, lifestyle, beliefs, geographic origin, economic status, and so on (37). But diversity training is often defined differently from organization to organization and from company to company, and many times training is defined by organizational leadership (38). This is problematic. Why would one assume that corporate or other organizational leaders, without proper education and training, are more knowledgeable about these issues than other U.S. citizens? Writing about the "academic relations of production," Faye V. Harrison (1999) contends that, at best, academic administrators are giving mixed messages about diversity issues. She characterizes diversity initiatives as being "politics of reception and reproduction" in which inclusion of minorities and women in the academic institution may be visible but still not represented in the "citation patterns and required reading list for core graduate seminars" (79, 82). It is a kind of accommodation that produces a critical mass while at the same time denying real inclusion and ultimately blaming the newcomers for "not producing" in the expected ways.

In a 1998 study on the effectiveness of diversity training programs, employees described diversity training as being too narrowly focused on categories protected by law—primarily race, gender, and disability—including affirmative action, equal employment opportunity, and sexual harassment. Training, according to the study participants, seems to be focused on "changing white males" (Kerka 1998, 1). These participants propose a more broadly inclusive definition of diversity, one that encompasses age, educational level, family structure, job function, sexual orientation, ethnicity, and values, among others. They believe that these variables must be considered within an additional focus on understanding and valuing the "varied perspectives and approaches to work" that people from all kinds of backgrounds bring (Kerka 1998, 1). Other participants, principally those from minority groups, see expanding the meaning of diversity as watering down the central problem, which they see as being fundamentally a race problem. As popular news commentator and journalist Julianne Malveaux concludes, black–white issues run the risk of getting "swallowed" in the diversity movement:

> Race has everything to do with diversity, but too many people are primed to forget it. The diversity movement is a direct outgrowth of the civil rights movement, and though diversity encompasses more than the simple issues of black–white racial differentials, from where I sit these differences are at the core of its meaning. (1994, 1)

Malveaux's concern is that race, as the ubiquitous issue of social inequality in the United States, will be relegated to the periphery of diversity concerns when lumped with issues of class disparity, sexual orientation, and disability—that is, when cast with the many differences that do indeed need to be addressed. Diversity training in employment and education, argues Malveaux, must first address the central issue of white male hegemony (1994, 3).

In the extensive study conducted by Wentling and Palma-Rivas already cited, diversity experts identified six organizational barriers that they considered most likely to inhibit the advancement of diverse groups in the workplace. They were negative attitudes and discomfort toward people who are different, discrimination, stereotyping, racism, prejudice, and bias (1997b, 7). This same study identified three additional barriers to preventing a *positive* outcome of diversity training. They were time, the lack of evaluation, and backlash from white males (1997b, 56). All of these can be seen as dimensions of racism if racism is understood as a system or structure of inequality and domination with ideological and material, as well as affective and instrumental, components. It seems reasonable that if the experts know that the greatest barriers to a successful work environment are racism, discrimination, and negative attitudes toward people who are different, then these should be the focus of diversity training. From our review of the literature, we are not sure this is the case.

It has been our experience that when it comes to confronting diversity issues, particularly the issue of race, top management wants to keep a low profile. There seems to be an overriding desire to convey the message "We are beyond that." This desire echoes a national fantasy that we have finally come to live the "color-blind theory," and any discussion to the contrary will somehow disturb that peace. But as Robert Staples reminds us, to believe that we have achieved a truly color-blind society "has as its main premise that after 365 years of slavery and legal segregation (at least for blacks and many Native Indians), only 25 years of governmental laws and action were necessary to reverse the historical systematic and legalized segregation and inequality in this country, and no further remedial effort is needed" (1993, 230–31). The fantasy seems fairly depicted in nearly every study about diversity training, for whatever the content of the training, the loudest and most virulent backlash against diversity training has come from white males, who invariably argue they are unfairly the targets of that training.

THE HEART OF THE MATTER:
RACE AS A POINT OF DEPARTURE

Most people in the United States either have no idea or have not thought of them in quite this way, but until recently the categories "white" and "male" were taken for granted. Research sociologist David Wellman contends that being white and male is not experienced by most white men as a privileged or advantageous category—no matter their class status (1997, 321). But for many people of color and women, being white and male has meant and still means automatic and exclusive entree. Wellman contends that in recent decades the rising numbers of women and people of color entering and competing in the workplace have made the status of being white and male problematic, challenging assumptions about race and gender once taken for granted, particularly assumptions about the competence of women and minorities. The result is that white men have "discovered what nonwhites and women living in a predominantly white male world have always known: Life in a racial and gendered category is not always comfortable" (321).

Given the European American experience, which is supposedly a nonracial experience, it is no wonder that programs designed to remedy past and current discrimination toward racial minorities *feel* like reverse discrimination for whites—but not because whites have experienced discrimination. We believe they have not. The reason is that, until recently, "equal opportunity" meant that white male Americans faced virtually no competition from racial minorities and women; white and male were the norm in the world of work. What it meant in actuality was white male exclusivity. In this context, Wellman argues that when white males lose the preferential treatment they traditionally enjoyed at the expense of racial minorities and women, they call it "reverse discrimination" (1997, 331–32).

Many observers agree that it is no accident that white males believe they are unfairly the brunt of diversity training. Human resource experts Michele Galen and Ann Palmer believe "that at the heart of the issue for many white males is the question of merit—that in the rush for a more diverse workplace, they will lose out to less qualified workers" (1994, 3). If this contention is correct, white males will have to come to terms with beliefs and assumptions that people of color as well as white women are less qualified for their jobs. Riccucci (1997) argues that the white male backlash to diversity initiatives in general and to diversity training in particular is in part due to the fact that white males have never come to terms with the 1978 U.S. Supreme Court decision in the *University of California v. Bakke*, in which the high court upheld the university's decision to deny Allen Bakke, who is white, admission even though his test scores were higher than some admitted minorities. The Court held that affirmative action in college admissions was justifiable because diverse student bodies produce better education and more stimulating campus communities. While Riccucci's position may be arguable, one outcome of *Bakke* is unquestionable. From the closely divided decision came the phrase *reverse discrimination*, which has become increasingly more popularized, believed, and litigated in both the educational arena and the corporate world. "Often for the first time in their lives, white males are worrying about their future opportunities. Outside the corporate sector white men are feeling threatened because of racial and gender tensions that have been intensifying in recent years" (Riccucci 1997, 2).

It is interesting that government and corporate officials appeared ill prepared for the backlash. According to Riccucci, conventional wisdom dictated that since the driving force behind diversity initiatives was not legal, as it was with affirmative action, but economic in terms of corporate competitiveness and viability, these strategies and programs would be accepted unconditionally by white males, their unions, and white male managers (1997, 3). This has clearly not been the case, demonstrated primarily by the nationwide assault on affirmative action and on any and all race-based or gender-based employment and educational programs. In the 1980s, when Clarence Pendleton, chairman of President Ronald Reagan's Equal Rights Commission, declared that racial equality had been achieved and that the race issue in the United States was a thing of the past, he provided fuel to the prevailing sentiment that minorities and women were making "too much" of the race–gender divide (Omi and Winant 1994, 5). But in her 1996 book *Privilege Revealed: How Invisible Preference Undermines America*, Stephanie Wildman argues that the Republican leadership at the time, using black voices such as Pendleton's, commandeered the popular discussion of race and gender so much so that the very concept of affirmative action became conflated with invidious preference and discrimination. Affirmative action, as well as the diversity initiatives that followed, were framed to be antithetical to the hopes of the nation to be a color-blind society. This strategy essentially undermined attempts to implement affirmative action as a corrective to historically white preferential treatment and instead promulgated affirmative action as the embodiment of preferential treatment for blacks and eventually other people of color (Russell 1997, 1).

WHITENESS UNDER THE
MICROSCOPE: DEVELOPING NEW GUIDEPOSTS

Understanding the current status of race and gender relations is paramount to understanding where we need to go. Labor historian David Roediger looks at the agency of working men in constructing the meaning of whiteness and believes that understanding this process is crucial. Using W. E. B. DuBois's argument in *Black Reconstruction* ([1935] 1962), Roediger's analysis of white male workers encompasses Du Bois's notion of "seeing the whiteness of the white worker in the broad context of class formation rather than in the narrow confines of job competition" (1991, 12). In its most simplistic light, DuBois's argument was that

European immigrants chose being white over their immigrant roots to differentiate themselves from Others. The heritage of slavery and racism led to whiteness replacing class in the struggle for wages. And at its root, according to Roediger, the notion of white superiority is perhaps the deepest injury that the exchange made (1991, 12–13). In a halting book chapter entitled "The Antidemocratic Power of Whiteness," law professor Kathleen Cleaver echoes DuBois's and Roediger's position that this "'passionate devotion' to white superiority partially explains the failure of the post–Civil War Reconstruction and the collapse of its legal framework for black freedom" (1997, 157–58). According to Cleaver, the analysis Roediger develops starts from a position that black scholars and writers have long articulated: the race problem is a white problem. The traditional theoretical approach to labor history will simply perpetuate an oversimplified view of race that sees whiteness as being natural, and it will do so until it recognizes how workers participated in the creation of their own racial identity (161).

But whiteness has only recently come under the microscope. In 1997, Peggy McIntosh, a professor at Wellesley College, published an article titled "White Privilege: Unpacking the Invisible Knapsack," in which she reflects on the unconscious privileges of whiteness. "White privilege," she contends, "is like an invisible weightless knapsack of special provisions, assurances, tools, maps, guides, code books, passports, visas, clothes, compass, emergency gear, and blank checks" (291). McIntosh warns that not only is white privilege unearned skin privilege but that whites have been "conditioned into oblivion about its existence" (292). This obliviousness is "kept strongly enculturated in the United States so as to maintain the myth of meritocracy, the myth that democratic choice is equally available to all" (297). This deeply embedded, seemingly unconscious acceptance of the dominance of the status quo is what Joyce King, an academic who works on diversity issues at the university level, calls "dysconscious racism," where many whites operate within a phenomenological framework wherein uncritical ways of thinking about race can persist:

> Uncritical ways of thinking about racial inequity accept certain culturally sanctioned assumptions, myths, and beliefs that justify the social and economic advantages white people have as a result of subordinating others. Anything that calls this ideology of racial privilege into question inevitably challenges the self-identity of white people who have internalized these ideological justifications. It is a form of racism that tacitly accepts dominant white norms and privileges. It is not the *absence* of consciousness but an *impaired* consciousness. (1997, 128)

Perhaps this is why proponents of critical race theory contend that it is time for us to "get real" about race and the persistence of racism in the United States and find ways of coping with it rather than finding strategies to eradicate it (Delgado 1995). McIntosh (1997) argues that the backlash to affirmative action and diversity initiatives by white males is an attempt to cover up the "systemic, unearned white male advantage and conferred dominance that characterizes racial hegemony in the United States."

> Just as co-opting the 1960s' color-blind language of Dr. Martin Luther King and the civil rights era in the 1980s created the myth that the race problem was solved, concerns about quality and merit remain incomplete discussions, ultimately protecting unearned white privilege and conferred dominance.

In an article entitled the "Unintended Negative Effects of Diversity Management," Teresa Foster, C. W. Von Bergen, and Barlow Soper conclude that white men "are being discriminated against solely based on the assumption that being white and male equals privilege and social power, an assumption which many impoverished white males could testify is absolutely untrue" (1997, 6). This is a point well taken, for many of us know personally some economically poor working- and middle-class white men who do not *feel* privileged by their whiteness. But compared to the legacy of racial minorities and women, the legacy of white male privilege continues to advantage them in the power structure and in the unspoken belief systems of individuals, even if they are personally unable to take advantage of it. "Unfortunately, for both whites and 'others,' this denial [of white privilege] continues to keep *the power of a few protected by the masses of whites who are themselves not powerful, but who are also primarily not black or Latino, either*" (McIntosh 1997, 212; emphasis added).

In *Displacing Whiteness*, Ruth Frankenburg seeks to "resituate whiteness" from its unspoken status, to displace it and then reemplace it; to demonstrate how whiteness operates in particular locales and webs of social relations (1997, 3). In nearly all cases, asserts Frankenburg, whiteness is not defined but left to remain "neutral" and "natural." Blind acceptance of whiteness places all things nonwhite in a particular unneutral and unnatural position—buffers between whiteness and everybody else. Perhaps no one expresses this position better than Nobel Prize–winning author Toni Morrison (1989):

> I feel personally sorrowful about black–white relations a lot of the time because black people have always been used as a buffer in this country between powers to prevent class wars, to prevent other kinds of real conflagrations. If there were no black people here in this country, it would have been Balkanized. The immigrants would have torn each other's throats out, as they have done everywhere else. But in becoming an American, from Europe, what one has in common with the other immigrant is contempt for me—it's nothing else but color. Wherever they are from, they would stand together. They could all say, "I am not that."

TRAINING PROGRAMS: A PLAN THAT GETS
TO THE HEART OF THE MATTER

In 1971, sociologist and civil rights activist Mark Chesler said, "Most of what is natural in American race relations is distrustful, oppressive, and separatist" and that "desegregation itself is a departure from our natural social patterns" (1971, 612). For the most part, this statement still rings true. In spite of the desegregation efforts of the 1960s and vast improvements in employment for blacks, other people of color, and women, many people—including whites, blacks, Asian Americans, Hispanic Americans, and Native Americans—still live virtually segregated lives and know one another tangentially at best. Racial bias and antagonism are more subtle, perhaps, but hardly eradicated. Jack Noonan, former president of Bloomfield College and fellow Fund for the Improvement of Postsecondary Education grant recipient, once said to us that "the problem today is not so much overt acts of racism, but the ignorance and obliviousness of well-meaning people—like us." As McIntosh reminds us, "It is not enough for white Americans to simply 'disapprove' of existing systems of dominance— a simple change of attitude won't solve the problem. Because 'white' skin privileges white people automatically, social systems will have to be redesigned." And this, she goes on to say, will require that whites first acknowledge "their colossal unseen dimensions" of advantage (1997, 292).

Knowledge of the history of race making in school curricula has been largely and purposefully absent as a way to maintain the myth of meritocracy and resultant notions of superiority by the white male power brokers of our society. Diversity training will, in essence, have to rewrite the 1915 silent-film epic *Birth of a Nation*, in which newly freed blacks are portrayed as being brutal and in which the Ku Klux Klan is seen as patriotic purveyors of white resistance to black insurgence. Whites will have to, quite literally, *see* how they have been lulled into unconsciousness about race. They will have to fully understand and appreciate that early European immigrants were raced in the way ethnicity was perceived at that historical moment—that is, Irish, Italian, Polish, Jewish, and so on—and while the "melting pot" concept essentially allowed European immigrants to transcend race and ethnicity, it was at a cost. The price of abandoning languages and other cultural markers, however, opened the door to the privilege of whiteness from which whites still benefit today (Gregory and Sanjek 1996).

The literature on diversity training is replete with suggestions on how to improve training outcomes. Experts believe that diversity training must be preceded by some type of needs assessment to diagnose the organizational conditions and diversity needs. This can be achieved by asking questions and seeking information and should be part of what the experts call the inquiry stage of the diversity initiative. Once the assessment is complete, organizations must determine the content of training. Wheeler suggests the following questions be answered in considering the content of training: What will be the focus of training? Is training about awareness? Should it be about race, gender, age, or all? What is the link between diversity and business? What do people know, and what don't they know? What is the makeup of the participant group (e.g., professional, nonprofessional), and to whom is the training focused (e.g., managers, employees) (Wentling and Rivas 1997a, 43).

CONCLUSION

People in the United States want to believe that we live in a racial democracy wherein plain old hard work (i.e., rugged individualism) can lead to economic success no matter your race, nationality, gender, or class. While litigation and the need for new laws have repeatedly proven this not to be the case, the national politics of both major political parties continues to create an aura within the nation that gives regular people, albeit mostly whites, reason to deny the fact that racial disparities persist as a national problem. In a recent article in the *Economist*, the author reminds us that Brazil, a nation that has lived under the myth of "hybrid harmony" for generations, now has to face the fact that racial democracy is not its reality. The solution, according to this article, "is not to ignore race but to plant it at the center of policies to overcome vast social and economic inequalities" (2003, 31). We agree. But in the wake of the September 11, 2001, terrorist attack on the World Trade Center in New York City, it is unlikely that U.S. politics will focus efforts on a human rights agenda in the United States. Instead, the current administration has promulgated a politics of necessity that justifies setting aside human rights concerns for those of so-called national security.

The large umbrella of "national security" notwithstanding, corporate and private sector executives still have license to make diversity a human resource priority in the workplace. In the 1980s, in a political atmosphere created to deny race as a problem, many large corporations and institutions of higher education still made diversity a priority. In the corporate sector, managers sought diverse consumer bases through marketing and recruiting; in the colleges and universities, administrators accepted the idea that a more diverse student body and faculty was good for attaining the mission of higher education. Regardless of what is going on in the political arena, corporate and private sector leaders can continue to focus on making the workplace more conducive to productivity through training and retraining on the issues of difference.

We maintain, however, that successful training presumes that top management abandon superficial and placating notions of "managing diversity" and get real about giving workers, and themselves, an opportunity to understand diversity by teaching our histories and providing the time it takes to learn from our past. We recognize, however, that one glaring obstacle to productive diversity training is the potential for dispelling myths about the Other. And we recognize that the ultimate obstacle to racial democracy is the potential for a shift in power relations, an extremely guarded position in the U.S. political, corporate, and private sector. We propose it anyway, even if only in the hope that some business entities and organizations in the United States and in other parts of the world might share the same sense of urgency that we do.

NOTES

1. *International Union of Anthropological and Ethnological Sciences Newsletter*, no. 58 (December 2001), University of Leiden, The Netherlands.

2. The first grant, received at Dominican College in New Orleans in 1979, was entitled "Enhancing Quality through Confrontation Strategies: A Change Model Response of a Historically White College to Its Minority Constituency." The second grant, received in 1985 at the University of Tennessee, was entitled "Dealing with Race in Teaching: Using Video as a Strategic Change Agent."

3. Formative and summative evaluations from the project in New Orleans and Tennessee indicate that most participants wanted *more* time, not less. They expressed that after eight weeks, they were just reaching a "point of departure," comfortable enough to share real experiences and begin to look at needed change.

4. One exception that we know of is the People's Institute for Survival and Beyond, a training group based in New Orleans, Louisiana, www.thepeoplesinstitute.org.

REFERENCES

Chesler, Mark A. 1971. Teacher training designs for improving instruction in interracial classrooms. *Journal of Applied Behavioral Sciences* 7:612–41.

Chesler, Mark A., and Kathleen Smith, eds. 1974. *Desegregation/integration: Planning for school change; A training program for intergroup educators.* Washington, D.C.: National Education Association.

Cleaver, Kathleen. 1997. The antidemocratic power of whiteness. In *Critical white studies: Looking behind the mirror*, ed. R. Delgado and J. Stefancic, 157–63. Philadelphia: Temple University Press.

Delgado, Richard, ed. 1995. *Critical race theory: The cutting edge.* Philadelphia: Temple University Press.

Diamante, Thomas, Charles Reid, and Leo Giglio. 1995. Make the right training move. *HR Magazine* 40 (March 1): 60–65.

DuBois, W. E. B. [1935] 1962. *Black reconstruction.* New York: Atheneum.

The Economist. 2003. Race in Brazil: Out of Eden. July 3, 31–32.

Foster, Teresa, C. W. Von Bergen, and Barlow Soper. "Unintended negative effects of diversity management," www.sosu.edu/bus/faculty/vonbergen/Unintended_Negative_ Effects_of_ Diversity_Management.htm (accessed March 23, 2001).

Frankenburg, Ruth, ed. 1997. *Displacing whiteness: Essays in social and cultural criticism.* Durham, N.C.: Duke University Press.

Galen, Michele, and A. T. Palmer. 1994. White, male, and worried. *BusinessWeek Online,* January 31, 50–55, www.businessweek.com/archives/1994/b335655.arc.htm (accessed March 20, 2005).

Gregory, Stephen, and Roger Sanjek, eds. 1996. *Race.* New Brunswick, N.J.: Rutgers University Press.

Harrison, Faye V. 1999. New voices of diversity, academic relations of production, and the free market. In *Transforming academia: Challenges and opportunities for an engaged anthropology,* ed. L. G. Basch, L. W. Saunders, J. W. Sharff, and J. Peacock, 72–87. Arlington, Va.: American Anthropological Association.

Johnston, William B, and Arnold H. Packer. 1987. *Workforce 2000.* Indianapolis, Ind.: Hudson Institute.

Kerka, Sandra. 1998. *Diversity training.* ERIC Trends and Issues Alerts, www.ericacve .org/docs/diverse.htm (accessed March 23, 2001).

King, Joyce. 1997. Dysconscious racism: Ideology, identity, and miseducation. In *Critical white studies: Looking behind the mirror,* ed. R. Delgado and J. Stefancic, 128–31. Philadelphia: Temple University Press.

Malveaux, Julianne. 1994. Do African American issues get swallowed in diversity movement? *Black issues in higher education,* July 28, 1994, 1–3

McIntosh, Peggy. 1997. White privilege and male privilege: A personal account of coming to see correspondence through work in women's studies. In *Critical white studies: Looking behind the mirror,* ed. Delgado and Stefancic, 291–99. Philadelphia: Temple University Press.

Mishel, Lawrence R., and Ruy A. Teixeira. 1991. *The myth of the coming labor shortage: Jobs, skills, and incomes of America's workforce 2000.* Washington, D.C.: Economic Policy Institute.

Morrison, Toni. 1989. The pain of being black. Interview by B. Angelo. *Time,* May 22, 1989, 120.

Nemetz, Patricia. 1996. The challenge of cultural diversity: Harnessing a diversity of views to understand multiculturalism. *Journal of the Academy of Management Review* 6:434.

Omi, Michael, and H. Winant. 1994. *Racial formation in the United States: From the 1960s to the 1990s.* 2nd ed. New York: Routledge.

Orfield, Gary, ed. 2001. *Diversity challenged: Evidence on the impact of affirmative action.* Cambridge, Mass.: Harvard Education Publishing Group.

Riccucci, Norma. 1997. Cultural diversity programs to prepare for workforce 2000: What's gone wrong? *Public Personnel Management* 26:35–42.

Roediger, David. 1991. *The wages of whiteness: Race and the making of the American working class.* London: Verso Press.

Russell, Margaret. 1997. Unpacking the knapsack. *Women's Review of Books* 14:15.

Staples, Robert. 1993. The illusion of racial equality: The black American dilemma. In *Lure and loathing: Essays in race, identity, and the ambivalence of assimilation*, ed. G. Early, 227–44. New York: Penguin.

Wellman, David. 1997. Minstrel shows, affirmative action talk, and angry white men: Marking racial otherness in the 1990s. In *Displacing whiteness: Essays in social and cultural criticism*, ed. R. Frankenburg, 311–31 (Durham, N.C.: Duke Univeristy Press).

Wentling, Rose Mary, and Nilda Palma-Rivas 1997a. *Diversity in the workforce: A literature review.* Diversity in the Workforce Series 1. ERIC Database (ED414473), www.eric.ed.gov.

———. 1997b. *Current status of diversity initiatives in selected multinational corporations.* Diversity in the Workforce Series 2. ERIC Database (ED414475), www.eric.ed.gov.

Wildman, Stephanie M. 1996. *Privilege revealed: How invisible preference undermines America.* New York: New York University Press.

· *13* ·

What Democracy Looks Like:
The Politics of a Women-Centered,
Antiracist Human Rights Coalition

Faye V. Harrison

CAN WE AFFORD TO TAKE DEMOCRACY FOR GRANTED?

In December 2002, a coalition of human rights organizations coordinated a series of direct actions in Miami, Florida. Protests at a public housing project, a Taco Bell, and the building housing the Immigration and Naturalization Service—now called the Bureau of Citizenship and Immigration Services within the government's more encompassing Department of Homeland Security—tied together social injustices related to housing and urban redevelopment, work conditions among migrant agricultural workers, and the discriminatory treatment of immigrants and refugees within a single framework that demanded a more robust conception of democracy and human rights. Despite the rain and, after the sun set, the dark, the boisterous crowd that raised its placards and sang its chants and protest songs across the street from the Immigration and Naturalization Service building was noticeably more vibrant than the demonstrations at the earlier sites. After several speakers had given rousing speeches, the multiracial crowd called out in classic call-and-response style:

> *What* does democracy look like?
> *This* is what democracy looks like!
> *What* does democracy look like?
> *We're* what democracy looks like!

Were the demonstrators, with all their vigorous chanting, merely posing a rhetorical question for the sake of public performance, or were they addressing an urgent problem that many more people in U.S. society should seriously ponder? Can we afford to take democracy and its constitutional rights for granted? Are those rights secure within American society? Do the Miami demonstrations and their organizers have significant lessons to teach us about recent shifts in American political climate and their implications for the well-being of diverse segments of the populace—including members of the middle class, who may feel very much entitled to the racial and class privileges they enjoy? People without those privileges who, as a consequence, bear the brunt of social injustice and its related suffering are compelled to negotiate the meanings and material groundings of age, gender, race, class, and national/transnational identity, as these dimensions of difference and inequality interact and play themselves out across the multiple domains of everyday life. These differences are also tremendous axes of power, which, as activist physician and anthropologist Paul Farmer points out, are the grounds upon which social disparities are seriously deepening and human rights are being violated (2003, 219).

My purpose in this chapter is to shed some critical light on the political project of a network of Southern-based activists, those responsible for organizing the direct actions described here. Those activists, women of color key among them, are critically conscious that their lived experiences, social locations, and identities are, in various ways, conditioned by a matrix of power within which overlapping hierarchies of race, gender, and class are central. Their understanding of the dynamics of that matrix has led them to implement strategies and tactics of political organizing that address human rights; interlocking inequalities, particularly those of race, gender, and class; connections among coexisting social movements; and, of increasing importance during an era of global restructuring, transborder networks and alliances across international terrain, especially the common ground that the U.S. South shares with the Global South.

Both September 11, 2001, and, right before it, the much-less-publicized but also controversial World Conference against Racism (WCAR) held in Durban, South Africa, are interrelated points of departure for understanding the evolving agenda of the network of organizations that I call by the pseudonym Southern Human Rights Activists Coalition (SHRAC).

ARE WE ENTERING AN ERA OF POSTDEMOCRACY?

Since September 11, 2001, and the launching of the war against terrorism in its immediate wake, Americans have become intensely anxious about national— or, should we say, homeland—security. This anxiety has led many to accept the ideological rationale for the USA Patriot Act, legislation that undermines the very democratic principles that the United States claims to model in the world community. The emergence of this kind of nativist patriotism has reinforced xenophobic responses to immigrants and refugees, particularly those who are

Muslim or from somewhere in the Muslim world. Of course, "the Muslim world" represents an imprecise designation in the paranoid imaginations of those considerable elements of the public lacking the geographical and cultural literacy to differentiate Arabs, South Asians, and any other swarthy foreigners or foreign-looking individuals suspected of being terrorists or harboring terrorists. Beyond intensifying the xenophobic and frequently racist treatment of new immigrants—who are more likely to be Asian, Latin American, Caribbean, or African than earlier generations of immigrants—the USA Patriot Act (along with additional legislation being considered to enhance it) also presents troubling possibilities to those who, without any question, were born and bred in the United States. The once-revered civil liberties guaranteed in the Bill of Rights are being reduced to expand and buttress the power of the state, rhetorically cast as the great protector of the nation and the free world in a conflict between "good and evil." Law enforcement authorities have been given sweeping new surveillance and detention powers that are not limited to fighting terrorism. These powers can be applied to criminal and intelligence operations that may implicate citizens in much the same way that 1950s McCarthyism persecuted innocent people, labeling them communists. In today's neoconservative climate now preoccupied with terrorists and those suspected of harboring them, even *liberal* is a bad word.

The attack on the civil liberties that mainstream Americans have long taken for granted raises serious questions about the status and meaning of human rights in U.S. society. This troubling trend endangers the very political and civil rights that have conventionally been placed in the foreground of American and, more generally, Western discourses on human rights. For the most part, political and civil rights have been put on a pedestal, at least in terms of public rhetoric, while social and economic rights have been adamantly refused recognition in a society where social mobility is claimed to be available to all who are willing to work hard and "pull themselves up by their own bootstraps." The American dream and the ideology of meritocratic individualism it enshrines place the onus on individuals to secure their own socioeconomic security in the "land of opportunity." While this model of society has held sway for some time, it has been redrawn in light of the recent context of economic restructuring, deindustrialization, welfare reform, cutbacks in educational benefits and in health and social services, and the virtual elimination of policies that would expand the market in affordable housing (National Center for Human Rights Education [NCHRE] 2000, 3; Thomas-Houston and Schuller n.d.). All of these interrelated trends, combined with the problematic policy and legal shifts accompanying the war on terrorism, have profound consequences for the state of democracy and human rights in both the United States and, in light of its superpower role, the whole wide world.

UNDERSTANDING THE SCOPE
AND CONTENTS OF HUMAN RIGHTS

Human rights are "the reasonable demands for personal security and basic well-being that all individuals" should be able to "make on the rest of humanity by virtue of being members of the species *Homo sapiens*" (Messer 1993, 222). They are "the liberties to which every human being is entitled to enjoy and to have protected, regardless of class, race, gender, age, ability, sexual orientation, nationality, ethnicity, religion, place of birth or citizenship" (NCHRE 2000, 2). Indeed, according to the National Center for Human Rights Education, an imperative right is the right to *know* what exactly your human rights are. Otherwise, you cannot claim, protect, and promote them.

In the United States, the concept of human rights dates back to the middle of the nineteenth century, when abolitionist Frederick Douglass protested the lynching of an African American man. He defined that heinous extrajudicial execution as a violation of human rights (NCHRE 2000). In view of the country's history of enslaving Africans, displacing and decimating indigenous peoples, and discriminating against other racialized ethnic minorities, including some European immigrants who did not originally have access to the privileges of whiteness, it is not at all surprising that human rights consciousness in the United States has long had a relationship with the struggle against racism.

Human rights consciousness among the majority of Americans is embarrassingly underdeveloped. In 1997 a national survey indicated that 92 percent of the sample had no knowledge whatsoever of the Universal Declaration of Human Rights (NCHRE 2000, 3). This ignorance may be related to the fact that the U.S. government externalizes human rights in its foreign policy with its double standards while refusing to acknowledge the severity of its own internal violations of international human rights standards. With such a low level of awareness, few Americans know that, increasingly, all over the world advocates for women, children, the racially subjugated, immigrants, refugees, and indigenous people are, in various ways, using the language, declarations, treaties, and organizing arenas of an international human rights system to build a global movement for justice. That human rights system includes growing networks of nongovernmental organizations (NGOs) and UN commissions and committees charged with monitoring compliance with the 1948 universal declaration and a host of more recent covenants and conventions (Harrison 2002a).

Having the status of treaties that ratifying states, at least theoretically, agree to proclaim and enforce, a number of covenants and conventions have been established to elaborate the principles delineated in the historic 1948 universal declaration and to clarify their implications for setting international standards for protecting and promoting human rights. As a result of decades of debate that has served to broaden the discourse and illuminate how humanness is conceived cross-culturally, the explicit meanings and scope of human rights have been expanded to include categories of people (e.g., women, children, migrants, and refugees) and contexts (e.g., the environment and development) that were previously neglected or left in the realm of the ambiguous and implied. Women's rights to equality and justice are now defined as human rights that warrant being specified at length in the Convention for the Elimination of All Forms of Discrimination against Women, a treaty that the United States has not ratified in the more than twenty years that it has existed. The standards for achieving the rights of people whose life chances have been constrained by processes of racialization have been elaborated in the International Convention on the Elimination of All Forms of Racial Discrimination. This is yet another treaty, one that is a decade older than the women's convention and, again, one with which the U.S. government has not been in compliance. This problematic human rights track record and the rationalizations for it became a volatile issue in summer 2001, when the United States refused to send an official delegation to the WCAR. This response was actually part of a longer pattern of refusing to participate in the UN's two earlier antiracism conferences. Reparations for slavery and colonialism and the Palestinian presence at the 2001 conference were the two major thorns in the U.S. government's side. Recognizing the potential ramifications of reparations, with its implications for debt relief, development, and the global redistribution of wealth, the United States simply refused to engage the issue. The United States was more vocal in its refusal to accept the Palestinians' claim that they are victimized by racist Israeli policies that are enabled and reinforced by U.S. foreign policy. The question of whether the Palestinians had a right or a legitimate reason to bring their grievances before an international conference on racism was an explosive issue on which the media concentrated its focus, neglecting the many others that were addressed by advocates for justice from all over the world. The controversial conference in Durban, however, was abruptly forgotten when public attention shifted to the tragic events of September 11.

The highly emotional and reactionary response to the catastrophic loss of life diverted attention from the legitimate grievances that many people in the Middle East and the larger global South have against U.S. foreign policy, both its overt and covert expressions as they contribute to the empire-building mission of the remaining superpower. This mission has led the United States to support oppressive regimes and overthrow progressive ones whose policies get in the way of U.S. interests, whether geopolitical or economic. Jeffrey Sluka (2000, 8) points out that many of the repressive, nondemocratic states that have deployed death squads against their citizens have been clients of the United States. As client nations, they have "received direct military and other assistance enabling them to establish and maintain authoritarian regimes prepared to resort to terror to pursue their interests and stay in power." Drawing on the political analysis of Noam Chomsky and Edward Herman (1980), Sluka advances the controversial position that the global rise in state-sponsored terrorism has been very much an outcome of U.S. foreign policy and its sphere of influence. Although the events of September 11 were certainly a crime against humanity, the issue of culpability is a much more complicated one involving a complex history of violence and counterviolence that protagonists and antagonists have enacted. That history implicates the United States' imperial agenda, a major obstacle to international human rights.

While important human rights work is being done across a growing number of world contexts—from grassroots mobilizations to regional coalitions and international forums—substantial numbers of Americans are completely unaware of these trends and their relevance to their lives. Granted, many Americans have enjoyed the privileges of living in a free and affluent society, and precisely because of these privileges they have been buffered from the rights violations and social sufferings that poor or racially marked people commonly experience. However, Pem Davidson Buck (2003, 39) warns that as "the stock market and major corporations go bust, dreams of retirement fade away, and the [U.S.] enters a state of permanent war," those taken-for-granted privileges are likely to wither away. Without having a substantive concept of human rights—one not fixated on abstract legalisms but informed by a contextually rich ethic of justice—it will be difficult to "defend and promote" "the basic standards [social, economic, and political] without which we cannot live in freedom and with dignity" (NCHRE 2000, 2). Without this critical consciousness, many Americans are vulnerable to succumbing to a xenophobic, racist patriotism that precludes their ability to understand the world and how issues of empire are implicated in many of the world's escalating conflicts.

In the context of these conflicts, human rights violations are intensifying, as are the widening inequalities in power, wealth, and health that engender them. Not surprisingly, the rights of people who are racially subordinated are being seriously undermined. Anthropologists are examining the wide range of settings in which major demographic, political, and economic shifts are working to the disadvantage of the world's peoples (e.g., MacClancy 2002). In my own research, I am particularly interested in how ordinary people negotiate and respond to the impact of global forces, among them the destabilizing effects of post–Cold War realignments and restructuring, the erosion of social welfare as a responsibility of states, the instability of international markets in the export commodities around which many peripheral economies are structured, the increasing internationalization of workforces, the formation of new diasporas and transnational communities of immigrants who have been twice or even thrice diaspora-ized, and the growing crisis of identities.

I am specifically interested in understanding the contours and dynamics of antiracist activism, the diverse forms that this activism assumes around the world, and the extent to which it is shaped by the class- and gender-specific ways that race is socially constructed in diverse cultural contexts. In an era of globalization, that coming both "from above" and "from below," another important question is whether local and national projects of antiracist mobilization are influenced by knowledge of struggles going on in other parts of the world and by that "movement of movements" that is perhaps most visibly crystallizing in the World Social Forum (Wallerstein 2003, 28). To what degree do antiracism activists situate themselves in webs of articulation with the struggles against sexism and class oppression? To what extent do they situate themselves within international and transnational arenas of human rights struggle? What are different ways that activists interpret and employ human rights instruments, such as declarations, covenants, treaties, and conference platforms for action? How are declaration- and treaty-based concepts grafted upon or integrated within various context-grounded ideologies and strategies for change? To what extent is domestic and international coalition building important in those political agendas? These are questions that I would like to answer through my ongoing research.

SEEKING PRELIMINARY ANSWERS FROM THE SOUTHERN HUMAN RIGHTS ACTIVISTS COALITION

I have begun to apply these research questions to the southeastern region of the United States, where I am starting to examine a network of human rights activists involved in a wide range of social and economic justice issues, all of which converge on antiracism in one way or the other. In light of its history as a major site for plantation slavery and postemancipation-era Jim Crow apartheid, the South is a particularly interesting place to study human rights violations and the patterns of mobilization against them. The Atlanta-based National Center for Human Rights Education (n.d.) points out that

> the South leads the country in the unfair application of the death penalty and in environmental racism. Underdeveloped educational systems, a massive prison-industrial complex and lack of unions . . . for low-wage workers perpetrate a caste system, the remnant of a slave-based economy. The exploitation of migrant farm workers and sharecroppers, and the brutality of police repression characterize living conditions for many Southerners. (N.d.)

The South is also an interesting focus of human rights research because of the more recent trends that characterize the new South. Today the region is much more culturally and racially diverse, and its changing demographic profile is based on the region's location within "the increasingly global labor market" (Smith 1998, 165). The new South has become a destination for foreign people as well as for foreign capital, which is drawn to the region because of "relatively low wages, a weak labor movement, and low taxes related to meager levels of social provision. The South appears extremely attractive [because it offers] First World amenities without First World costs" (171). The region is also a "point of departure for traditional, low-wage industries seeking lower costs [and bigger profits] in other countries" only a generation after having moved to the South from the deindustrializing North. These political-economic ebbs and flows are creating conditions that demand new approaches to organizing for change—new consciousness, new alliances, and new strategies.

The specific coalition of organizations I am examining, the Southern Human Rights Activists Coalition (SHRAC), is only eleven years old, but it has organized five biennial regional conferences (SHRAC I-V) that over the years have grown to involve participants from all over the United States as well as those from abroad. For instance, at SHRAC III there were participants from as far away as New England and California. Although some had been invited to present in workshops and plenaries, most of the non-Southerners attended because of the wider significance and urgency of the issues that the conference addressed. These issues included environmental racism, the death penalty, racial profiling, hate crimes in the workplace, unethical sterilization, assaults against immigrant women, HIV/AIDS, and how to get involved in the then-upcoming WCAR. The role that SHRAC III played as a preparatory conference for the 2001 Durban NGO Forum made it particularly significant in its attempt to provide an important bridge linking Southern and, more generally, U.S. activists to the global arena that UN conferences provide. By effectively publicizing the conference with kindred organizations all over the country (e.g., Women of Color Resource Center in Oakland, California, and the Kensington Welfare Rights Union in Philadelphia), the audience for SHRAC's conferences was considerably expanded and diversified.

FROM LOCAL TO GLOBAL
BY WAY OF REGIONAL COALITION BUILDING

Besides situating itself on national terrain, SHRAC III was also a cosmopolitan event, positioning itself globally. Its participants included activists from Canada, Brazil, Zimbabwe, and India as well as from transnational immigrant communities in the U.S. South, principally its major cities. One of the plenaries at SHRAC III featured a representative from India's National Federation of Dalit Women. She exposed the audience to the injuries of untouchability and the caste system. As a member of an NGO dedicated to the plight of women, she spoke poignantly of the particular social sufferings, notably rape, that Dalit women endure. Her presence signaled a type of international exchange that is a continuing part of the legacy of India's, particularly Gandhi's, influence on the civil rights movement. Martin Luther King Jr.'s civil disobedience strategy was inspired by Gandhi's example. Indians, particularly Dalits (meaning "the oppressed"), have also been influenced by the African American struggle for dignity and freedom. An excellent instance of this lies in the Dalit Panthers' movement, which drew upon the symbols and ideology of the Black Panther Party.

The plenary presentation on the plight of Dalits anticipated the strong presence that Dalit NGOs would have a year later in Durban, where they dramatically publicized casteism as a parallel or even a variant of racism. The cross-cultural connections and parallels that the National Federation of Dalit Women spokesperson illuminated are not entirely new to antiracists in the South. During the Jim Crow era, especially during the 1930s depression, the concept of caste was commonly used by scholars (Davis, Gardner, and Gardner 1941; Dollard 1937) to elucidate the complexities and rigidities of "American apartheid" (Collins and Veskel 2000). Whereas caste was an *etic* concept, a heuristic tool rather than a native category, that American social scientists used to situate the properties and dynamics of the birth-ascribed system constructed around "race" in the United States, in present-day India, Dalit activists and intellectuals use race in much the same way, as an analogous concept to interrogate, contest, and contextualize the structures and experiences of India's caste hierarchy (see Channa in this volume, chapter 2). This reciprocal, dialogic relationship speaks to the importance of situating local and regional discourses on invidious social distinctions within international and cross-cultural contexts that allow for potentially insightful cross-references and comparisons.

As Southern activists become more involved in the international human rights arena—such as through the UN's preparatory conferences for the WCAR and through the WCAR itself—they have learned that their "issues are critical issues for marginal peoples all over the world" (Gay McDougall, member of the UN Committee for the Elimination of Racial Discrimination, speech presented at SHRAC III, 2000). The internationalization of domestic issues in black Southern activists' experience appears to have the effect of transfiguring them from members of a racial minority to members of a new majority with enormous potential strength. This understanding of the potential to forge a new majority offers a hopeful context for situating regional experiences and struggles, especially those of African Americans, within a larger context. Indeed, the multiple contexts that SHRAC's leadership emphasizes are those of the African diaspora and the larger global South. Once abstract notions without immediate practical political significance for many, the concepts of diaspora and the global South have gained human faces and multilingual voices for those activists who have had the chance to travel outside of the United States; to participate in international conferences where black people from the Caribbean, Latin America, and Europe have been present; and to be a part of the SHRAC conferences, which have come to play an important educational and consciousness-raising role. The networks cultivated from these exchanges have enriched many activists' thinking, making them more aware of the importance of globalizing the local and localizing the global. SHRAC seeks to build bridges that link multiple localities within a Southern regional framework that is in turn articulated to wider national and international arenas of consciousness raising, debate, lobbying, and leveraging for meaningful substantive change.

Human rights language, consciousness, and legal and organizational instruments allow activists to reposition themselves internationally among potential allies as well as against an enemy or network of enemies that is larger than localized or even nationalized structures. Although conventionally human rights instruments have been limited by statist concerns (i.e., assuming that the state is the primary culprit held responsible for protecting citizens from human rights violations), increasing numbers of human rights advocates are becoming more aware of nonstate and of supra- and transnational offenders, including corporations, the International Monetary Fund, and the structural violence of unsustainable development and abject poverty.

BEYOND CIVIL RIGHTS TO THE MULTIPLE DIMENSIONS OF HUMAN RIGHTS

SHRAC members see themselves as providing the necessary if not sufficient conditions for a human rights movement that builds on the political grounds that the civil rights movement cleared. Many of the organizations within SHRAC's network are part of the legacy of that historic movement. SHRAC attempts to enable its core member organizations "to expand their programmatic vision beyond civil rights to human rights" (program of SHRAC III, December 2000, 2). As one veteran civil rights activist put it, "Every one of the issues [of struggle] must be translated into human rights [terms]" (SHRAC III speech given on December 1, 2000, at Clark-Atlanta University, Atlanta, Georgia). In his view, a human rights approach offers a language with an international frame of reference. Working closely with the Southern regional office of Amnesty International, which has a noticeably multiracial and multinational staff, SHRAC has as its primary goal to "equip a culturally diverse community of activists, community-based and nonprofit organizations with the knowledge, skills, materials, and resources needed to effectively participate in the national and international human rights movement."

SHRAC's biennial conferences have brought civil rights activists together with their counterparts working on issues related to labor (especially black and Latino labor), women (especially racial minority and immigrant women), youth, immigrants and refugees (especially those that are racially marked), gay/lesbian/transgendered persons, education, welfare rights, poverty, criminal injustice and the death penalty, environmental justice, and health disparities (such as those manifest in the HIV/AIDS epidemic, which is especially wreaking havoc on communities of color). SHRAC activists are making an effort to build bridges that link parallel movements that otherwise operate separately and competitively. To counter that tendency, SHRAC works to establish "collaborative partnerships" that help to expand the view that many activists formerly had of their specific struggles. This strategy was evident in the organization and contents of the conferences held in 2000 and 2002; however, in SHRAC IV, the strategy was taken to a new level with the direct action in Miami. The local organizations involved in that event had never worked together before the SHRAC conference and the opportunity it provided for local and translocal partnership.

The juxtaposing of multiple rights and struggles has been conducive to an intersectional approach to making connections and forging alliances across differences, whether the differences being negotiated are domestic or international. The language of intersectionality—which originally came out of a dialogue between feminist activists and scholars, particularly between women of color (e.g., Collins 1990; Crenshaw 1991) and white women—is now being used by a number of people in SHRAC as a basis for understanding interrelationships among social injustices as well as for political strategy.

WAR AT THE BORDERS

While SHRAC III focused on educating its participants about the issues and procedures that would be key to the WCAR and about the global scope of the human rights struggles that affect the U.S. South, the 2002 SHRAC conference emphasized the problems that have been especially relevant since September 11 and the onslaught of the war on terrorism. A number of sessions and plenaries dealt with the intensification of human rights abuse in the United States and

the enduring climate of crisis and militarism that the war on terrorism manu-
factures. The dismantling of due process, the extension of powers of surveillance
and detention, the repudiation of international law, and the dangerous reinter-
pretation and revision of domestic law all contribute to a political climate that
threatens the human rights of both citizens and immigrants, especially the most
vulnerable, which include Arabs, Haitians, and Mexicans.

Repressive border-control policies and the mistreatment of immigrants
who violate the current sense of needed security were a major focus of discussion. Representatives from a number of organizations in Florida, the Southwest, and elsewhere addressed this issue and the urgent need to demilitarize the
border. For instance, the experiences of Haitian detainees in Florida and of
Haitian immigrants living in the Dominican Republic were discussed in
graphic terms. Local activists were especially concerned about the conditions
faced by a group of more than one hundred refugees who made it to the coast
of Florida early in December 2001. These Haitians were still in detention a
year later, without much access to attorneys and others who are assisting them
with asylum claims and requests for release. The conditions in the detention
facilities are deplorable and dangerous. Sexual abuse is not uncommon, and
there are no recreational facilities and educational services, not even for the
children. The demoralization the refugees suffer is exacerbated by the fact that
families are separated—husbands from wives, and parents from children—and
dispersed across four different sites in the Miami area. The situation for Haitian immigrants in the Dominican Republic is equally precarious. An activist
who put herself through law school after raising six children spoke of the laws
that prevent Haitian immigrants and their Dominican-born children from se-
curing citizenship and being integrated into Dominican society.

The experience of Mexican immigrants in the Southwest, especially
Mexicans and Mexican Americans of largely indigenous descent, was addressed
by activists from Arizona who are organizing for defense against hate and vig-
ilante groups, paramilitary units that "assist" Homeland Security officials in se-
curing the border against the "invasion" of "anti-American *reconquistas*." The
vigilantes, many of whom are former members of the military's special forces,
recruit reinforcements from outside the state to hunt illegal aliens as though
they are dangerous wild animals. The results of this protracted hunting season
are found all over the desert: dead bodies, often unidentifiable and typically
abandoned on indigenous lands. One grassroots organization that works on
these issues is Alianza Indígena sin Fronteras (Indigenous Alliance without
Borders). Alianza sees the national boundary separating the U.S. Southwest
from Mexico as an artificial barrier dividing indigenous communities that have
the potential to share a common sense of peoplehood in light of their common history and culture in the colonial and precolonial past. Accordingly,

Alianza identifies itself, its constituency, and its objectives as being essentially transnational. The human rights of migrants and indigenous peoples intersect in their agenda.

In light of the national security panic that the war against terrorism sustains, SHRAC IV's major focus was on the human rights implications of border militarization and on neoliberal globalization's role in producing the desperate conditions that force people to seek alternative circumstances for personal and family survival. Unfortunately, some of those alternatives end up being just as bad as what refugees are trying to escape, especially when migration leads to detention centers, desert hunts, and farmwork marked by near-slavelike conditions.

CONSCIOUSNESS-RAISING TOURS OF ACTION

The many poignant presentations, testimonies, and discussions at SHRAC IV painted a very different picture of terror, its perpetrators, and victims than what most Americans view when they turn on the evening news. The conference program, which spanned over four days, reached its symbolic and emotional culmination with what the conference moderator had referred to all Saturday morning as a "surprise procession," as she built up the audience's anticipation. The surprise turned out to be a group of about thirty Guatemalan men, women, and children who were escorted into the auditorium by organizers and students working with farmworkers' alliances such as the Coalition of Immokalee Workers. Welcomed by a roaring standing ovation, the guests—mainly comprising Guatemalans, referred to as Mayan by one of the American Indian speakers—were migrant worker families involved in the coalition's campaign to boycott Taco Bell, has a corporation that benefited from tomato producers' exploitation of migrant labor. The four-year boycott ended in March 2005 when Taco Bell agreed to improve work conditions. Earlier in 2002, the coalition had organized a "truth tour" to galvanize support for the Taco Bell boycott in several cities all over the country. The march began in Florida, where the participants walked more than two hundred miles. They then followed an itinerary to a number of cities, including Chicago, Denver, San Francisco, and Oklahoma City. The tour ended in Memphis, where Martin Luther King Jr. was assassinated. The audience was reminded that he had traveled to Memphis to lend his support to the sanitation workers' strike and to the broader cause of economic justice. In December 2002, months after the completion of the tour, some of the activists and workers involved in that campaign brought the spirit of their truth tour to SHRAC IV. After viewing a film on the Taco Bell truth tour and listening to another series of talks and discussions on case studies of oppression, most of the conference attendees boarded yellow buses that took them on a "tour of shame" around Miami.

The tour began in Liberty City, a historically black neighborhood, where a rally was held on the grounds of a public housing project. The protest was in support of poor families, mainly poor black women, and it was organizing against Hope VI, the most recent version of urban removal (colloquially called "Negro removal"). From there, the buses went to a different part of Miami, the vicinity in which the building for Immigration and Naturalization Service— now Homeland Security—is located. Before the crowd made its way in front of the building, it gathered in a nearby place that was only a block away. On that site was a Taco Bell restaurant, the focus of a demonstration that brought attention to the boycott and its attempt to link everyday consumption choices to the exploitative conditions of production that deny migrant workers a living wage and healthy conditions of work, which are basic needs and rights. Finally, the demonstrators made their last stop on the tour, the Immigration and Naturalization Service building, which focused the demonstrators' attention on the human rights violations that deny Haitians and other refugees their rights as human beings. That day, SHRAC practiced what it preached by revealing in a four-hour period the mutual relationships that can and should be built to link the struggles of poor inner-city African American families, Guatemalan families working in migrant labor camps, and Haitian families separated under the demoralizing conditions of indefinite detention. SHRAC IV had offered some moving lessons in human rights education through its workshops, plenaries, and the "service learning" experience that was built into the tour of direct action. Strengthening the kinds of solidarities that SHRAC's direct action only symbolized is integral to the political response necessary to defend human rights—not just in the word of law but in the concrete conditions of everyday life—at a moment when civil liberties are under attack. Under the war on terrorism as the Bush administration defines it, democracy cannot be taken for granted.

CENTERWOMEN MOBILIZING FOR CHANGE

It is no accident that the principal activists who have brought perspectives on multiple oppressions into SHRAC's work have been women of color, primarily African American women who have reached out to others, both women and men, who share their view of the world and the importance of establishing links with the global movement for human rights justice and social transformation.

The founder of SHRAC is a charismatic African American woman. A veteran of the civil rights movement, she went back to school in her forties to study law so that she could acquire the skills to advance the social and economic rights of black workers in Mississippi and other areas of the Deep South. Her work for workers' dignity and humanity has included struggles against the particular indignities and assaults that women face in work settings—for instance, sexual harassment, women being fired from their jobs for resisting their supervisors' advances.

Her involvement with Amnesty International and the Southeastern office of the Center for Constitutional Rights gave her a context to establish an extensive regional and national network that came to include another African American activist, one who has worked around black women's reproductive rights for nearly thirty years. She was politicized as a result of her own personal experience with sterilization abuse. Her outrage and pain led her to a political trajectory that moved her focus from sterilization abuse to broader issues of reproductive freedom and sexual health, including abortion rights and the right to protection from sexual violence. In her view, it is important for activists to protect women's and particularly racialized women's right to have or not have children. Reproductive rights among people of color are germane to the survival of entire communities that historically have been subjected to eugenics policies designed to restrict the growth of poor people, various immigrants, and racial minorities, who were seen as fetters to national development. Racist and xenophobic biases also informed the early birth-control movement, which advocated "choice for white middle class women . . . and [cast] sterilization [as] a moral obligation for the indigent, disabled, and uneducated women and for women of color" (Choi 2001).

One of this activist's close comrades in SHRAC is a public health practitioner and activist who organizes women of color around the health disparities that racism engenders, especially HIV/AIDS as it affects black women in particular. Within the past several years, her work has expanded to include the building of exchanges and partnerships with women's organizations in South Africa.

These three women have played a central role in sustaining SHRAC's political project as a regional organization with networks that extend its links throughout the country, as well as outside of it, to other parts of the global South, especially to those parts where black people are struggling for dignity and justice. At SHRACs III and IV, these women's presence was strongly felt, along with that of several other women who represented organizations committed to such issues as environmental justice, housing rights, the abolition of the death penalty, economic justice, and electoral reform. Included among the women was a charismatic union organizer from a catfish plant in Mississippi who participated in the NGO Forum. In a powerful voice reminiscent of the late Fannie Lou Hamer, she brought gender, class, and subregional underdevelopment (i.e., the economic poverty of the

Mississippi Delta) into the discussion on racism and related intolerance. SHRAC IV featured members of the group Low Income Families Fighting Together (LIFFT). These women are struggling against having their homes and community displaced by the latest round of the government's housing policies, which supports privatization and gentrification. A dynamic woman from the organization Haitian Women of Miami was also a key player in SHRAC IV, especially in organizing the demonstration at the Immigration and Naturalization Service. Another woman from the Haitian diaspora who was on the program of SHRAC IV and is part of SHRAC's African diaspora network is a lawyer from the Dominican Republic who founded Asociación Pro-Desarrollo de la Mujer y Medio Ambiente (Association for the Development of Women and the Environment), a grassroots organization of Haitian women who organize against deportation and other assaults against Haitian immigrants' rights in the Dominican Republic. Like the founder of SHRAC, she had put herself through school during her middle age. She was able to undergo this important transition after she had raised six children and perfected the values and skills of organizing kin, which she managed to extend into public domains of struggle.

SHRAC's core network is made up of African American and other African-descended women activists, but it extends beyond this center to connect with others, including Latina and indigenous women (e.g., the representative from Alianza Indígena sin Fronteras) as well as progressive, antiracist white women. It is important to note that there are also ethnically diverse men who are integral to SHRAC and the SHRAC conferences. However, the individuals who appear to be the most pivotal in mobilizing networks and resources on behalf of the coalition and in setting its political tone and articulating its vision and goals are African American women—veterans of civil rights, women's, and labor struggles. These women's wider identity as women of color has inspired them to reach out and build solidarities with an ethnically and racially diverse pool of organizations and movements in the South and the broader, global South. Their praxis serves to situate SHRAC within the same translocal and transnational political field as that of California's nationally recognized Women of Color Resource Center (Oakland), Arizona's Alianza Indígena sin Fronteras (Tucson), and the Haitian Dominican Asociación Pro-Desarrollo de la Mujer y Medio Ambiente.

These women's leadership is consistent with significant trends that are developing in peoples' movements worldwide. In these contexts, women are playing key roles linking their "scattered resistances" and "counterhegemonic struggles," and in the process they are developing "connections between social, political, economic, and environmental issues and diverse coalitions" (Naples and Desai 2002, 41). In many cases, the main tools and skills they deploy in their struggles are the same as, or are built upon, those that women have traditionally employed to do the work of kinship and community organizing. In these settings, women mobilize social power anchored in the extended family–based values and skills that enable and empower them "to engage in effective communication, goal and priority setting, decision making, and conflict mediation and resolution" (Harrison 1997, 461). Karen Brodkin Sacks (1984) has characterized women who bring these kinds of familial practices into workplace struggles and other public arenas as *centerwomen*. Centerwomen, as the term suggests, are in the middle of social networks that can be mobilized for social action. The women are not necessarily recognized as leaders or official spokespersons, but the part they play in mobilization is nonetheless central. At the current moment, in the context of what is often referred to as "new social movements," increasing numbers of centerwomen are coming to voice and taking their rightful place in the forefront of their respective struggles. This certainly appears to be the trend that SHRAC is following. As part of the interlocking legacies of both the civil rights movement and the women's movement, SHRAC has managed to create a supportive space where women's voices, issues, and leadership abilities can be exercised without antagonizing or—according to a patriarchal gaze—"emasculating" men. This accomplishment reflects the effective implementation of a multiaxial strategy for organizing across differences with the tools that diversity affords.

CONCLUSION

In this chapter, I address the significance of a regional human rights coalition's attempts to oppose racism, xenophobia, and sexism as experienced by the increasingly diverse people in the contemporary U.S. South, the *new* South. The specific historic moment within which I have observed this organization has been conditioned by the worldwide mobilizations that culminated in the WCAR and by the aftermath of the September 11 catastrophe, the war on terrorism. The xenophobic climate manufactured through the political intensification of "homeland security" has enabled the passage of legislation that undermines the civil liberties guaranteed in the Bill of Rights—all in the name of patriotism but in the interests of an elite willing to breach constitutional and international law to stake claims to expanded power on domestic and international fronts.

SHRAC challenges this erosion of democracy with a strategy based on cultivating connections with the global human rights movement and the system of UN standards, treaties, monitoring mechanisms, and conferences. The coalition's concern for human rights takes on special resonance now for at least four reasons. First, this is a time when First Amendment protections are being dismantled within the United States purportedly for the greater end of national security and antiterrorism. Second, human rights violations are intensifying worldwide under a neoliberal regime spread through the mechanisms of global restructuring. Despite the claims it makes for state minimalism and free markets, neoliberalism is not monolithic or consistently implemented across the board. For example, in July 2003 the World Trade Organization chastised the United States for refusing to eliminate tariffs on imported steel, a move made to protect the U.S. industry and to stimulate "an unprecedented level of consolidation and restructuring" (*International Herald Tribune* 2003, 5). The United States has, however, imposed market deregulation on other countries through the strings attached to its aid and the clout it exercises through multinational institutions such as the International Monetary Fund and World Bank. The imposition of structural adjustment programs and export-driven economic growth strategies on debt-ridden countries has resulted in severe forms of austerity that repudiate the social and economic rights delineated in the International Covenant on Economic, Social, and Cultural Rights, which is theoretically a legally binding treaty rather than a declaration. The widening gaps in wealth, health, and power—including military power—that globalization engenders have grave implications for this category of rights as well as for political and civil rights. These two categories of rights have a mutual, complementary relationship. Many of the conflicts around the world that states attempt to manage through repressive means ultimately implicate the diminished subsistence security and deepening poverty that global integration exacerbates (Nash 1994). Farmer points out that "the more spectacular forms of violence that are uncontestedly human rights abuses" are often "punishment for efforts to escape [the] structural violence" of "extreme and relative poverty" and other social inequalities (2003, 8).

The third reason that SHRAC's project is so significant now is closely related to the second. Although the worst of structural violence may be suffered in the global South, the North has not escaped its own variants of it. Social, cultural, and economic security and well-being have been under intensified assault in the United States, with welfare reform, litigation against affirmative action, and referenda opposing unregistered immigrants' access to health and education. Also, economic restructuring according to the global values of free market culture and flexible accumulation has repositioned the South in the new international order, opening it up to accelerated flows of capital and labor, reconfiguring its social and cultural landscape, and complicating its struggles for social and economic justice.

The fourth reason that SHRAC resonates so strongly is that increasing numbers of grassroots organizations, social movements, and coalitions all over the world are using human rights language and tools for their political purposes. The political processes that culminated in the WCAR and that continue to unfold in its aftermath have set an important precedent for framing racial oppression and forming strategies for combating it in the terms offered by international human rights declarations, treaties, and conference plans of action. However, it appears that SHRAC—and, I suspect, other political organizations in other parts of the world—translates abstract and often legalistic ideas about universal rights into a language informed by historically contingent and politically variable experiences. Such a grounded interpretation of international human rights standards may be able to offset the decontextualizing, top-down approach that inhibits well-intentioned human rights NGOs from sufficiently taking into account the complex political dynamics and structural processes that shape the specific contours of human rights cases (Wilson 1997). "Codifying accounts" that fail to deconstruct "abstract, natural rights" belonging to "universal individuals" are inadequate for dealing with the "abuse, social suffering, and structural violence" that limit and undermine human well-being (Harrison 2003, 22).

In my view, SHRAC's centerwomen attempt to reconcile the two competing ideological tendencies and strategies that political analyst Manning Marable (2002) claims are operating within the forces of antiracism in the United States and throughout the world. On the one hand, there is the liberal, populist tendency that uses a discourse of rights and calls "for civic participation, political enfranchisement, and the capacity building of institutions to promote civic empowerment and multicultural diversity" (15). It also promotes "constructive engagement" with globalization and the peaceful "building of political cultures of human rights." On the other hand, there is the radical egalitarian tendency that calls for

> the abolition of poverty, the realization of universal housing, health care, and educational guarantees. . . . *It is less concerned with abstract rights and more concerned with concrete results.* It seeks not political assimilation in an old world order, but the construction of a new world from the bottom up. (16; emphasis mine)

SHRAC emphasizes the building of bridges across differences, including ideological differences. However, within its leadership and membership, there are radical egalitarians who recognize the need to seek an alternative to "capitalism's failed experiment" and to the expanding "American empire," as one SHRAC IV speaker underscored. Although these ideas may not be part of a coalitionwide consensus, there is within the network's discursive repertoire a stream of thought that brings a notion of rights into dialogue with demands for concrete results.

The human rights framework appeals to SHRAC activists for several reasons: its internationalism; its holistic matrix for connecting and acknowledging the mutual relationships among the multiple categories of rights, including individual and collective rights; and the legitimacy that the international human rights system lends to struggles for social justice and change, despite the weaknesses and mixed record of the UN, especially vis-à-vis the United States' superpower politics. This latter point may be especially important in the post–Cold War period, when free market ideology triumphantly claims that there is no alternative to neoliberal capitalism. Human rights discourse may fill a space in the ideological vacuum produced by the purging and assassination of earlier radical political activists (e.g., Black Panthers and communist labor organizers in North Carolina) who raised similar issues and demands.

I have used the example of SHRAC to demonstrate how activists in the U.S. South are coming to respond to the constraints as well as the new opportunities of an increasingly globalized world. I am also interested in their deployment of a human rights–based strategy for organizing a power base with a web of connection that extends throughout the country as well as beyond national boundaries. My first phase of investigation has been largely restricted to examining two SHRAC conferences, focusing on their form, content, and cast of characters as windows onto the shifting sociopolitical field. In future research, I hope to investigate this cast of characters and their organizations in greater detail. Perhaps at that point, I will be able to answer my questions concerning the role and sustainability of the coalition in the interim between the biennial meetings and the influence of SHRAC's consciousness raising on the organizing routines within the local settings that the coalition hopes to connect in both theory and practice. I am particularly eager to find out whether the "tour of shame" made any lasting impressions on the Miami activists who helped to organize it under the moral and political support of SHRAC. Are those organizations finding ways to continue working together? Will SHRAC find ways to pursue its vision of democracy and inspire more people to question what it should look like, especially now in the midst of war and a new ideological rationale for war? Is the war at home and abroad being waged against terrorism or against democracy?

NOTE

I would like to express my thanks for the assistance that Nancy Anderson gave me in audiotaping parts of the SHRAC III program, especially sessions I was unable to attend. I must also thank the centerwomen who took time out of their busy schedules to correspond and talk with me both in person and in long-distance telephone calls.

REFERENCES

Amin, Samir. 2003. Confronting the empire. *Monthly Review* 55 (3): 15–22.

Anderson, Carol. 2003. *Eyes off the prize: The United Nations and the African American struggle for human rights, 1944–1955.* Cambridge: Cambridge University Press.

Buck, Pem Davidson. 2003. 1984: 9/11 and the mediation of the loss of white privilege, part II. *Anthropology News* 44 (5): 39–40.

Choi, Jung Hee. 2001. Our bodies, our communities: Women of color activism and reproductive health rights. In *Time to rise: Women of color—issues and strategies* (report to the United Nations World Conference against Racism), ed. Maylei Blackwell, Linda Burnham, and Jung Hee Choi, 61–71. Oakland, Calif.: Women of Color Resource Center.

Chomsky, Noam, and Edward Herman. 1980. *The Washington connection and Third World fascism.* Boston: South End Press.

Collins, Chuck, and Felice Veskel. 2000. *Economic apartheid in America: A primer of inequality and insecurity.* New York: New Press.

Collins, Patricia Hill. 1990. *Black feminist thought: Knowledge, consciousness, and the politics of empowerment.* New York: Routledge.

Crenshaw, Kimberlé. 1991. Mapping the margins: Identity politics, intersectionality, and violence against women of color. *Stanford Law Review* 43:1241.

Davis, Allison, Burleigh Gardner, and Mary Gardner. 1941. *Deep South: A social anthropological study of caste and class.* Chicago: University of Chicago Press.

Dollard, John. 1937. *Caste and class in a Southern town.* New Haven, Conn.: Yale University Press.

Farmer, Paul. 2003. *Pathologies of power: Health, human rights, and the new war on the poor.* Berkeley: University of California Press.

Harrison, Faye V. 1995. The persistent power of "race" in the cultural and political economy of racism. *Annual Review of Anthropology* 24:47–74.

———. 1997. The gendered politics and violence of structural adjustment: A view from Jamaica. In *Situated lives: Gender and culture in everyday life*, ed. Louise Lamphere, Helena Ragoné, and Patricia Zavella, 451–68. New York: Routledge, 1997.

———. 2002a. Subverting the cultural logics of marked and unmarked racisms in the global era. In *Discrimination and toleration: New perspectives*, ed. Kirsten Hastrup and George Ulrich, 97–125. The Hague: Martinus Nijhoff.

———. 2002b. Unraveling "race" for the 21st century. In *Exotic no more: Anthropology on the front lines*, ed. Jeremy MacClancy, 145–66. Chicago: University of Chicago Press.

———. 2003. Justice for all: Meeting the challenge of advocacy research in the global age. Delmos Jones Visiting Scholar Lecture. Graduate Center, City University of New York, April 11.

International Herald Tribune. 2003. WTO rules U.S. tariffs on steel are illegal. July 12–13, 1, 5.

MacClancy, Jeremy, ed. 2002. *Exotic no more: Anthropology on the front lines.* Chicago: University of Chicago Press.

Marable, Manning. 2002. The political and theoretical contexts of the changing racial terrain. *Souls: A Critical Journal of Black Politics, Culture, and Society* 4 (3): 1–16.

Messer, Ellen. 1993. Anthropology and human rights. *Annual Review of Anthropology* 22:221–49.

Naples, Nancy A., and Manisha Desai, eds. 2002. *Women's activism and globalization: Linking local struggles and transnational politics.* New York: Routledge.

Nash, June. 1994. Global integration and subsistence insecurity. *American Anthropologist* 96 (1): 7–30.

National Center for Human Rights Education. 2000. *Bringing human rights home: Linking individual dignity with mutual destiny; 1996–2000 report on program activities.* Atlanta, Georgia: National Center for Human Rights Education.

———. n.d. National Center for Human Rights Education website, www.nchre.org/about/shron.shtml (accessed April 2003).

Sacks, Karen Brodkin. 1984. Computers, ward secretaries, and a walkout in a Southern hospital. In *My troubles are going to have trouble with me: Everyday trials and triumphs of women workers,* ed. Karen Brodkin Sacks and Dorothy Remy, 173–90. New Brunswick, N.J.: Rutgers University Press.

Sluka, Jeffrey A. 2000. *Death squad: The anthropology of state terror.* Philadelphia: University of Pennsylvania Press.

Smith, Barbara. 1998. The postmodern South: Racial transformations and the global economy. In *Cultural diversity in the south: Anthropological contributions to a region in transition,* ed. Carole E. Hill and Patricia D. Beaver, 164–78. Athens: University of Georgia Press.

Thomas-Houston, Marilyn, and Mark Schuller, eds. N.d. *Homing Devices: The Poor as objects of public policy and planning.* Lanham, Md.: Lexington Press.

Wallerstein, Immanuel. 2003. U.S. weakness and the struggle for hegemony. *Monthly Review* 55 (3): 23–29.

Wilson, Richard A. 1997. Representing human rights violations: Social contexts and subjectivities. In *Human rights, culture, and context,* ed. Richard A. Wilson, 134–60. London: Pluto Press.

• *14* •

Confronting Hegemony, Resisting Occupation

Fadwa El Guindi

*I*n a compelling television interview on the subject of gender and resistance carried out recently, Laila Khalid expressed support for al-Muqawama (Arabic for "the resistance") in all its forms and by both sexes. She is the Muslim Palestinian heroine who nonviolently hijacked two commercial airliners in 1972, taking the world by surprise regarding the resilience of Arab womanhood (El Guindi 1992b) and steadfastness of Palestinian resistance. In the interview, Khalid eloquently describes how Israeli and U.S. bombs and bullets do not distinguish age or gender, indiscriminately killing men, women, children, and elderly. She points out that it is neither fair nor right that men sacrifice their lives to liberate land from occupation and restore dignity to the people while women sit back and later reap the fruit of men's sacrifices. Women, like men, can sacrifice their lives and boldly resist in various forms to accomplish the same end—liberation. She considers all forms to resist occupation and liberate one's land to be legitimate, which should be the responsibility of the entire society. It is a universal and legitimate right. A colonized people have the internationally legal right to resist occupation of their land.

PALESTINE

Laila Khalid succeeded in putting at center stage of worldwide politics and consciousness the long-muted Palestinian *nakba* (Arabic for "catastrophe")—a term and a remembrance associated with the coercive formation of Israel on Palestinian land in 1948. The *nakba* was a forgotten and muted issue in global politics, U.S. domestic academics, and diplomatic circles—an illusion. The Palestinian Arabs and the rest of the Arabs and Muslims would

251

never buy into this Zionist-constructed illusion. Palestinians are real, and their tragedy is historical. Their story is not memories, their roots not mythical, and their community not imagined. Whether in refugee camps or elsewhere after fleeing by coercion, threat, or intimidation since 1948, they still carry their home keys—awaiting return. It would have remained an illusion, as Zionism wishes it to be, had it not been for the resistance by women like Laila Khalid and the *kaffiyeh*-wearing youth (*kaffiyeh*—Arabic for men's checkered headscarf worn by Palestinians, which is now a universal symbol of Palestinian steadfast struggle for liberation; for more, see El Guindi 2005b) of the Intifada (Arabic for uprising against Israeli occupation of Palestine) throwing stones at the Israeli colonists, the Istishhadiyyun (men and women who weaponize their own bodies by choice as the ultimate form of sacrificing one's life for one's country), along with *'amaliyyat fida'iyya* (armed struggle).

Israel is engaged in practices muted by the media: massacres and genocides, trafficking of human organs, genetic experimentations, inhumane torture. It has repeatedly ignored UN resolutions, the Geneva Convention, all peace accords, international law, and human rights over and over. It is the only country colonially planted in the midst of the Arab world that possesses weapons of mass destruction. Until occupation ends and Palestinians return, the issue of Palestine will remain at the center of the Arab-Islamic region's tension with the United States. Palestinian resistance is confined within the borders of Palestine 1948, yet the problem is linked to the overall resistance movement in the Arab and Islamic world. Attempts by Israel and the United States to delink the Palestinian problem from the Arab regional context have failed.

SEPTEMBER 11: SHOCK AND AWE

On September 11, 2001, the American people saw an unprecedented kind of attack in Manhattan, New York, and the nation's capital (see Chomsky 2001, 2003), in which the United States was powerless to prevent or contain an attack on two monuments—the World Trade Center and the Pentagon—representing two pillars of American global power: the economy and the military. This sent shock waves across North America. The American people were traumatized by shock and awe. They felt grief, guilt, depression, and anger. Many American people were reported to have depression.

President Bush set the tone for the U.S. response. A paradigm posing both good versus evil and civilized values versus desperate terrorism was unleashed by the administration as it simultaneously demanded unquestioned public loyalty, by flying flags and resuming consumerism, "buying and flying normally so we win this war against terrorists who are attacking our freedom and lifestyle." He framed the events as those perpetrated by evil forces lurking in the shadows and that America will take revenge so that good (Christian America) prevails over evil (Arabs and Muslims). President Bush initially used the term *crusade*, which sent alarm bells to all Arab and Muslim states, and although he corrected it afterward, it had instantly captured evangelist imagery and pleased the Christian extremists, particularly the Armageddonists.

The trauma experienced by the American public is not unique, nor is the condition that produced it—the September 11 attacks. The reaction complex fits an identifiable universal pattern of behaviors in similar circumstances. According to the National Academy of Sciences terrorism subpanel report (2002), the textbook manifestations of cultural trauma include a heightened group consciousness, emotional numbing, collective mourning, national brooding, and reference to the sacred. However, there are many invasion-produced traumas around the world and many ground zeros—many caused by the United States and Israel. Israel, since its colonial beginnings, has been displacing Palestinians and violating sovereignty of Arab states and human rights of Muslims. But when in 1967 Egypt was defeated in a preemptive strike by Israel, the Egyptian people were traumatized, their psyche shattered. They became a public in despair. In their despair, Egyptians saw apparitions of Virgin Mary—a religious figure central to the theology and morality of Christian and Muslim Arabs. When the United States invaded Afghanistan and began to threaten invasion of Iraq next, again apparitions of Virgin Mary were seen in Egypt, this time in the south. Muslims and Christians traveled daily to the south to catch a view of her—a sign of hope and peace.

In their despair after September 11, the American people began to see an apparition of the devil. The image of a form resembling the devil appeared to people in the rubble of the twin towers of the World Trade Center and was circulated widely in cyberspace. It represents the evil half of the paradigm of polarity—good and evil, god and devil, with us or against us, or the famous Bush Jr. cowboy edict, "I want him dead or alive." America's apparition reflects the U.S. response to the crisis—retaliation and revenge.

In response to September 11, Americans flew U.S. flags (some Jewish Americans flew Israeli flags), and they assaulted immigrants, brown-skinned people, and those appearing to be of Arab or south Asian descent. They also went to church more frequently. Resorting to faith in times of crisis fits the overall pattern of such reactions by many societies throughout recent history. Assaulting other Americans because of their different ethnic origins, or brown-skinned immigrants for the color of their skin or appearance, is racist—plain and simple.

HOMELAND SECURITY AND INSECURITY

America, in revenge, declared a war on terror, one without borders and no end. At home, the climate became that of fear and intimidation. The process that had already begun a few years before September 11, by which racial profiling targeted Arabs and Muslims, gained a framework, a legitimacy, and an institution—namely, Homeland Security and Patriot Acts I and II. A sweep of civil liberty violations took the United States by storm, as the public and the Senate were in a state of shock and fear. Opposing such measure or war would be construed as being unpatriotic. Flag waving and bigotry permeated the landscape. Human rights and civil rights were being violated. High values such as "freedom, liberty, and the pursuit of happiness" were phrases used alongside images of high-tech warplanes by corporations such as Lockheed. The link between militarism, patriotism, and all-American values was made. Dress codes, from Sikh turbans to *kaffiyeh* to women's headcovers, became targets of assault (see El Guindi 1999c and 2005b for details on origins and meaning of Muslim and Arab dress). Many were detained. In the eleven months after the September 11 attacks, 762 aliens were detained for immigration offenses, including overstaying their visas and entering the country illegally.

According to an internal Justice Department investigation, cited in the Council on American-Islamic Relations report (2002), "significant problems" were found with how detainees were treated in U.S. facilities in the wake of the September 11, 2001, attacks. The problems included physical and verbal abuse, extended detention without cause, and unacceptable conditions of incarceration. It also referred to officials' imposing a communications blackout for September 11 detainees immediately after the terrorist attacks, one that lasted several weeks. After the blackout period ended, the September 11 detainees became designated "witness security" inmates, a move that frustrated efforts by detainees' attorneys, families, and even law enforcement officials to determine where the detainees were being held. Frequently people who inquired about a specific September 11 detainee were falsely told that the detainee was not held at a certain facility.

The Council on American-Islamic Relations report also mentions that the American Civil Liberties Union saw the report as quite clearly being action against immigrants. "Immigrants weren't the enemy," ACLU executive director Anthony Romero said in a statement. "But, the war on terror quickly became a war on immigrants. The inspector general's findings confirm our long-held view that civil liberties and the rights of immigrants were trampled in the aftermath of 9/11."

ARAB AND MUSLIM AMERICANS

In the aftermath of September 11, the climate of fear, bigotry, intimidation, violation of civil liberties, and suspicion affected Arab and Muslim Americans the most—a situation worsened by the absence of adequate education about them. According to the fifty-page study alluded to earlier—*Stereotypes and Civil Liberties*, released by the Washington-based advocacy organization Council on American-Islamic Relations (2002)—Muslim Americans are facing serious discrimination in the form of ethnic and religious profiling, detentions, and interrogations. This worsened the climate for Muslims and tacitly encouraged their official and public targeting. Anti-Muslim incidents nearly tripled during the twelve-month period ending March 2002. The report mentions twelve hundred Muslims that were unjustifiably detained and presumed to be terrorists by immigration officials, five thousand legal visa holders submitting to "voluntary interrogations," and fifty thousand detained for giving donations to charity and relief organizations that got shut down by the government after September 11. The cartoon by Danziger in figure 14.1 depicts this scenario quite well.

Arab Americans had been lobbying actively to seek a separate classification for Arabs so that they could access benefits such as social and economic services

Figure 14.1.

or simply produce research data. In this atmosphere, some Arab Americans are now quite comfortable with checking the box labeled "white," fearing that a separate classification of "Arab" or "Muslim" would be a government attempt to identify them for profiling purposes. There is a general reluctance reminiscent of pre-Holocaust Jewish fears in Europe of being classified or numbered for fear of possible abuse by government or law enforcement agencies. Many now fear that in the present political climate, adding an "Arab American" category on any government form can be used in current campaigns to round up those who check the box. Tensions rise as the multiple-pronged conflict in the Middle East intensifies. Arab and Muslim Americans directly experience these conflicts in their lives.

Arab and Muslim Americans had already been suffering from racism and discrimination not unlike some other ethnic/racial groups in America (African American, Japanese American). But the problem has become deeper and the relationship more complex. Conspicuously, there is not one studies program or center (plans are considered at the Dearborn campus of the University of Michigan) dedicated to the study of, research on, or the teaching about Arab and Muslim Americans, an American ethnic and religious group that has grown into a population exceeding ten million, now well organized and quite active in American public and political life and directly related to America's most volatile area of foreign policy.

The bias extends to academics and scholars of the same origin, especially in the social sciences, few of whom hold positions in Islamic and Middle East studies, contrary to the nationwide initiative to recruit African Americans for African American studies, Jews for Jewish studies, and Asians for Asian and Asian American studies. Ironically, Jews tend to be recruited (without scrutiny for likely bias against Arabs and Muslims) to teach Middle East and Islamic studies. You will not find many, if any, Muslim scholars occupying Jewish chairs in Jewish studies. Is it not time to institute Arab and Muslim American studies in the curricula of major universities? Arabs and Muslims constitute the only segment of the American ethnic landscape officially left out of academe (see El Guindi 2003).

CONSTRUCTING AN ENEMY

The enemy was described as the amorphous evil that lurks in the shadows. Terrorism is the enemy. It has no borders, no timetable, no place. But America's might comes from superior military air power designed for conventional war. To take revenge and destroy the enemy, the United States needed a concrete embodiment of evil, a person and a place. The process began with words. September 11 was framed as an act of terrorism and a declaration of war against the United States. An enemy without borders allows the United States to have endless wars chasing the phantom. Defining it as a "declaration of war" allowed the United States to escape the charge of preemption. This would correspond to a literalist simplistic framing of U.S. foreign policy. It cannot deal with intangible movements resisting hegemony. The enemy has to be in a form that America understands: cells, active and sleeper. It is a concrete logic that U.S. foreign policy use a strategy to turn a people's resistance into enemies that it can fight conventional wars with and win. But there were no wars. The disparity in power and the act of preemption and its illegality make them invasions, not wars. These invasions, just like the medieval Crusades, are driven by narrow religious ideologies and for economic gain, carried out in the name of security and a mission for liberation and democratization. Beyond the euphoria and false patriotism, the question becomes Has the United States won? Certainly not. So, what has the United States achieved?

FROM OSAMA BIN LADEN (AFGHANISTAN)

In an effort to prevent war, the Muslim world and the UN called for a conference to discuss terrorism and produce a unified body of resolutions and actions to take. Egypt favored this path. But the United States would not accept it; it was ready for revenge, immediate and spectacular. Long-term consequences for the United States were not well thought out. Other factors took priority: corporate profit, direct access to oil, control of oil pipelines, demonstration of superpower status, domestic partisan politics, creating consumers and markets for U.S. military weapons and consumer goods to satisfy an insatiable corporate appetite, and pleasing Israel. The United States coercively globalizes markets, homogenizes cultures, and tries to pacify people who resist.

In the Gulf War, constructing the enemy for the American people and the world was much easier. This time, however, a phantom had to be made concrete using Christian vocabulary and hegemonic language. By adding a phrase of collective punishment, "terrorists *and* those who harbor them," the Anglo-American axis gave itself the go-ahead to attack one of the poorest nations in the world and a people who have been suffering for decades from resisting the Soviet invasion, droughts, civil unrest, power struggle, and extreme poverty.

Bin Laden was made the symbol of evil and terror perpetrated on the United States. To others elsewhere, however, he was a messenger of resistance to tyrannical and greedy globalized power, chiefly by the United States. The place was called *al-Qa'da* (Arabic for "the base"). The location was Afghanistan. The phrase "terrorists and those who harbor them" widened the

targeted landscape to encompass countries, particularly oil-rich or economically strategic countries, such as Afghanistan. The Taliban were charged with
harboring terrorists who trained in a camp run by bin Laden and his follow-
ers. Al-Qa'da is a term used by the United States to refer to a training camp
in Afghanistan for people from all over the world but primarily Afghan Arabs.
Al-Qa'da and the Taliban are not the same thing. The Taliban form a local
Afghani group engaged in post-Soviet civil war and struggle for power. They
were gaining ground in the civil war. It is interesting that, as one listens care-
fully to all of bin Laden's early messages and tapes in the original language
(Arabic), the term Qa'da was never a term he or any of his companions used.
It could possibly be a term created by U.S. intelligence to construct a tar-
getable entity, referring to this general training that may not have been as localized nor centralized as we were led to believe.

In his op-ed column, Thomas Friedman states that the "real reason" for
this war, which was never stated, was that after September 11 America needed
to hit someone in the Arab-Muslim world (*New York Times*, June 4, 2003, A31).
Terrorists are Muslim. It is Islamic terrorism. There is a factor of racism here.
Note that Timothy McVeigh, the man charged with bombing the federal
building in Oklahoma, was never labeled as a terrorist, let alone a Christian terrorist. The media never talked about Christian terrorism after that tragedy. Nor
did America bomb McVeigh's hometown.

Friedman writes that America attacked "because we could." This "might-
as-right" must have been the drive behind the Mongols' sweep across the Middle East in violent destructive conquests. However, one must heed lessons and
irony from history. The Mongols conquered, ravished, destroyed, and then converted to Islam and vigorously carried the message of Islam wider and deeper.

Other nations found it handy to imitate the United States and call their
enemies "terrorists." Resistance became terrorism. Chechnyans became Rus-
sia's terrorists, and Palestinians became Israel's terrorists. Calling its target a "terrorist" permitted atrocities and justified gross violations of human rights. Israel
engaged in racist and inhumane practices against Palestinians. Still, as Friedman
puts it, Afghanistan was not enough. The United States invaded using high-
tech firepower from faraway distances, and troops simply walked into Baghdad.
It was one-sided. The United States attacked Iraq. There was no war and no
victory.

TO SADDAM HUSSEIN (IRAQ)

Undermining resistance to hegemony, Friedman outlines what I consider to be
a roadmap to the abyss, justifying endless wars against Arabs and Muslims. He

refers to a "terrorism bubble" that poses a real threat and has to be punctured. He seems to argue for endless, elusive wars, oblivious that these would bleed America's economy and deplete its moral capital around the world.

He goes on to say that the only way to puncture that bubble is for American soldiers, men and women, to go into the heart of the Arab-Muslim world, house to house, and make it clear that we are ready to kill, and die, to prevent our open society from being undermined by this terrorism bubble. Smashing Saudi Arabia or Syria would have been fine. But we hit Saddam for one simple reason: because we could, because he deserved it, and because he was right in the heart of that world. Friedman's piece is a call for vendetta, an eternal one, and seems to serve Zionist rather than U.S. interests. Friedman may be right about U.S. intent, but he is wrong about Arab and Muslim discontent.

Now two Arab countries are occupied: Palestine under Israeli occupation since 1948 and Iraq under Anglo-American occupation starting in 2003. Intellectuals must wonder whether the postmodernist notion of postcolonialism is of any value, being merely an intellectual ploy in polemics and an exercise in denial, since coloniality is real and continues in its original form. To refer to a postcolonial phase is to deny that people and lands (Palestine and Iraq) are occupied by colonial powers and, hence, to deny their right to liberation.

Despite the gross disparity in power between U.S. unprecedented might and Iraq—a devastated developing country—the resistance in Iraq at the time of invasion succeeded in bringing down invading Apaches, Cobras, and tanks, and it took prisoners of war. Since the occupation, Iraqis continue to down Apaches and F16s, ambush troops, and kill marines. The Anglo-American occupying force in Iraq is not wanted there. In Palestine, resistance has been going strong for years. Both Palestinians and Iraqis are determined to continue the resistance as long as their land, homes, and resources are occupied.

Could the first Gulf War have been prevented? The Arab countries tried. They had in fact reached a mediated solution, a *sulha* (Arabic for "reconciliation") building on traditional institutions of *khuwwa* (Arabic for "brotherhood") between both parties of the original conflict, Iraq and Kuwait. But the United States was determined then, as in the recent invasion, to go ahead with war. The Anglo-American war machine had been greased. The same pattern is repeated. A Pakistan-mediated offer made with bin Laden's approval to submit to international procedures of trial and justice was ignored, as again the Anglo-American military machine was unleashed in 1990 and on October 7, 2002, and again in March 2003. In between, there were many strikes (the Sudan) and frequent bombings (daily bombing of Iraq).

The war of 2003 could also have been averted. A UN-sponsored inspection team had demonstrated that Iraq did not possess weapons of mass destruction, but America insisted on war, shifting pretexts from regime change, to WMDs, to a al-Qa'da link. The world, countries and people, objected. But the United States moved ahead with another invasion, this time preemptively, against human rights, against the United Nations, against the Geneva Convention, and against the peoples of the world who demonstrated daily in every city in every country—the World Street (more on this later) spoke loudly against the war. The U.S. attack was preemptive, unilateral, unsupported by the international community, and in violation of international law and universal human rights; it took place despite disapproval of the United Nations and against the will of all the peoples of the world, as seen in the worldwide protests by women and men against the war.

It is as if Iraq had not suffered enough. A decade of sanctions and continual attacks since the devastating Gulf War had caused inhumane suffering for the people and destruction of society and services. Other than the damage from direct attacks ongoing since 1990, according to reports by the United Nations (n.d.) and the International Action Center (n.d.) each month a conservative estimate of about 6,000 Iraqi children perished from sanction-related causes. For instance, at least 133 children each day, nearly 50,000 a year, had died from complications from malnutrition and sewage-contaminated water; from diarrhea and pneumonia; and from diseases such as polio, cholera, and typhoid. I have not included the genetic deformities of an entire generation caused by depleted uranium. The proportional equivalent for the United States would very conservatively be 69,000 children dying each month. Compare this figure with the one-time event of fewer than 3,000 deaths at the twin towers for perspective on ground zero and tragedies.

Despite this bleak picture of extreme human suffering, the United States invaded Iraq, without any legitimacy, armed with unconvincing pretexts and the disproportionate weight of vengeance—a long-awaited reprisal for all the humiliations experienced by the United States at the hands of elusive groups or individuals in Yemen, Somalia, Saudi Arabia, Iran, Lebanon, and so on. It is a war that the United States began but has no power now to end.

WAR AGAINST CIVILIZATION

Former prime minister Margaret Thatcher of England, former president George H. W. Bush, former secretary of state Madeleine Albright, and current U.S. president George W. Bush have all described Iraq as being barbarian and needing to join the civilized world. This is colonial vocabulary and racist thinking that are part of an attitude reminiscent of the nineteenth- and early-twentieth-century scheme that put societies on a ladder from savagery to barbarism to civilization. This scheme is empirically wrong. Archeologists know what civilization is and that these claims are racist misuses of well-defined terms. Why have archeologists remained silent? Anthropologists know about violence and about the value of heritage for peoples with civilizational culture. Why have anthropologists remained silent? Samuel P. Huntington (1998) used the phrase "clash of civilization." Politicians used it to promote their strategies. But where is anthropology? There is a technical definition for the notion of civilization, which if applied would discredit the scenario of a clash altogether, since the term represents a stage in the developmental history of human societies, its cradle being Mesopotamia and Egypt (now the Arab world), culminating in the development of industrialized and electronic technologies. Civilization does not characterize the Western level of development. It marks the revolutionary developments of the East—Mesopotamia, Egypt, and so on. The clash is not conducted between civilizations but rather is created by a militaristic, unilateralist, preemptive, hegemonic force from the West *against* civilization in the East (El Guindi 1991). The West has not shown any moral, social, or cultural superiority over the East. It has only demonstrated its hegemonic force. It is particularly ironic when U.S. missionaries rush to Iraq to convert the original Christians.

What complicates the picture is that although power shifted from the East to the West, most vital natural resources coveted by the West are present in abundance in the East. In today's world, countries trade on the basis of international laws and agreements. Instead of "civilized" trade relations, America in racist arrogance wants to acquire these resources by a hegemonic use of force and invasions to remove sovereign regimes, which results in killing and destruction.

Recurrently throughout history, peoples from land or sea invaded settled prosperous civilizations and ravished, killed, and conquered seeking wealth and resources. Today we have U.S. invasions by air using weapons of mass destruction, part of the largest arsenal in the world, which can incinerate the world over in minutes. It seems as if, other than being motivated by greed, America is also trying to eliminate or deface the evidence of a civilizational record. What happened to Iraq's antiquities and civilizational heritage in damage and loss, under U.S. occupation and in the presence of U.S. forces, attests to this view. There was no effort to prevent thefts, and more evidence suggests complicity. These are antiquities that have survived seven thousand years despite invasions and conquests. There was theft by colonizing countries of valuable items that ended up in European and American museums. The Iraqi regime is to be credited for preserving its heritage despite all of that. The antiquities of Iraqi heritage are part of Iraq's sovereignty, although knowledge about it belongs to the world. The United States is a country with might but with no civilization now destroying a country that began and preserved civilization for the world but has might of resistance against being colonized.

WOMEN, *BURQU'*, *HIJAB*

Feminists may be proudly counting the number of U.S. women in the service, but is sisterhood served when U.S. women invade and kill invaded women and children? A commentary by James Flanigan ran in the *Los Angeles Times* (April 16, 2003, C1) with the title "U.S. Policy on Iraq Is Banking on Women." The word *banking* rings alarm bells—it smells of corporate greed sending its tentacles to women. This runs shivers down my spine. Women and feminists on both sides are again exploited for power and wealth for a selected few and for corporate gain. In this story, Flanigan takes us to women on the invaded side, the other side of the war equation. He writes how Iraq was an advanced society in which women participated at all levels—studies, observations, and statistics bear this out. Even the notorious deck of cards drawn by the U.S. Pentagon to identify the most wanted from Iraq's Baathist regime has a number of women at the highest level of positions in science.

Deterioration in health and status for women, as for men, can be traced to the regional war; United States–imposed sanctions; deprivation of food, medicine, and services; and invasions by the United States—and it is not caused by the Iraqi regime, Islam, or Arab society or culture. We know that Iraq's regional war against Iran cannot be blamed on Iraq alone but mainly on the United States' role in arming both sides, with the goal of "dual containment," as it is called in vocabulary intended to sanitize the destructive character of such strategy.

Middle East women are considered the center of sacred and ordinary Arab and Muslim life and culture. They are the pivots that hold together the family, the core of the social group (El Guindi 1985, 1986a). What women do and what happens to women become of concern to those in charge of society and religion. In times of threat, instability, and crisis, women are subjected to restrictions and controls that have no basis in scripture (El Guindi 1992a). These are historical behaviors in historical times. In the context of Islamic groups seeking state control or power, as in the Islamic revolution of Iran in 1979, rigid restrictions are initially enforced at every level of society. In its third decade as a successful revolution, liberalization takes place. We are familiar with this process, which was theorized in anthropology in the 1960s. So if we look at movements of change, such as the Islamic movements in the Middle East, we need to take a longitudinal, processional approach in which we witness how the movement passes through different phases until reaching the phase of routinizing, stabilizing, and liberalizing its measures.

This takes us to the *burqu'*. There is a difference between *burqu'* (Arabic for "face mask") and *Hijab* (Arabic for "women's Islamic headcover"; for a full discussion, see El Guindi 1995, 1999c, 2005a). The burqu' is secular tradition.

In the most sacred space of worship, as during pilgrimage i.
would not be allowed. It is not Islamic. Hijab is Islamic; bur.
ing the woman's face is not permitted in Islam's most sacred m
ship. In approaching Islam, one had better not separate religion
but rather talk about Islam as that lived, experienced, reformed, anc
Muslims. What Muslim women wear or do not wear, or do or do   ao, is
the concern of the women and their families and cultures (El Guindi 1983,
1987, 1995, 1999b). The feminist majority spearheaded an intense campaign
against the women's burqu' in Afghanistan that served the goals of military
campaigns. Intervention, particularly hegemonic provocations such as that by
the feminist majority and evangelist missionaries, which tend to precede military attacks, serves only to foster anger. Such actions are based on ignorance
and arrogance. I ask, How can we discuss gender and the role of women in the
Arab and Islamic region without discussing the hegemonic role of United
States–driven wars and colonial occupation by the United States in Iraq and
that by Israel of Palestine and the related roles of hegemonic fundamentalist
Western Christian missionary work and hegemonic feminism? U.S. feminism
must liberate itself from the hold that hegemony has over it.

ISLAM AND ISLAMIC RESISTANCE

And then there is Islam. There is a tendency to frame it in boxes. After September 11, President Bush reiterated the box approach to Islam. He drew a geography of evil, encouraging Israel to call the resisting Palestinians terrorists
and then attack them, their mosques, their homes, and their olive trees, mercilessly.

President Bush began to carve Islam into good Islam and bad Islam. The
bad is, of course, the one that does not agree with the United States and its
military and economic encroachment plans. Good Muslims (the term is moderate) are the Stepford wives, docile citizens who attend to their worship. This
is at a time when fanatic televangelist Christians called Islam a religion of violence and its prophet a terrorist. They found the devil in Islam but also in
Harry Potter. Clearly, they are possessed and obsessed by the devil.

Indeed, simplistic American foreign policy imagined it possible to press the
button and turn Muslims on, then off. When we needed them to fight the Sovi-
ets, as did Reagan with the mujahideen, we found Islam useful, giving Muslims
the right kind of energy to implement our plans, so we lavished arms and funds
on them and their activities. After they won the war for us, we decided to pacify
them, assassinate their leaders, destroy people's lives and cultures, and reconfigure
Islam itself. Afghanistan now has an American-made/American-guarded leader,

n economy of opium, German-issued banknotes, refugees all over the world, poverty, disintegration, and disruption. Despite all the intervention, to the total bewilderment of the feminist majority, Afghan women, exercising their freedom, continue to wear the burqu'. Another ignorance, another miscalculation.

Oversimplification is new neither to U.S. policy nor to the all-American worldview: this worldview combines immediacy in action (short-sightedness), immediate gratification, and simple polarity. Polarity is fundamental to the American psyche, not simply a model of policy: black and white, cowboy and Indian, civilized and barbaric, good and evil—it is fundamentally Christian and American. The real world is much more complex than that, but who has time for complexity? Or for knowlege? The Bush administration shoots first and finds information later. It struck Afghanistan before demonstrating to the world persuasive evidence of perpetrators, and the soldiers blew up a wedding because the local Afghanis shot rifles in the air in celebration, as is the custom throughout the region.

Despite the secondary status of many Islamic countries and the poverty of many Muslims, Islam is the fastest growing religion in the world today, larger than Catholic Christianity and larger than Protestant Christianity. Let us imagine, as schoolteacher David Smith (2002) asked students to do, the globe, which has over six billion people, as one village of a hundred people, while maintaining the ratios equivalent to the demographics of world ethnicities, nationalities, religions, and languages. Who would be in this village? It would have 19 Muslims, 16 Catholics, 13 Hindus, 6 Protestants, and 1 Jew. How are dominance and power, food and wealth, and general discontent distributed? In the answer to this question lies the key to what the United States ought to be doing but is not.

Let me share a few simple points and general observations about Islam. First, it is unproductive and inaccurate to approach Islam as if there were many Islams or as if there were cultural variants. There is only one Islam. Not understanding this point leads to core misunderstandings of the unified notions of community, identity, religious language, and individual and collective worship. In general, religion in the Middle East plays a central role in people's daily, ordinary lives. Islam's modern role in politics of identity and resistance is a function of modern historical events and situations of conflict, appropriation, and confrontation. It is important that we (and, particularly, U.S. political decision makers) understand how conditions of colonial occupation and legacy, the imposed U.S. military bases, and the imposition of Western consumerist values become largely responsible for creating climates of anger and discontent, leading to resistance and globalized confrontations. There is also the inhumane United States–imposed sanctions and bombing of Arab and Muslim countries and groups. I must stress in particular the occupation of Palestine and the human and international rights violations against the Palestinians. As observers of Middle East politics point out, before 1948 the United States had no enemies in the Arab world.

RESISTANCE TO HEGEMONY: ARAB STREET BECOMES WORLD STREET

The resistance to hegemony is worldwide—without borders, without governments. In media interviews, I had spoken of the phenomenon of the Arab Street. I had also mentioned the notion to President Clinton during a meeting in the Cabinet Room of the White House, with scholars and activists of Arab origin brought together to discuss domestic and foreign policy issues (see El Guindi n.d.).

The Arab Street is a spontaneous expression of protest by the people without the mediation of politically controlled election booths (which, as seen during the presidential election of Bush Jr., is not foolproof) or other rigid political structures. The Arab Street is a truly an alternative democratic expression. Bin Laden himself predicted its rise, in one of his taped messages.

Now there is an emergent World Street. The world has joined the Arabs and Muslims in protesting U.S. might and Israeli colonial occupation. We have seen its passionate expression in vigorously protesting war and U.S. economic domination, on the television screens through European and Arab satellite channels. Peoples all over the world protested the Anglo–American wars. There is a worldwide rift between peoples and states. If history teaches us anything, we learn that resistance is not managed by single leaders. Once the idea is adopted, killing the leader or ideologue does not kill the idea. Christianity itself attests to that.

The power of the street lies in its very nature, its very character—it is intangible, it is prevalent, it is passionate and popular. It has no borders, no states, no politicians. Egyptian president Hosni Mubarak told President Bush, when Bush was determined to invade Afghanistan and "get" bin Laden, that killing bin Laden would give birth to thousands of bin Ladens, that they would sprout everywhere. This caution captures the nature of the Islamic current that began in the 1970s and the Islamic resistance that was born in Egypt to confront regional hegemony of politics and products in order to end Israeli colonial occupation and put a check on their complicit governments (El Guindi 1981a, 1981b, 1982a, 1982b, 1982c). Islamic currents are popular. Arab states today are fully aware that allowing truly free elections will lead to Islamic parties, if not Islamic governments. Algeria tried and reneged (El Guindi 1998). The United States today has just discovered this in Iraq. The people are demanding elections and demanding an

Islamic state. If America is to export democracy and free elections as it promised to do, it has to expect an Islamic state in Iraq. To prevent this from happening, the United States dictates, it controls, and it kills. The Shiites, along with all elements of the majority of the Iraqi population, want America out of Iraq. They are demonstrating daily against U.S. occupation. U.S. troops respond by shooting them. Muslims throughout the region are on the road of a Shiitization—the answer to U.S. hegemony and Israeli brutal occupation.

But U.S. thinking on the Middle East is literalist, simplistic, dualistic, evangelistic, and concretistic. America and Israel use the same model and the same tactics searching for "leaders" and "cells" because they cannot deal with ideas, movements, and streets. They motivate their attacks by false arguments of national security. And both extend their revenge by collectively punishing an entire people, a nation, a region, and a civilization. Although he himself made such mistakes (El Guindi 1993), President Mubarak of Egypt wisely reminded the United States, in response to U.S. threats of war, that "Egypt was subjected to many actions of terror, and I myself was subjected to terrorist attacks. I do not respond in retaliation by unleashing the wrath of military power on an entire nation. There are other ways." Israel knows no other way. America should consider alternatives.

DATES AND ARABIC COFFEE DIPLOMACY

What can such trigger-happy policy produce? More anger, more hate. What is the consequence of humiliating, defeating, crushing, killing, dislocating, and silencing? Those who do not own B52s and other killing machines will use whatever they can get their hands on. America experienced September 11—fear, depression, withdrawal, shock, humiliation, and anger. But the American people have not experienced starvation or devastation from homes bombed mercilessly in the name of freedom, as those in Afghanistan and Iraq have.

Instability, famine, humiliation, and occupation can only breed anger and rage. The United States cannot expediently censure resistance against foreign occupation, or dissent against injustices by labeling such legitimate processes as terrorism. The Arabs, in in their lively debate since September 11, which can be heard on Arab satellite television, have come up with a more realistic identification and a set of more sophisticated distinctions about terrorism.

How can the situation be different? From an unquestioned position of power, America can learn to understand, have the patience to dialogue, demonstrate respect to poor nations, establish normal relations with weaker countries—in effect, end its own occupation of Iraq and Israel's violations of Palestinian land and integrity, seek resources and labor by trade and not by invasion, and allow negotiation by diplomacy through the United Nations during crises. In a recent media interview, I was asked what I thought would be an alternative U.S. foreign policy in the Middle East, an alternative to heavy-handedness and hegemony. My reply was phrased with ethnographic imagery: "dates and Arabic coffee" diplomacy. Diplomacy is invented to deal with situations in which the parties are trying to resolve conflict. Sit with any Arab leader and discuss matters of trade and compliance, even friendship and partnership, and make deals, as guest and host both enjoy the most delicious Arabic dates and coffee. This will make the difference between a world stately power leading the world and a corporate-run bully out of control.

REFERENCES

Chomsky, N. 2001. *9-11*. New York: Seven Stories Press.

———. 2003. *Power and terror*. New York: Seven Stories Press.

Council on American-Islamic Relations. 2002. Executive summary: The status of Muslim civil rights in the United States. In *Stereotypes and Civil Liberties*. Washington, D.C.: Council on American-Islamic Relations.

El Guindi, Fadwa. 1981a. Is there an Islamic alternative? The case of Egypt's contemporary Islamic movement. *Middle East Insight* 1 (4): 19–24.

———. 1981b. Veiling infitah with Muslim ethic: Egypt's contemporary Islamic movement. *Social Problems* 28 (4): 465–85.

———. 1982a. Die Ruckkehr zum Schleier: Vom unaufhaltsamen Siegeszug eins konservativen Symbols. *Nahost in Flammen, Der Monat* 285:165–78.

———. 1982b. The emerging Islamic order: The case of Egypt's contemporary Islamic movement. *Journal of Arab Affairs* 1 (2): 245–62.

———. 1982c. The killing of Sadat and after: A current assessment of Egypt's Islamic movement. *Middle East Insight* 2 (5): 20–27.

———. 1983. Veiled activism: Egyptian women in the Islamic movement. *Peuples Mediterranéans* (Special issue: Femmes de la Mediterranée) 22–23:79–89.

———. 1985. The status of women in Bahrain: Social and cultural considerations. In *Bahrain and the Gulf: Past perspectives and alternative futures*, ed. J. B. Nugent and T. H. Thomas, 75–95. Sydney: Croom Helm.

———. 1986a. The Egyptian woman: Trends today, alternatives tomorrow. In *Women in the world, 1975–1985: The Women's Decade*, ed. L. Iglitzin and R. Ross, 225–42. Santa Barbara, Calif.: Clio Press.

———. 1986b. The mood in Egypt: Summer heat or revolution? *Middle East Insight* 4 (4–5): 30–39.

———. 1987. Das islamische Kleid "al-hidschab." In *Pracht und Geheimnis: Kleidung und Schmuck aus Palastina und Jordanie*, ed. G. Volger, K. V. Welck, and K. Hackstein, 164–67. Koln, Germany: Rautenstrauch-Joest-Museum der Stadt Koln.

———. 1991. Images of domination, voices of control. *International Documentary: Journal of Nonfiction Film and Video* (Spring).

———. 1992a. Feminism comes of age in Islam. Commentary. *Los Angeles Times*, February 17, B5.

———. 1992b. Waging war on civilization: Report on the archeology of Mesopotamia. In *War Crimes: A Report on United States War Crimes against Iraq*, ed. Ramsey Clark. Washington, D.C.: Maisonneuve Press.

———. 1993. Mubarak should call an election and step aside. Op-ed. *Los Angeles Times*, March 26, B7.

———. 1995. Hijab. In *The Oxford encyclopedia of the modern Islamic world*, 108–111. New York: Oxford University Press.

———. 1998. UN should act to protect Muslim women. *Newsday*, April 13.

———. 1999a. Veiled men, private women in Arabo-Islamic culture. *ISIM Newsletter* 4.

———. 1999b. Veiling resistance. *Fashion Theory: The Journal of Dress, Body, and Culture* 3 (1): 51–80.

———. 1999c. *Veil: Modesty, privacy, resistance.* Oxford: Berg.

———. 2003. Arab and Muslim America: Emergent scholarship, new visibility, conspicuous gap in academe. *American Anthropologist* 105 (3): 631–34.

———. 2005a. Hijab. *Encyclopedia of clothing and fashion*, ed. Steele. Detroit: Charles Scribner's Sons.

———. 2005b. Kaffiyeh. *Encyclopedia of clothing and fashion*, ed. Steele. Detroit: Charles Scribner's Sons.

———. n.d. Personal webpages. White House meeting, www-bcf.usc.edu/~elguindi/WhiteHouse.htm. AAA public policy forum: Violence against the middle east, www.bcf.usc.edu/~elguindi/AAAPublicPolicyForum99.html. Accessed March 30, 2005.

Huntington, Samuel P. 1998. *The clash of civilizations and the remaking of world order.* New York: Simon & Schuster.

International Action Center. n.d. Why We Are Opposing the US/UN Sanctions on Iraq. www.iacenter.org/oppsan99.htm (accessed March 30, 2005).

National Academy of Sciences. 2002. *Subpanel on psychological, social and behavioral aspects of terrorism.* Washington, D.C.: National Academy of Sciences.

Smith, David. 2002. *If the world were a village: A book about the world's people.* Toronto: Kids Can Press.

United Nations. n.d. Sanctions against Iraq. www/globalpolicy.org/security/sanction/indexone.htm (accessed March 30, 2005).

Index

About the Contributors

Subhadra Mitra Channa is professor of anthropology at the University of Delhi. She earned a doctorate in social anthropology from Delhi University in 1982. Her research has focused on the low castes of Indian society and on cross-cultural perspectives on gender and its intersection with caste and class. She has vast fieldwork experience in Northern India and has published extensively. In 2000, she was awarded the Charles Wallace Visiting Fellowship at Queen's University, United Kingdom, and in 2003–2004 she received a Fulbright Visiting Lectureship to the United States. She was president of the Indian Anthropological Association from 1998 to 2000. She is currently cochair of the Commission on the Anthropology of Women in the International Union of Anthropological and Ethnological Sciences.

Jan Delacourt works as an applied anthropologist in migrant services in Northern Italy. She grew up in what was Rhodesia before going to England to study psychology and education at the University of Sussex. She taught in London for more than twenty years, at most levels between classes of five-year-olds and in-service education for head teachers and advisory staff. In 1999, she earned a master of arts in social and cultural anthropology from the California Institute of Integral Studies, San Francisco. She then moved to Northern Italy, where she "went native." Since 1998, she has been a core member of the International Union of Anthropological and Ethnological Sciences Commission on the Anthropology of Women.

Fadwa El Guindi is on the faculty of anthropology at the University of Southern California. She has retired from the University of California, Los Angeles, where she was a professor from 1972 to 1978. She holds a bachelor of arts in political science and a doctorate in anthropology. She has conducted field research in Mexico, Nubia, Egypt, and in Arab and Muslim America. She is widely published and lectures internationally. Her expertise on the Middle East was sought at a White House meeting with President Clinton, at the U.S. Senate, and by the media. Her most recent book, in its second printing, is *Veil: Modesty, Privacy, and Resistance.* She is a past president of the Middle East Section of the American Anthropological Association.

Cheryl Fischer received her bachelor of arts in English from Xavier University in New Orleans and her master of arts in teaching from Reed College in Portland, Oregon. Ms. Fischer worked on a doctorate in Chinese literature at Ohio State University in Columbus, Ohio, and learned Chinese and Japanese, even though she did not complete the degree. She has worked with many social justice organizations in the United States as well as in Sweden, Switzerland, and Japan. Currently, she coordinates the Kuumba Human Rights Focus Group in Springfield, Missouri, and documents civil and human rights issues in that area.

Melissa D. Hargrove received a Ph.D. in cultural anthropology at the University of Tennessee, Knoxville. Her dissertation is on spatial segregation and cultural politics among the Gullah/Geechee of the U.S. Southeast's Sea Islands. Her scholarly and teaching interests include the African diaspora, the local impact of tourism and development, race as a social construct, the cultural meaning of space and place, and critical whiteness studies.

Faye V. Harrison is professor of African American studies and anthropology at the University of Florida and has taught at the University of Tennessee, Knoxville. She earned a doctorate in anthropology from Stanford University in 1982. She has done fieldwork in the United States, the United Kingdom, and Jamaica examining urban poverty, the informal economy, drug trafficking, grassroots politics, and local impacts of global restructuring. She has published extensively on these issues as well as on race, gender, and the history and politics of anthropology. Since 1993 she has chaired the International Union of Anthropological and Ethnological Sciences Commission on the Anthropology of Women. She is currently completing a book, *From the Outside Within: Reworking Anthropology as a Labor of Love.*

Diana Hayman has worked in the federal government for over twenty-eight years in the field of higher education. She is the product of a military family and has traveled widely. She has a bachelor of arts in English and a master's degree in business and management and has served as board president of the National Society for Experiential Education. She has been both a consumer and a critic of diversity training throughout her career and presents on the topic of diversity at the Federal Management Institute in Washington, D.C. She is a member of the American Anthropological Association.

Camille Hazeur is currently assistant to the president and director of the Office of Equity and Diversity Services at George Mason University in Fairfax, Virginia. She has received two grants from the U.S. Department of Education's Fund for the Improvement of Postsecondary Education to work with faculty and staff to develop and implement a program called a Change Model. The Change Model provides group participants with an opportunity to spend several weeks together discussing diversity issues and how they affect classroom interaction. In addition to spending several years working in higher education at a variety of public, private, and two- and four-year institutions, she spent ten years the University of Tennessee, Knoxville, as director of diversity resources and educational services. She holds a bachelor of arts in sociology and a master of arts in counseling and has done graduate work in anthropology.

Devaki Jain is a development economist and feminist activist. She graduated in economics from Oxford and taught at Delhi University for six years. Since then, her academic research and advocacy, influenced by Gandhian philosophy, have focused on issues of equity, democratic decentralization, people-centered development, and women's rights. She has been an active member of the women's movement, at its local, national, and international levels. She has published extensively and is the author of *The Vocabulary of Women's Politics*.

Fatma Jiddawi Napoli is a mother, a professional woman, and a community advocate born and raised in Zanzibar, Tanzania. She was educated at the University of Dar-es-Salaam in Tanzania and later earned an MBA from Boston University. She is an advocate for women and against all forms of social oppression. In Tanzania, she provided educational support for projects devoted to urban and rural women's socioeconomic empowerment. She is cofounder of Zanzibar America Cultural Alliance, an organization still in its infancy geared at assisting immigrants and mobilizing awareness in Boston on their issues. She currently lives in Cambridge, Massachusetts, with her husband and four children.

Esther I. Njiro works as a senior researcher, anthropologist, and gender specialist for the Council for Science and Industrial Research, based in Pretoria, South Africa. She holds a doctorate in anthropology from the University of Nairobi. Her research has taken her to many African countries where she has studied sustainable livelihoods in rural areas and the cultural opportunities and constraints operative in community development, particularly in mountain settings. She is the African region coordinator for Celebrating Mountain Women, an event of the International Year of the Mountains, and the African regional editor for the journal *Mountain Research and Development.* She founded the Centre for Gender Studies at the University of Venda in South Africa. From 1998 to 2003, she was cochair of the Commission on the Anthropology of Women in the International Union of Anthropological and Ethnological Sciences.

Philomina E. Okeke is an associate professor of women's studies at the University of Alberta, Edmonton, Canada. Her research and teaching focus on gender and development in Africa; the social dynamics of race, class, and gender in North American communities; and Africa in the globalization process. Her publications in journals and books reflect a continuing contribution to debates in these areas. Dr. Okeke is also actively involved with other scholars in building linkages between researchers and social activists working in Africa.

J. Maria Pedersen teaches Aboriginal studies at the University of Notre Dame, Australia (Broome Campus). She has a bachelor's degree in indigenous Australian studies from the same university and is completing a master's in indigenous Australian studies. For many years, she has been actively involved in social justice issues for Aboriginal people in the areas of youth suicide, substance abuse, family violence, and education, as well being a sole, full-time parent to four sons.

Helen I. Safa is professor emerita of anthropology and Latin American studies at the University of Florida. She was director of the Center for Latin American Studies at the University of Florida and president of the Latin American Studies Association. She has published numerous books and articles focused on gender, race, development, and urbanization in the Americas, including her two monographs: *The Myth of the Male Breadwinner: Women and Industrialization in the Caribbean,* a comparison of women industrial workers in Puerto Rico, Cuba, and the Dominican Republic; and earlier *The Urban Poor of Puerto Rico: A Study in Development and Inequality.* She has a doctorate in anthropology from Columbia University, where she has held a visiting appointment. She has also held Fulbright fellowships at the Universidade Federal da Bahia, Brazil, and the Universidad Pompeu Fabra in Barcelona.

Mohamed Ahmed Saleh was born in Zanzibar. He has been active in the struggle for the restoration of democratic rights and civil liberties in Tanzania in general and Zanzibar in particular. He holds a master's degree and a diplôme d'etudes approfondies in social anthropology from the Ecole des Hautes Etudes en Sciences Sociales in Paris. He is currently completing his doctoral research, entitled "The Zanzibari Diaspora: Identity and Nationalism." He has done fieldwork on fishing communities in Zanzibar as well as on identity and marriage among Swahili living in East Africa, the Comoros, and Europe. He has also worked with French public television (France 3), producing documentary films on the Eastern Caribbean and Zanzibar for the television program *Thalassa*.

Gina Ulysse is an assistant professor of anthropology and African American studies at Wesleyan University. She received a doctorate in anthropology from the University of Michigan in 1999. She is currently completing a book based on her dissertation, *Downtown Ladies: Informal Commercial Importing and Self-Fashioning in Jamaica*. She has done research on gender, race, and class dynamics in cultural production, politics, and economic practices in Jamaica, Haiti, and South Africa.

She is also a poet and spoken-word performer. Her poetry has appeared in *The Butterfly's Way: Voices from the Haitian Diaspora in the United States*, edited by Edwidge Dandicat, and *Women on the Verge of Home*, edited by Bilinda Straight. She has also published work in *Jouvert: Journal of Postcolonial Studies*; *Meridians: Feminism, Race, and Transnationalism*; and *Ma Comere*, journal of the Association of Caribbean Women Writers and Scholars.